MASTERING GLOBAL STUDIES

SECOND EDITION

James Killoran
Social Studies Supervisor, New York City

Stuart Zimmer
Social Studies Teacher, New York City

Mark Jarrett
Former Social Studies Teacher, New York City

JARRETT PUBLISHING COMPANY

East Coast Office
19 Cross Street
Lake Ronkonkoma, NY 11779

West Coast Office
2524 Highgate Drive
Richmond, CA 94806

(516) 981-4248 • 1-800-859-7679 • Fax (516) 588-4722

This book is dedicated to our children...Christian, Carrie, Jesse, Todd, Ronald, Alexander and Julia.

ISBN: 1-882422-04-X

Printed in the United States of America
Second Edition

ABOUT THE AUTHORS

James Killoran is an Assistant Principal at Jamaica High School in New York. He has written *Government and You, Economics and You, Mastering U.S. History and Government, The Key To Understanding Global Studies, The Key To Understanding U.S. History and Government, Mastering Ohio's 9th Grade Citizenship Test, Mastering Ohio's 12th Grade Citizenship Test, Comprende Tu Mundo: Su Historia, Sus Culturas,* and *Los Estados Unidos: Su Historia, Su Gobierno.* Mr. Killoran has extensive experience in test writing for the New York State Board of Regents in Social Studies and has served on the Committee for Testing of the National Council of Social Studies. His article on social studies testing was recently published in *Social Education,* the country's leading social studies journal. In addition, he has won a number of awards for outstanding teaching and curriculum development, including "Outstanding Social Studies Teacher" and "Outstanding Social Studies Supervisor" in New York City.

Stuart Zimmer is a Social Studies teacher at Jamaica High School in New York. He has written *Government and You, Economics and You, Mastering U.S. History and Government, The Key to Understanding Global Studies, The Key To Understanding U.S. History and Government, Mastering Ohio's 9th Grade Citizenship Test, Mastering Ohio's 12th Grade Citizenship Test, Comprende Tu Mundo: Su Historia, Sus Culturas,* and *Los Estados Unidos: Su Historia, Su Gobierno.* Mr. Zimmer has served as a test writer for the New York State Board of Regents in Social Studies, and has written for the National Merit Scholarship Examination. He has presented numerous demonstrations and educational workshops at state and national teachers' conferences. In addition, he has been recognized by the New York State Legislature with a Special Resolution noting his achievements.

Mark Jarrett is a former Social Studies teacher and a practicing attorney at the San Francisco office of Baker & McKenzie, the world's largest law firm. He has written *Mastering U.S. History and Government, The Key to Understanding Global Studies, The Key To Understanding U.S. History and Government, Mastering Ohio's 9th Grade Citizenship Test, Mastering Ohio's 12th Grade Citizenship Test, Comprende Tu Mundo: Su Historia, Sus Culturas,* and *Los Estados Unidos: Su Historia, Su Gobierno.* He has served as a test writer for the New York State Board of Regents, and has taught at Hofstra University. Mr. Jarrett was educated at Columbia University, the London School of Economics, the Law School of the University of California at Berkeley, and Stanford University, where he is a doctoral candidate in history.

Acknowledgments

Cover design by Peter R. Fleck. Illustrations by Ronald Scott Zimmer. Manor illustration by Alex Gardega. Maps created by Morris Kantor. Layout and typesetting by Maple Hill Press, Huntington, New York.

We wish to acknowledge use of the Global Studies syllabus of the State Education Department of New York State.

The authors also wish to thank our colleagues and good friends — Joel Fischer for his insightful comments, and Hanna Kisiel for her suggestions on the final manuscript.

The authors alone are responsible for the contents of this book and any errors it may contain.

Finally, we wish to thank our wives, Donna, Joan and Goska, without whose help this work would not have been possible.

HOW THIS BOOK HELPS YOU
TO PASS GLOBAL STUDIES EXAMINATIONS

It is no secret that learning about our world today can be quite demanding. How can you be expected to learn and remember so much about so many parts of the world? With this book as your guide, you should find it less difficult and even fun to learn. *Mastering Global Studies* not only teaches you about the world around you, but gives you a framework to help you answer any test question about the subject. The following chapter-by-chapter explanations will give you an overview of the approach used in this book.

CHAPTER 1: STUDYING FOR SUCCESS

This first chapter provides general techniques to help you learn and remember key terms, concepts, and people. It is important to follow the instructions in this chapter when reading the rest of the book, if you want to do your very best. The key is to read, to understand what you have read, and then to write down what you understand in your own words and to illustrate it with a picture. Using this technique, you will be surprised at how much more successfully you can learn.

CHAPTERS 2-10: THE CONTENT AREAS

This section contains brief reviews of the most important facts you need to know about each of the areas found in the Global Studies curriculum: Africa, Latin America, the Middle East, South and Southeast Asia, China, Japan, the Commonwealth of Independent States and Europe. There is an important additional chapter that examines major "global" concerns and trends facing the world today.

Several features in each chapter are designed to help you read, understand and remember the material. Each content chapter is broken down into identical sections:

CHAPTER OPENERS. Each chapter opens with a silhouette of the content area surrounded by a mini "table of contents" giving an overview of the main topics and themes. Each chapter also contains:

- **A Photo Montage** of the area, showing important aspects of its history, people and culture.

- **Think About It** sections that provide a thought-provoking question, encouraging you to reflect about one aspect of the area you will be reading about. In addition, the most important terms and concepts are highlighted.

- **Analysis** sections ask you to think more fully about key terms and concepts or to relate them to the outside world. These sections allow you to interact with the text, and often encourage you to state your opinion about crucial events or controversial issues in global studies.

- **Summary** sections close each content section by reviewing the essential information you have just learned about.

- **Thinking It Over** sections ask you to re-examine some aspect of the information you provided in the opening **Think About It** section.

- **Checking Your Understanding** concludes each section with multiple-choice and essay questions about the most important terms, concepts and people.

- **Vocabulary Cards** require you to fill in the essential information about the most important terms and concepts in the text. Diamonds (◆) appear in the margins to help you to locate the information to complete these cards.

GEOGRAPHY. This section uses text and maps to familiarize you with how the major physical features, climate, resources, and geography of the region have affected its history and culture.

HISTORY. This section contains the most important historical events and developments that you are expected to know and understand. The number of detailed facts is limited, so that you will be better able to understand and remember those main developments that really are important.

SYSTEMS. This section explains how people in the region live, work, and govern themselves. It deals with the principal governmental, economic, social and religious systems of the area. A special section on the arts then helps you understand something about the culture of the region.

IMPORTANT PEOPLE. There are a small number of individuals who have played a significant role in shaping the history of every region. This section presents, in a newspaper-style format, these key people in short biographical paragraphs containing information about their contributions.

CONCERNS. Each area of the world today is affected by problems and concerns. Knowledge of these issues is essential to a fuller understanding of the area. This section contains the most up-to-date information about these concerns, providing you with maximum understanding of world problems and current events.

SUMMARIZING YOUR UNDERSTANDING. Most high school students make the mistake of studying for a test just by reading. To do your best on a test, you must practice *applying* the knowledge that you have learned. This section helps you to do this by having you summarize the key terms, concepts, and other important information discussed in the content area. Several features help you to recall the material:

- **Puzzles** — crossword, word scrambles, word circling — help you remember the definitions of the most important terms, concepts and people you read about in the chapter.

- **Paragraph Frames** provide you with a paragraph about the chapter, with certain key words removed. You must find and insert these words in the proper part of the paragraph.

- **Visual Organizers** sharpen your recall skills by asking about the most important causes, results, and explanations found in the chapter.

- A **Describing Historical Events** organizer helps you review the "who," "what," "where," "when" and "why" of important events explained in the chapter.

TESTING YOUR UNDERSTANDING. Each chapter ends by testing your understanding of the material found in the unit. The test consists of short-answer questions and essay questions similar to those found on most school and statewide comprehensive tests.

SPECIAL FEATURES. Three special features are included in each content chapter:

- **Skill Builders** help you to understand the various kinds of data-based materials found on global studies examinations — maps, tables, political cartoons, bar graphs, line graphs, pie charts, time lines, and readings. These skills are developed gradually, with one type of Skill-Builder in each chapter.

- **Test-Helpers** look at the major themes that run through the content areas — geography, historical events, the impact of technology, the role of religion, and the problems of developing nations. Each **Testing Your Understanding** section then applies what you have learned by requiring you to answer an essay question on that particular theme.

- **Checklists** present the major terms, concepts and people found in the chapter. You are asked to mentally review each item in the checklist before going on to the next chapter. Items that you may have forgotten or are unsure about should be re-read.

CHAPTER 11: A FINAL REVIEW

How much can you recall about each of the areas you have read about? This chapter reviews the major vocabulary, people, events, and religions you have learned about, by using charts and graphic organizers. A **Glossary** section then provides a comprehensive list of key terms and concepts you should know.

CHAPTER 12: A FINAL PRACTICE TEST

How much have you learned? This section allows you to inventory your knowledge of Global Studies by providing you with a practice examination. If you have carefully read through this book and completed all the exercises and chapter tests, you should do well on the test. We recommend that you take this final practice test under "real" test conditions. Take it with your class in a quiet place, and re-view your answers with your teacher or tutor. Once you have passed this practice exam, you will feel confident about taking any school or statewide comprehensive test in global studies.

By paying careful attention to your teachers at school, by completing your homework assignments, and by preparing for school or statewide global studies examinations with this book, you can be confident that you will do your best.

TABLE OF CONTENTS

STUDENT ACTIVITIES

MAPS

MAP OF THE WORLD

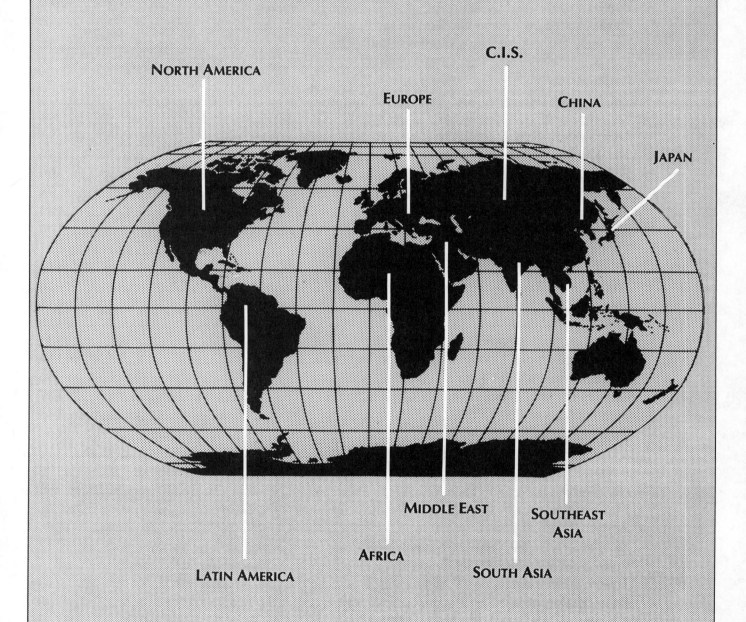

CHAPTER 1

STUDYING FOR SUCCESS

In order to graduate from high school, many students must take and pass a course in global studies. This means that you will need to pass a number of global studies examinations. It would be nice if just wanting to pass these exams were enough, but it is not. You have to work hard to prepare for them. Most of the examinations contain questions that require knowledge of important terms, concepts and people. This chapter contains techniques to help you learn and remember this information.

REMEMBERING IMPORTANT INFORMATION

KEY TERMS

Terms are the basic units of history. They are words or phrases that refer to specific things that have happened (*World War II*) or existed (*the United Nations*). These terms are of several different basic types. The following chart is one way of classifying them. Complete the chart by filling in the right-hand column.

TYPE	EXAMPLE	ANOTHER EXAMPLE (FILL IN)
Society	Egyptian	_____
Place	Africa	_____
Document	Magna Carta	_____
Event	World War II	_____
Group	Serfs	_____
Policy	Containment	_____
Organization	United Nations	_____
Time Period	Middle Ages	_____
Religion	Islam	_____

■ **What To Focus On When Learning A New Term**. Although each test question usually asks that you know **what** the term is, test questions may also ask for different kinds of things depending on the type of term. It is therefore important to understand different things about each type of term. For example:

TYPE OF TERM	WHAT TO FOCUS ON
Place	its location or significance
Document	its purpose or effect
Event	its causes / effects
Group	its goal / living conditions
Policy	its goal / purpose
Organization	its goal / purpose
Time Period	its characteristics
Religion	its beliefs

ANALYSIS

Please complete:

Term: **What to focus on:**

- Judaism   • _____

- French Revolution   • _____

- Creoles   • _____

- Japan   • _____

■ **Using Index Cards**. One reason many students find history to be such a difficult subject is because they do not know how to study properly. Simply reading and re-reading the pages of a book will not help you to learn and remember the many facts, dates and events that you encounter. You have to take a more active approach, deciding what is important, and thinking about it. One of the best ways to learn a new term is to use an index card. In this book, we will ask you to prepare index cards on some of the most important terms at the end of each section.

- You will be directed to write some information about the term on the front of the card. You will be asked to identify the term, and — depending upon the type of term — its special focus points.

- You will then turn over the index card and draw a picture of what you think the term should look like. This turning of written information into a **picture** helps clarify the meaning of the term. To change a person's ideas about a term from one medium (**words**) to another (**pictures**) is only possible if that person truly understands the term. By "seeing" the key points of a term you have created an impression in your brain. This process helps you remember the term. Look at the following example:

SOUTH AFRICA

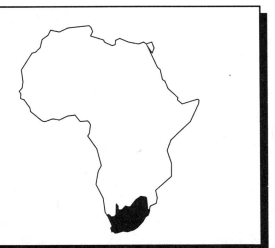

What is it?
It is one of the largest countries in Africa.

Location: It is located at the southern end of the African continent.

Note: Your drawing can appear on the front of the card as shown, or on the back of the card. If the pictures are only on the back of the cards, you can study by looking at the pictures and trying to recall what the other side of the card says.

KEY CONCEPTS

In most global studies courses, there are also important key **concepts** for you to learn and remember. Concepts are the building blocks of knowledge — they are ways of grouping individual things, rather than the things themselves. Concepts give a name to things that may be ideas, systems or patterns. Some examples of concepts are:

IDEAS	SYSTEMS	PATTERNS
Ethnocentrism	Democracy	Imperialism
Animism	Mercantilism	Balance of Power
Monotheism	Capitalism	Revolution
Machismo	Communism	Isolationism
Developing Nations	Nazism	Social Mobility
Pollution	Totalitarianism	Extended Family

Most questions about concepts ask you either to give

- the *meaning* or *definition* of the concept, or
- an *example* that shows what the concept is.

When you learn a new concept, it will therefore be helpful for you to know both the definition of the concept and an example that illustrates what the concept is.

Your memory will again be helped if you translate this information about the concept into picture form. Each time you read about an important concept, you should therefore fill out an index card similar to the following example:

CULTURE

Definition: Culture describes a people's language, attitudes, customs and beliefs.

Example: Masks are used in many African societies. They are worn during dances and tribal ceremonies. They are part of the culture of these societies.

(Your drawing may appear on the front, as shown, or on the back of the card.)

KEY PEOPLE

There are many famous individuals in world history for you to learn about and remember. Most questions will ask you why they are famous. It will therefore be helpful when you learn about a new person if you learn and remember:

- where and when the person lived
- the person's major beliefs or actions
- the person's impact (*how the person affected other people, ideas or events*)

Again, one of the best ways to learn and remember this information is to translate it into picture form, as shown in the example on the following page:

KARL MARX

Where and When: Europe, 1800s.

What Marx Believed:
1. Workers were taken advantage of by the owners of private property.
2. Workers rather than employers should own the means of production.
3. This could be achieved through revolution.

Impact:
1. His beliefs came to be known as Communism.
2. Some countries adopted Communism as a way of life. For example, China is a Communist nation.

(Your drawing may appear on the front, as shown,
or on the back of the card.)

Once you have learned the key terms, concepts and people, start to think about how they relate to each other. Which terms illustrate the concepts you have learned? Which people were involved in which events?

HOW TO ANSWER
MULTIPLE CHOICE QUESTIONS

Once you have learned the key terms, concepts and people, you will be ready to take a test. However, to do your best on any test, it helps to know something about the form of the test questions. This section reviews some of the main types of multiple choice questions found on global studies examinations.

RECOGNITION OF TERMS, CONCEPTS AND PEOPLE

You are responsible for knowing the major characteristics of important terms, concepts and people. Here are some examples of the many ways these questions may be worded (keep in mind that the terms shown in brackets will change).

- Which is a major goal of the [*United Nations*]?
- Which is an essential feature of [*democracy*]?
- Which statement about [*Gandhi's beliefs*] is most accurate?

To help you recognize the major terms, concepts and people, each chapter will present the major terms, concepts, and people in **boldfaced** print.

COMPARE AND CONTRAST

We often compare and contrast two things in order to understand how they are *alike* or how they are *different*. Compare-and-contrast questions might appear as follows:

- A similarity between the political system of [*the United States*] and that of [*India*] is that both ....
- [*Islam, Judaism, and Christianity*] are similar in that they all ....
- The actions of [*Lenin and Castro*] were strongly influenced by ....

> As you read through the chapters in this book, test yourself by comparing and contrasting **new** names and terms with those you already know. Try to understand and remember what these things have in common and how they differ.

CAUSE AND EFFECT

Cause-and-effect questions test your understanding of the relationship between the **cause** of (*the reason for*) an action and its **effect** (what happened directly *because of the action or event*). Be careful to understand which question is being asked for — cause or effect. Remember also that each event often has several causes and several effects. These types of questions might appear as follows:

- Which was a cause / result of [*World War I*]?
- Which was a significant cause / result of [*colonialism*]?
- Which development led to the other three?

> To help you focus on cause-and-effect type questions, important cause and effect relationships are identified and stressed in each chapter of this book.

DATA-BASED QUESTIONS

These questions are based on some form of data presented as part of the question. The data may appear in maps, tables of information, political cartoons, line graphs, pie charts, bar graphs, and timelines. But no matter what type of data you find, there are usually two major types of questions you will be asked.

■ **Comprehension Questions.** These questions ask you to find a specific item, figure or number presented in the data. A comprehension question may take different forms; here are two examples.

- The [*eagle*] in the cartoon is a symbol representing ....
- In which year was [*auto production*] the greatest?

■ **Conclusion Questions.** These questions ask you to make a conclusion by putting together several elements from the data presented. A conclusion question may take different forms; here are two examples.

- Which statement is correct?
- Which statement is best supported by the data in the chart?

> To help you answer data-based questions, special **Skill Builder** sections are found throughout this book.

TOOLS FOR IMPROVED LEARNING

To help you organize your thoughts and remember the most important terms, concepts and people, the following features are found throughout this book:

ANALYSIS
These special sections reinforce your understanding of key terms, concepts and people by asking you to think more fully about them or to relate them to the outside world.

VOCABULARY CARDS
At the end of each section of every chapter, you will find *Vocabulary Cards* to fill in. They are similar to index cards. By using these cards or by creating your own set of index cards, you will build up a group of cards that are extremely helpful in preparing for class tests and examinations.

MULTIPLE CHOICE QUESTIONS
At the end of each section, multiple choice questions help you to see what you've learned and what you may need to review.

CHECKLIST
Following the content section of each chapter is a *Checklist*, containing the essential terms, concepts and names in the chapter. You are asked to check the items that you are able to recall and explain. If you cannot remember an item, you are referred back to the page that explains it. If you do this consistently at the end of each chapter, you will greatly reinforce your understanding of the most important material.

GRAPHIC ORGANIZERS
Following the content section of each chapter, there is a *Summarizing Your Understanding* section. In this section you will be asked to complete a series of activities that are designed to reinforce your understanding of the material.

TESTING YOUR UNDERSTANDING
Each chapter contains a *Testing Your Understanding* section. In this section you will be tested on the most important terms, concepts and people appearing in that chapter.

GEOGRAPHY

- Size and Location
- Geographic Features and Their Effects

CONCERNS

- South Africa and Apartheid
- Tribalism versus Nationalism
- Hunger and Famine

HISTORY

- Early Civilizations
- Slavery and the Slave Trade
- European Imperialism in Africa
- Africans Gain Their Independence

CHAPTER 2

SUB-SAHARAN AFRICA

IMPORTANT PEOPLE

- Jomo Kenyatta
- Nelson Mandela
- Desmond Tutu
- F. W. de Klerk

SYSTEMS

- Government
- Economy
- Society
- Religion
- The Arts

What do these pictures show you about Africa? _____
_____
_____
_____
_____

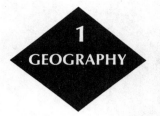

In this section you will read about the major geographic features of sub-Saharan Africa, and how these features have affected its people and its history.

THINK ABOUT IT

Look at the map of Africa on page 12. What do you think it shows us about Africa's major geographic features? _____

_____

_____

Important Terms: As you read this section, look for the following terms:

◆ **Sub-Saharan Africa**   ◆ **Sahara Desert**
◆ **Nile River**   ◆ **Savanna**

To help you find these terms, the ◆ symbol appears in the margin where the term is explained.

SIZE AND LOCATION

Africa is the second largest **continent** (*large land mass*), and contains more than 50 different nations. In the north, Africa is separated from Europe by the Mediterranean Sea. To Africa's east lies the Red Sea and Indian Ocean. On the west, Africa is bordered by the Atlantic Ocean.

◆   Many geographers classify Africa into two regions, North Africa and **sub-Saharan Africa** (*Africa south of the Sahara*). They consider sub-Saharan Africa — with its different climate, land features and life styles — as a separate region.

MAJOR GEOGRAPHIC FEATURES AND THEIR EFFECTS

Global studies examinations often contain several kinds of data-based questions. Knowing the different types of data and learning how to interpret them will be a regular feature found in every chapter of this book. This section contains a map of the physical features of Africa. Learning how to read this and other maps is the focus of the following **Skill Builder**.

SKILL BUILDER:
READING
A MAP

WHAT IS A MAP?

A map is a small diagram of an area of land. Many maps show the political divisions between countries, or the major geographic features of an area, but there is almost no limit to the different kinds of information that can be shown on a map. Different types of maps can be found in a special reference book called an **atlas**.

KEYS TO UNDERSTANDING A MAP

First, look at its major parts:

Title. The title will usually tell you what information is found on the map. For example, the title of the map on page 12 is "GEOGRAPHY OF AFRICA." It shows the main physical features — deserts, mountains, rivers — of Africa.

Direction. A direction indicator that often looks like a small compass shows the four basic directions: **north**, **south**, **east** and **west**:

Most maps show north at the top and south at the bottom. On our map of Africa, the direction indicator is in the upper right corner.

Scale. The scale — usually a marked line — tells the size of an area shown on a map. For example, at the very bottom of our map you will see a line marked **Scale of Miles**:

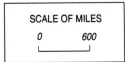

This line is about ¹/₂" (half an inch) long. Notice also that the scale indicates that ¹/₂" is equal to **600 miles**. Here the mapmaker is telling you that the distance between two points ¹/₂" apart on this map would be 600 miles. If two points are 2 inches apart in the map, then they are (600 x 4) = 2400 miles apart in the real place.

Legend or Key. The legend or key unlocks the information found on a map. It lists the symbols used and tells what each symbol represents. The "key" in our map on page 12 tells you that all the gray-shaded areas are Africa's savanna regions:

⊞ SAVANNA REGION

INTERPRETING A MAP

Read the title, to know what type of map you are looking at.

➤ If it is a political map, the lines show the political boundaries between countries, while black dots or circles are often used to indicate major cities:

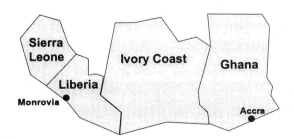

➤ On other maps, the legend or symbols are a key to unlocking the meaning. Maps may show population density, climate, geographic features, or a nation's history.

As you read the following geographic descriptions, see how many of them you can find on the map on page 12.

DESERTS

Deserts are extremely dry regions, generally unsuitable for humans to live in. There is not enough water to drink or to grow crops. The **Sahara Desert**, which takes up most of North Africa, is the world's largest. This desert has separated Africans living north and south of it, because people had trouble crossing it. For many centuries, the Sahara isolated sub-Saharan Africa from the rest of the world.

SAVANNAS

Much of Africa is **savanna** (*land where tall, wild grasses grow*). The savannas are the best land in Africa for growing crops and raising livestock. Most Africans live in the savannas, or along the coasts where fishing provides food.

TROPICAL RAIN FORESTS

The hot and humid African rain forests get from 60 to 100 inches of rainfall a year. This climate produces thick forest and jungle areas, making travel difficult. Rain forests are home to many types of plant and animal life not found elsewhere.

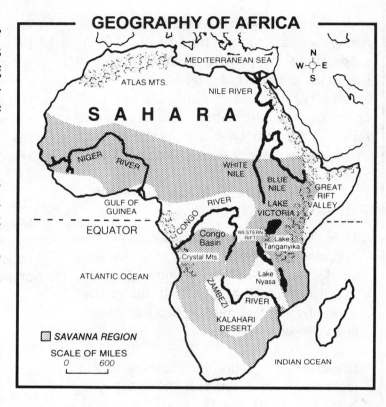

RIVERS

Africa has several major rivers — the Nile, Zaire (Congo), Zambezi and Niger. Rivers provide fresh drinking water, and water for agriculture, industry and hydroelectric power. In Africa, river systems are hard to use for travel because they are not connected to each other and have many rapids and waterfalls along their course. The **Nile**, the world's longest river, flows 4,150 miles from central Africa to the Mediterranean. The banks of the Nile provide some of Africa's richest farmland, and the Nile river valley was once the home of one of the world's oldest known civilizations — the Egyptians.

COASTLINE

Africa has few natural harbors (*places in which ships can dock safely*). As a result, trade between Africa and the rest of the world has been difficult.

GEOGRAPHIC BARRIERS

Africa's mountains, deserts, lakes and rivers have kept different groups of people apart. As a result each African group or tribe developed its own separate culture, language and traditions.

CLIMATE

Most of Africa is warm, with hot summers and mild winters. The amount of rainfall differs greatly; desert areas receive too little rain for planting crops, while other areas receive too much rain. The amount of rainfall an area receives usually determines whether it becomes a jungle, desert or grasslands area. These conditions affect where people live, what they eat, and how they dress.

RESOURCES

Africa is rich in many resources, especially diamonds, gold and oil. These resources attracted European imperialist powers in the late 19th and early 20th centuries. These minerals and other natural resources make up the major exports of Africa, providing a basis for its future economic growth.

Picture at right: Workers in a South African diamond mine

ANALYSIS

Deserts, savannas and tropical rain forests are all found in Africa. Which of these regions do

you think you might want to live in? _____ Explain your answer:

_____

_____

SUMMING UP: GEOGRAPHY

Africa is the second largest continent in the world. Its varied geography and climate help to explain some of the differences in the ways the people of Africa live.

THINKING IT OVER

Now that you have read this section, what items can you add to your list (from page 10) of Africa's

major geographic features? _____

_____

SUB-SAHARAN AFRICA

Describe it: *The area south of the Sahara Desert.*

Difference from North Africa: *It has different climates and land features; its people have different histories and lifestyles.*

SAHARA

Describe it: _____

One effect it had on Africa's people: _____

_____

NILE

Describe it: _____

One effect it had on Africa's people: _____

_____

SAVANNA

Describe it: _____

One effect it had on Africa's people: _____

_____

1 The Zaire, Niger, and Nile are the names of
  1 mountain ranges
  2 rivers
  3 lakes
  4 deserts

2 "Sub-Saharan Africa" refers to those countries that are
  1 south of the Sahara Desert
  2 in the Sahara Desert
  3 largely rain forest
  4 largely desert

3 One effect of the Sahara Desert on Africa has been to
  1 unite all Africans against a common enemy
  2 separate sub-Saharan Africans from northern Africans
  3 develop hydro-electric power for Southern Africa
  4 provide a vacation resort for Africans

4 Which item would tell us the most about Africa's geography?
  1 a study of famous African business leaders
  2 a novel about the transatlantic slave trade
  3 an outline map of Africa's coastline
  4 a dictionary

5 A person living on Africa's savanna would most likely work at
  1 cutting lumber
  2 mining gold
  3 raising livestock
  4 deep-sea fishing

6 Preserving the rain forest is important to Africans because rain forests
  1 provide a source of water for desert regions
  2 are the home of many forms of animal and plant life
  3 increase the amount of fertile farmland
  4 protect Africans from foreign invasions

In this section you will read about the major historical developments in Africa, from its earliest civilizations to its present role in the world community.

THINK ABOUT IT

Look at the maps of Africa on pages 17 and 18. What do you think they tell us about Africa's history?

_____

_____

_____

Important Terms: As you read this section, look for the following terms:

◆ **Early African Empires**   ◆ **Atlantic Slave Trade**
◆ **Imperialism**   ◆ **Nationalism**
◆ **Cultural Diffusion**   ◆ **Organization of African Unity**

TIMELINE OF HISTORICAL EVENTS							
1870s	**1902**	**1948**	**1957**	**1964**	**1986**	**1990**	**1991**
"Scramble for Africa" begins	British defeat the Boers in South Africa	South Africa begins apartheid	Ghana becomes independent	Nelson Mandela sent to prison	Wole Soyinka first African to win Nobel Prize in literature	Nelson Mandela freed	Africa has 54 independent nations; South Africa announces end of apartheid

EARLY CIVILIZATIONS

ANCIENT AFRICA

Some scientists believe that Africa was the birthplace of humanity. Since few written records exist, little is known about ancient Africa's culture and civilization. The first known African civilization was ancient Egypt. You will read more about this civilization in the chapter on the Middle East. The ancient Egyptians had important trading links with several cultures further south on the Nile River, including the Kush in the Sudan and the Axum in Ethiopia.

Since the terms "culture" and "civilization" will be used frequently, it is important that you understand them:

➤ **Culture** describes a people's language, attitudes, customs and beliefs. Every group has its own culture, or ways of doing things.

➤ **Civilization** is an advanced form of culture. It usually includes people who (1) lived in cities and (2) had some form of writing.

◆ EARLY WEST AFRICAN EMPIRES

Between 500 and 800 A.D. several empires developed in West Africa. (If you have trouble understanding dates and time periods, see a full explanation of them starting on page 242.) The wealth and power of these empires came from controlling the trade routes between north and western Africa. Three of the most important empires were:

➤ **Empire of Ghana** (500-1200): Profits from selling gold and salt to Arab traders (*people north of the Sahara Desert*) made this kingdom very prosperous.

➤ **Empire of Mali** (1200-1400): Its riches came from selling gold, iron and copper. This kingdom was known for the wealth of its most famous king, Mansa Musa. The Mali people were proud of their university at Timbuktu, which was a center of Muslim scholarship.

➤ **Songhai Empire** (700-1600): This empire's wealth was based on trade and agriculture. With its merchants, doctors and scholars it became a showcase of advanced civilization, attracting caravans of traders from Europe and Asia to its cities.

EARLY CENTRAL AFRICAN KINGDOMS

Other important states developed in central Africa. **Benin** was a powerful kingdom in present-day Nigeria, known for its artworks. **Zimbabwe** was a kingdom to the south. Its wealth was based on its control of valuable gold mines.

SLAVERY AND THE SLAVE TRADE

Slavery has existed in Africa since ancient times. As Africans gradually came into contact with other cultures, trading of slaves increased. Arab traders in East Africa helped spread the Islamic religion and extended the slave trade. European explorers sailed along the coast of West Africa in search of new ocean routes to Asia. Their explorations led to the start of the slave trade across the Atlantic in the 1500s.

◆ THE ATLANTIC SLAVE TRADE

Africans were captured in raids by other African tribes, and then sold to European traders to provide slave labor in North and South America. The captured Africans were chained in the holds of slave ships, tightly packed together. Many Africans died because of these conditions during the trips across the Atlantic Ocean. People made large profits trading enslaved people for guns and bullets. The enslaved people were forced to work long hours on sugar, cotton or tobacco plantations.

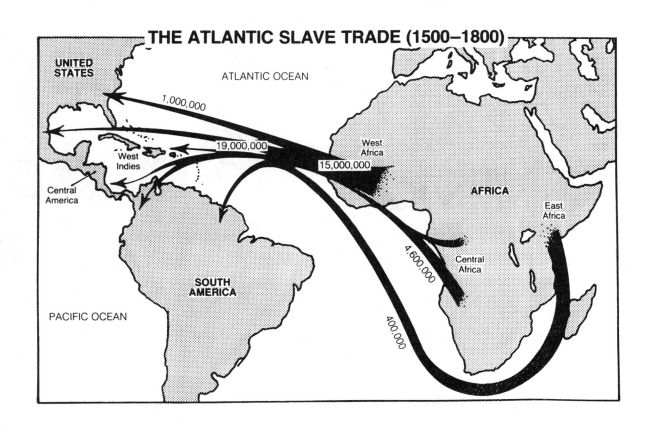

THE ATLANTIC SLAVE TRADE (1500–1800)

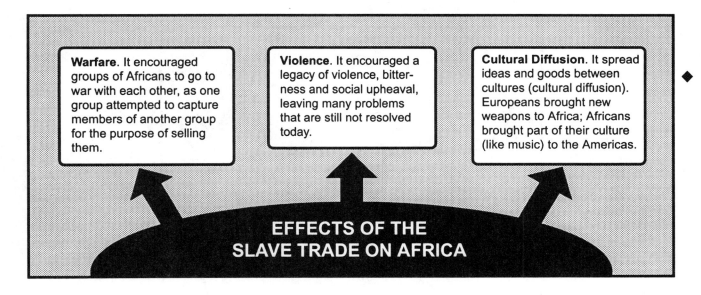

Warfare. It encouraged groups of Africans to go to war with each other, as one group attempted to capture members of another group for the purpose of selling them.

Violence. It encouraged a legacy of violence, bitterness and social upheaval, leaving many problems that are still not resolved today.

Cultural Diffusion. It spread ideas and goods between cultures (cultural diffusion). Europeans brought new weapons to Africa; Africans brought part of their culture (like music) to the Americas.

EFFECTS OF THE
SLAVE TRADE ON AFRICA

THE SLAVE TRADE ENDS

World-wide opposition to slavery slowly grew. Reformers, declaring slavery to be immoral, worked until slavery and the slave trade were ended by the mid-1800s. However, the end of the slave trade was followed by a period of European imperialism in Africa.

EUROPEAN IMPERIALISM IN AFRICA

◆ **Imperialism** is the political and economic control of one country or area by another. The area being controlled was called a **"colony,"** and the imperial power was sometimes called the "mother country."

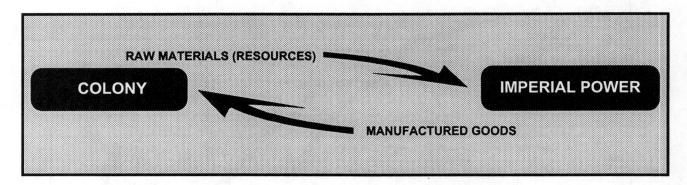

Between 1870 and 1890, European countries took control of almost all of Africa, which mostly contained various tribal homelands. This period has been called Europe's "**Scramble for Africa**." For example, the area of present-day Nigeria and Egypt became colonies of Great Britain. Other parts of Africa came under the control of other European countries.

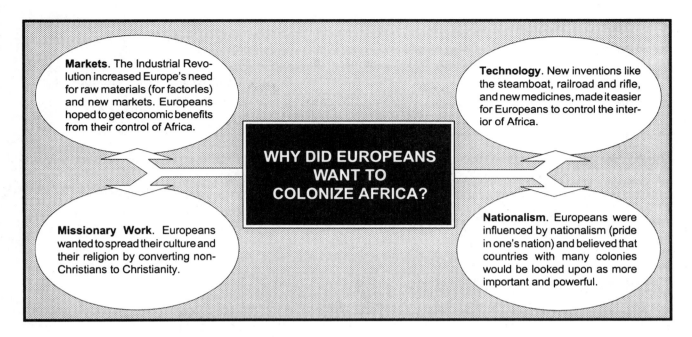

Markets. The Industrial Revolution increased Europe's need for raw materials (for factories) and new markets. Europeans hoped to get economic benefits from their control of Africa.

Technology. New inventions like the steamboat, railroad and rifle, and new medicines, made it easier for Europeans to control the interior of Africa.

WHY DID EUROPEANS WANT TO COLONIZE AFRICA?

Missionary Work. Europeans wanted to spread their culture and their religion by converting non-Christians to Christianity.

Nationalism. Europeans were influenced by nationalism (pride in one's nation) and believed that countries with many colonies would be looked upon as more important and powerful.

EFFECTS OF EUROPEAN IMPERIALISM

European imperialism had many important effects on Africa:

➤ **Economic**. Europeans took many of Africa's resources. Many Africans were forced to work long hours for low pay. Some improvements were made in transportation and communication, and some new job opportunities were made available. But on balance, European rulers probably received more economic benefits than they gave back in return.

➤ **Political**. Europeans divided Africa into different colonies, without regard to local tribal or cultural boundaries. People who belonged to the same tribal or ethnic group were separated. Later, when these colonies became independent nations, differences among tribal groups in the same country caused problems. The Nigerian Civil War of 1967-1970 between the Hausa people of northern Nigeria and the Ibo people of southern Nigeria illustrates this problem.

➤ **Social**. Many Europeans acted as if they were better than Africans. Some Europeans attempted to force their way of life on Africans. This tended to weaken traditional African family and tribal group ties.

➤ **Health**. Europeans brought their ideas about medicine and health to their African colonies. This often prevented diseases and resulted in longer life for Africans. However, in some cases Europeans brought diseases which Africans had never been exposed to, causing many deaths.

AFRICANS GAIN THEIR INDEPENDENCE

After World War II, Africans moved to bring about an end to imperialism. The feeling of nationalism arose throughout Africa. **Nationalism** is the belief that people who share common characteristics ◆ (language, customs and history) should have their own nation. The spread of nationalism brought about the desire among Africans to put an end to European rule, and to govern themselves.

CAUSES OF AFRICAN NATIONALISM

Because Africans had helped fight European dictators like Adolf Hitler in World War II, many of them refused to accept European rule after the war. Also, the independence of India from Great Britain helped spread ideas about freedom. In addition, the European nations were too weakened by the loss of lives and property in World War II to resist the movements for independence.

INDEPENDENCE

During the 1950s and 1960s most African nations gained their independence. The first of these was the Gold Coast, a British colony in West Africa. In 1957 the Gold Coast became the independent nation of Ghana — named after the ancient African kingdom. Most African nations obtained their freedom peacefully. In a few cases, however, independence was only gained after bloody civil war. The **Organization of African Unity (O.A.U.)** was founded in 1963 to promote African unity and to provide a place where African nations could discuss their common problems.

PROBLEMS FACING THE NEW NATIONS

Most of the newly independent African nations faced many problems. As you remember, the European imperialists divided Africa in a way that was convenient for them. Traditional groups (or tribes) were split up into different colonies. At the same time, tribes with a history of conflict between them were sometimes forced to live side by side in the same area. When African countries gained independence, serious problems faced the new leaders who had to unite these tribal groups. In addition, most countries were left with underdeveloped economies and few skilled workers. As a result, dictatorships were established in many of these countries, leading to rebellions and civil wars.

SUMMING UP: HISTORY

Many scientists believe that Africa was the birthplace of humanity. There were some very important ancient African kingdoms. Africa's development suffered greatly from the Atlantic slave trade and the "scramble" for African colonies. Since the 1950s, most African nations have achieved independence.

THINKING IT OVER

What additional items about sub-Saharan Africa's history can you now add to your list (from page 15)? _____

CHECKING YOUR UNDERSTANDING

Directions: Complete each of the following cards. Then answer the multiple choice questions that follow.

IMPERIALISM

Definition: *When one country takes control of another.*

Effects on Africa: *Europeans built roads and hospitals but took many natural resources from Africa.*

EARLY AFRICAN EMPIRES

Their names:_____

What did they control?_____

_____

ATLANTIC SLAVE TRADE

What was it? _____

Effects on Africa: _____

_____

NATIONALISM

Definition:_____

Effects on Africa: _____

_____

CULTURAL DIFFUSION

Definition: _____

Example: _____

_____

ORG. OF AFRICAN UNITY (O. A. U.)

What is it? _____

Its purpose: _____

_____

---

1 Which event occurred first?
  1 African nations became independent from Europe.
  2 The Mali civilization began.
  3 The Atlantic slave trade ended.
  4 Africa was colonized by Europeans.

2 The term "imperialism" refers to the
  1 division of a nation into smaller states
  2 unification of a people under a central government
  3 political and economic control of one nation by another
  4 military system of any country

3 During the 1500s and 1600s Europeans were interested in Africa because
  1 it had important spices
  2 oil was discovered in South Africa
  3 they wanted slaves for the "New World"
  4 it had food to export

4 In looking at the history of most African nations, one sees that
  1 they have been colonized by European nations
  2 they have fought a war at one time against the United States
  3 democracy has been the main type of government
  4 they share a common language

5 A major purpose of the Organization of African Unity is to
   1 end European colonialism in Africa
   2 develop overseas empires for African countries
   3 encourage cooperation among African peoples
   4 increase the birth rate in Africa

6 An African listening to Michael Jackson's latest song is an example of
   1 nationalism
   2 cultural diffusion
   3 imperialism
   4 self-determination

7 Which would be an example of African nationalism?
   1 African nations entering organizations with their former colonial rulers
   2 European nations increasing the number of their colonies in Africa
   3 African nations breaking away from their former colonial rulers
   4 European nations dividing the African continent among themselves

8 Which term is used to describe a people's language, customs and beliefs?
   1 urbanization   3 culture
   2 sectionalism   4 imperialism

3
SYSTEMS

In this section you will read about sub-Saharan Africa's major political institutions, economic development, social structure, religions and art.

THINK ABOUT IT

Find the meaning of "extended family" and "tribe" in this section or in the glossary (at the back of the book). These terms will help you understand the following section.

Extended Family: _____

_____

Tribe: _____

_____

Important Terms: As you read this section, look for the following terms:

◆ subsistence farming   ◆ animism
◆ nationalized   ◆ urbanization

GOVERNMENT

In the period following national independence, the leaders of many African countries allowed only one political party. Very often these countries were ruled by the same nationalist leaders or military leaders who had helped win independence. The army played an important role in keeping such rulers in power. Most people had few rights, and real elections were never held. Recently, there has been a move towards more democratic government. Popular elections have been held in Angola, Mozambique, Tanzania, and many other African nations. Voters in these nations can now choose between candidates from opposing political parties with different policies.

ECONOMY

Providing people with higher standards of living is a major task for most African nations. Many Africans do **subsistence farming** (*growing just enough food to meet the needs of their own families*). Often ◆ traditional farming methods lead to the erosion of the soil. After independence, African leaders tried to encourage the growth of industries. Some borrowed money from banks around the world, while other leaders **nationalized** (*took control of property which formerly belonged to private citizens*) ◆ businesses, banks and factories. These attempts at industrialization were only partly successful. Efforts to improve the economy were also hurt by rapid population growth, unfavorable changes in climate, and the spread of diseases in some African nations. In many African countries, living standards are no better now than they were 30 years ago.

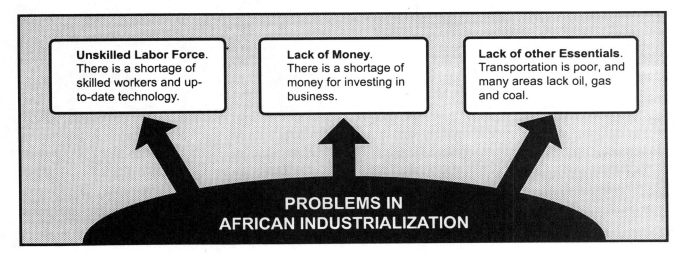

SOCIETY

People of many races live in Africa. Most are black, but large numbers of Africans are Arabs. Smaller numbers come from Europe and Asia. In traditional African society, most people lived as part of an **extended family**, which includes many relatives —aunt, grandparents, cousins — living together in ◆ the same village. Villagers who spoke the same language and shared the same customs formed a **tribe**. ◆ Today, many Africans still feel a greater sense of loyalty to their tribe than to their nation.

Efforts at industrialization in Africa have caused **urbanization** (*people moving from rural villages to* ◆ *the cities, in search of jobs and better living conditions*). This urbanization movement is leading to important social changes.

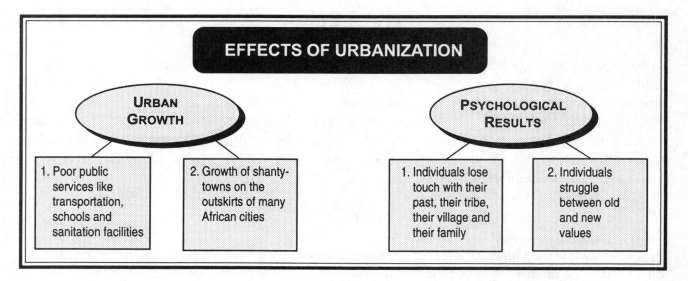

RELIGION

Traditional religions, practiced by Africans since ancient times, are still widespread today. An important part of many of these religions is **animism** (*the belief that every object in nature has its own spirit, and that people's ancestors in the spirit world watch over them in the living world*). Traditional African life was filled with religious customs and ceremonies. Islam has also had an important influence on Africans. Today, as many as one in four Africans is **Muslim** (*a believer in the Islamic faith*). Most African Muslims are Arabs, living north of the Sahara. Europeans spread Christianity in Africa, and there are now about as many Christians as Muslims.

African Muslims praying at a mosque in Mali

THE ARTS

The arts played an important role in traditional African social life. Many Africans consider art a form of communication with the spirit world. Various art forms gave each tribe its own identity. The most famous art forms are the mask and figurine. Africans are also famous for their music and dance, based on drum rhythms. These art forms have strongly influenced Western music and dance, especially jazz and rock music.

(*Picture at left: Gold alloy pendant made by the Akan people of the Ivory Coast.*)

SUMMING UP: AFRICA'S SYSTEMS

GOVERNMENT. Since independence many African countries have been ruled by military dictators, who allow only one political party to exist. Recently, some African nations have introduced more democratic forms of government.

ECONOMY. Standards of living in Africa remain low. African leaders are attempting to bring about greater industrialization.

SOCIETY. Africa is a land of many races. In sub-Saharan Africa, the majority of Africans are black, but there are other important minorities. Many Africans follow traditional ways of life. However, the movement to the cities, increased schooling and improved communications are leading to important changes in African lifestyles.

RELIGION. Animism is common among the traditional religions practiced by many groups of Africans. Islam's influence is growing. There are also large numbers of African Christians.

THE ARTS. The arts, especially music and dance, play an important role in traditional and modern-day Africa.

THINKING IT OVER

After reading this section about Africa's systems, what other important terms besides "extended family" and "tribe" do you think should be included? _____

_____

_____

CHECKING YOUR UNDERSTANDING

Directions: Complete the following cards. Then answer the multiple choice questions that follow.

SUBSISTENCE FARMING
What is it? _____
Result: _____
_____

NATIONALIZED
Definition: _____
Result: _____
_____

ANIMISM

Define it: _____

Major beliefs: _____

_____

URBANIZATION

Define it: _____

Importance: _____

_____

---

1 The term "urbanization" is best defined as
   1 an educational system found in cities
   2 a way of earning a living
   3 the movement of people from rural areas to cities
   4 government ownership of all property

2 A subsistence farmer would probably
   1 use modern farm machinery
   2 grow large quantities of crops
   3 produce just enough to meet family needs
   4 export large amounts of crops

3 Which idea is basic to animism?
   1 separation of church and state
   2 belief in only one God
   3 belief that objects in nature have spirits
   4 belief in reincarnation

4 An extended family in present-day Africa would most likely include
   1 grandparents, parents, and their children
   2 a husband, wife, and their children
   3 several wives and a husband
   4 two parents, some of their adult friends, and all of their children

5 The influence of African art forms can best be seen today in Western
   1 music and dance   3 political ideology
   2 family patterns   4 technological advances

6 Which would be an example of nationalization?
   1 a group asks for national independence
   2 the government declares ownership of private banks
   3 a leader makes himself a dictator
   4 force is used to end tribal disagreements

4 IMPORTANT PEOPLE

In this section you will read about some of the people who have played a key role in shaping the history of sub-Saharan Africa.

THINK ABOUT IT

What do you think makes a person a great leader? _____

_____

Important Names: As you read this section, look for the following names:

◆ **Jomo Kenyatta**   ◆ **Nelson Mandela**
◆ **Desmond Tutu**   ◆ **F.W. de Klerk**

THE AFRICAN TIMES

Volume II   **No. 7**

JOMO KENYATTA

While growing up in Kenya, Jomo Kenyatta became angry with the acts of discrimination blacks were suffering under British rule. He soon emerged as a leader for independence against British rule in Kenya. Accused of leading a bloody uprising, he was arrested by the British in 1952 and sent to prison until 1961. In 1963, Great Britain granted independence to Kenya. Kenyatta became its first president, a post he held until his death in 1978. He came to symbolize the independence movement in Africa.

NELSON MANDELA

In 1964, Nelson Mandela was sentenced to life in prison for his activities in the African National Congress (A.N.C.), an organization opposing apartheid (*separation of races*) in the Republic of South Africa. Soon he became the symbol of black resistance to apartheid. Released from prison after 27 years, Mandela still leads

the fight to achieve equality for black South Africans. (For a fuller discussion of Mandela, see the top of page 30.)

DESMOND TUTU

Tutu is a black Anglican archbishop who won the Nobel Peace Prize in 1985 for his efforts to bring about a non-violent end to apartheid in South Africa. He repeatedly called on the countries of the world to pressure the government of South Africa to end its policy of apartheid. Tutu's hope is to bring about social change in South Africa without civil war or violence.

F.W. DE KLERK

De Klerk, a white South African, was elected President of South Africa in 1989. He announced that his goal was to bring about the equal treatment of all citizens in South Africa. He is trying to bring about the peaceful introduction of black majority rule with safeguards for the interests of the white minority. Despite his desire to reduce racial tensions and hatred, he faces much opposition. Some white South Africans feel he is introducing changes too quickly, while many black South Africans believe he is not making changes fast enough. (For a fuller discussion of de Klerk, see page 30.)

SUMMING UP: IMPORTANT PEOPLE

Leaders of nations can often bring about important changes in their country. Jomo Kenyatta was a leader in the movement for African independence. Nelson Mandela and Desmond Tutu have shown great bravery in fighting for the rights of black South Africans. F.W. de Klerk is trying to reform the political structure in South Africa. All three have helped bring about important recent changes in South Africa.

THINKING IT OVER

Based on your definition of what makes a great leader, do any of the people you just read about deserve to be called "great?" (Yes ___ No ___) Explain who deserves the title and why.

_____

_____

CHECKING YOUR UNDERSTANDING

Directions: Complete the following cards. Then answer the multiple choice questions that follow.

JOMO KENYATTA

Where and when: _____

What he believed: _____

His importance: _____

NELSON MANDELA

Where and when: _____

What he believes: _____

His importance: _____

DESMOND TUTU

Where and when: _____

What he believes: _____

His importance: _____

F. W. DE KLERK

Where and when: _____

What he believes: _____

His importance: _____

1 Nelson Mandela and Desmond Tutu are similar in that they both sought to
   1 make Africa more industrial than agricultural
   2 run for political office
   3 put an end to the policy of apartheid
   4 achieve their goals using military force

2 Nelson Mandela is most closely associated with
   1 removing European imperialists from Africa
   2 fighting for equality for black South Africans
   3 eliminating waste in government
   4 writing African poetry

3 Mandela, Kenyatta and De Klerk are best known as
   1 economic theorists   3 political leaders
   2 military commanders   4 guerrilla fighters

4 Nelson Mandela and F.W. de Klerk are similar in that both
   1 converted their nation to Christianity
   2 have tried to expand political and human rights
   3 introduced Western technology into South Africa
   4 resisted change in South Africa

5
CONCERNS

In this section you will read about some major problems facing Africa today: apartheid, tribalism and hunger.

THINK ABOUT IT

What do you think is the greatest problem facing Africa today? _____

_____

Important Terms: As you read this section, look for the following terms:

◆ **Apartheid**   ◆ **African National Congress**
◆ **Tribalism**   ◆ **Desertification**

SOUTH AFRICA AND APARTHEID

BACKGROUND
The Dutch began to settle in South Africa in the 1600s. However, by 1898, Great Britain gained control. In 1833, Britain had ended slavery. The Dutch speaking people (called Boers), wanting to continue the practice of slavery, moved to a different area in South Africa. When the Boers discovered gold and diamonds in their new homeland, the British claimed the territory. This led to the **Boer War** (1899-1902), which the British won. In 1934, South Africa won its independence from Britain.

POLICY OF APARTHEID
Blacks, coloreds (*the South African word for people of mixed racial groups*) and Asians had little say in the newly-independent South African government. In 1948, a Dutch-speaking government was elected. This new government announced a policy known as **apartheid** (*keeping races separate*). This ◆ policy made racial segregation legal in South Africa. Apartheid prevented non-whites from traveling where they wished, living in white neighborhoods, going to school with whites, and marrying someone of a different race.

RESISTANCE TO APARTHEID

Many people, both inside and outside of South Africa, attempted to bring an end to apartheid. One
◆ group, the **African National Congress (A.N.C.)** headed by Nelson Mandela, led the fight against
apartheid. The A.N.C.'s opposition to apartheid has sometimes resulted in violence, as in 1976 in
Soweto township (*townships: places where blacks have been forced to live in South Africa*). During
the 1980s, many nations took actions against South Africa to try to bring an end to apartheid. For
example, the United States limited its trade with South Africa, and refused to lend it money.

A NEW SOUTH AFRICAN GOVERNMENT BRINGS REFORM

In 1989, white South Africans elected a new President, **F.W. de Klerk**. De Klerk has taken a number
of actions that promise hope for a better way of life for non-white South Africans.

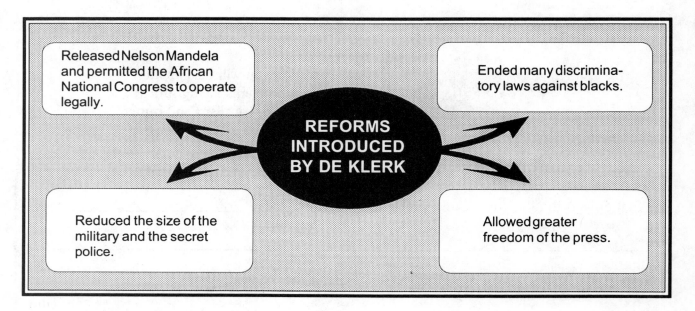

Released Nelson Mandela and permitted the African National Congress to operate legally.

Ended many discriminatory laws against blacks.

REFORMS INTRODUCED BY DE KLERK

Reduced the size of the military and the secret police.

Allowed greater freedom of the press.

THE FUTURE OF SOUTH AFRICA

South Africa's future is uncertain. Although there are many more blacks and coloreds than whites,
white South Africans still control the government. De Klerk has proposed a new South African constitution that would give black South Africans the right to vote. A transitional Executive Council
will oversee the government of South Africa until these elections are held. Another problem is violence between the A.N.C. and the **Inkatha** movement, a rival black South African group. Inkatha
members, some of whom have been friendly to white government leaders, have fought with the
A.N.C. over who should speak for black South Africans.

TRIBALISM VS. NATIONALISM

European imperialist nations divided up the African continent without regard to Africa's ethnic or
tribal boundaries. These colonies later became independent countries. This has created problems,
◆ since many Africans feel more loyal to their tribe than to their nation. **Tribalism** (*loyalty to one's
tribe*) has caused political disunity throughout much of Africa. Different tribes within the same
country often do not get along, weakening those nations.

HUNGER AND FAMINE

One of the most important problems facing Africa is hunger and **famine** (*widespread shortage of food*). Making this problem worse is the fact that while there is less food, Africa's population is constantly increasing. There are many reasons behind Africa's continuing food shortages, including **desertification** ◆ (*a desert region grows larger and farmland is lost, due to lack of rain*).

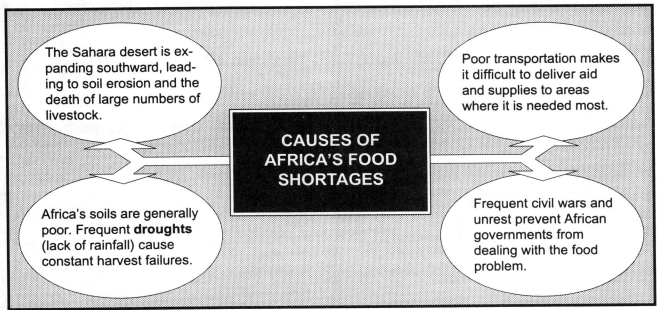

The Sahara desert is expanding southward, leading to soil erosion and the death of large numbers of livestock.

Poor transportation makes it difficult to deliver aid and supplies to areas where it is needed most.

CAUSES OF AFRICA'S FOOD SHORTAGES

Africa's soils are generally poor. Frequent **droughts** (lack of rainfall) cause constant harvest failures.

Frequent civil wars and unrest prevent African governments from dealing with the food problem.

One example of Africans facing hunger is found in **Somalia**, at the northeastern end of Africa. Rebel warlords drove out Somalia's dictator in 1991. The rebel groups, of different tribal backgrounds, were unable to cooperate to establish a new government. Civil war and several years of drought threatened millions of Somalis with starvation. In December 1992, a U.S.-led United Nations force landed in Somalia to open supply routes and to provide starving Somalis with food and medical supplies.

SUMMING UP: CONCERNS

Africa's future, while filled with hope, is uncertain. The people of South Africa must decide how power will be shared between the non-white majority and the white minority. Other countries must decide how they will build strong nations with prosperous economies.

THINKING IT OVER

Based on what you have just read, would you change your mind about what Africa's greatest problem is? (Yes____ No____) If yes, what do you *now* think is the greatest problem? _____

_____

If no, explain why: _____

_____

CHECKING YOUR UNDERSTANDING

Directions: Complete the following cards. Then answer the multiple choice questions that follow.

APARTHEID

Define it: _____

Effects on South Africa: _____

_____

_____

AFRICAN NATIONAL CONGRESS (ANC)

What is it? _____

What is its goal?_____

What should it do to achieve this goal? _____

_____

TRIBALISM

What is it? _____

Effects on Africa's political life: _____

_____

_____

DESERTIFICATION

What is it? _____

Effects on Africa's people: _____

How would you deal with this problem? _____

_____

---

1 In South Africa, the term "apartheid" refers to
   1 colonialism   3 landowners
   2 racial segregation   4 traditional farming

2 A major problem facing Africa today is
   1 the high birth rate   3 foreign colonialism
   2 Communist control   4 cultural diffusion

3 The major problem facing the Republic of South Africa today is
   1 racial inequality   3 foreign domination
   2 rising inflation   4 illegal drug traffic

4 The term "tribalism" refers to an African's
   1 loyalty to his or her tribe
   2 adoption of European customs
   3 desire to change his or her tribe
   4 attempt to unify a nation

5 Today, the main effect of tribalism in Africa is
   1 imperialism   3 disunity
   2 harmony   4 socialism

6 The political boundaries of most African nations have been most influenced by
   1 Africa's traditional tribal divisions
   2 patterns of European imperialism
   3 increased urbanization
   4 religious beliefs

7 National unity in some African nations has been hard to achieve because of
   1 the size of its population
   2 environmental reasons
   3 Communist-led rebellions
   4 loyalty to tribes

8 Why did United Nations forces intervene in Somalia in December 1992?
   1 to help victims of famine
   2 to defeat Communism
   3 to establish new colonies
   4 to stop the expansion of Somalia

SUMMARIZING YOUR UNDERSTANDING

CROSSWORD PUZZLE

Building Your Vocabulary. Use your reading of the information in this chapter and the clues below to complete this crossword puzzle.

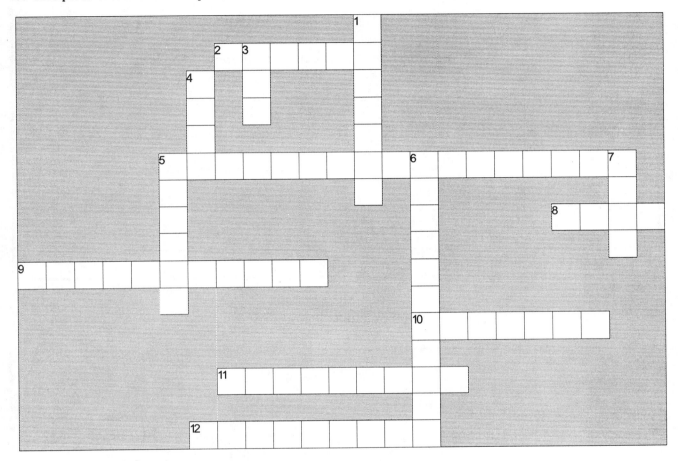

ACROSS
2. World's largest desert, located in north Africa
5. The act of exchanging different ideas between different cultures
8. Early African kingdom
9. The love a person has for his or her country
10. A religious belief that every object in nature has its own spirit
11. Policy followed in South Africa of keeping the races separate
12. Feeling of loyalty to a tribe rather than to a country

DOWN
1. Leader of anti-apartheid forces in South Africa
3. Initials for an organization opposed to apartheid
4. Anglican archbishop working to end apartheid in South Africa
5. An area controlled politically and economically by another country
6. Acquiring and controlling an overseas empire
7. World's longest river, located in northeast Africa

PARAGRAPH FRAME

Directions: Complete the blank lines in the following paragraph with information that you have learned about Africa.

WHAT IMPACT DID THE SLAVE TRADE HAVE ON SUB-SAHARAN AFRICA?

The Atlantic slave trade had a major impact on life in sub-Saharan Africa. It _____

_____ (name an effect)_____

A second effect was _____

_____

Lastly, _____

_____

Directions: Fill in the information in the organizer below.

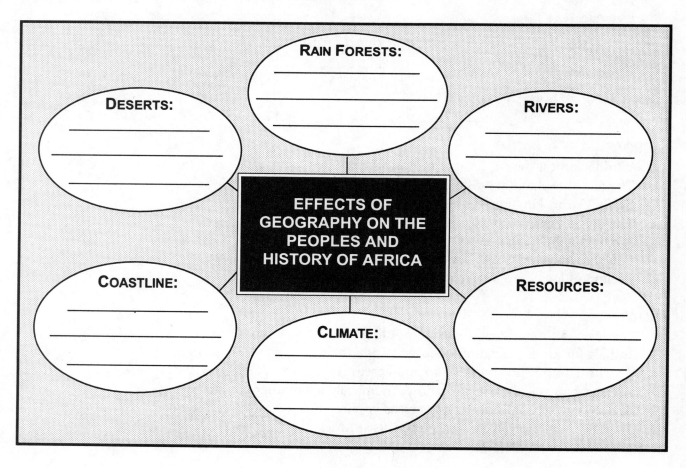

DESCRIBING HISTORICAL EVENTS

Directions: The following chart requires that you describe fully an important historical event you learned about in this chapter. Complete the chart by filling in the information called for in each box. (In this chart, some of the items have been filled in to help get you started.)

WHO was involved?
European nations and African tribes
_____
_____
_____

WHEN did it happen?
_____
_____
_____
_____

EUROPEAN IMPERIALISM IN AFRICA

WHERE did it take place?
Throughout the continent of Africa
_____
_____
_____

WHAT were its main causes?
_____
_____
_____

RESULTS:

1. _____

2. _____

3. _____

4. _____

Each chapter of this book ends with a test. Before each test there is a special "Test-Helper" section that will prepare you to answer certain kinds of questions. This section takes a look at geography questions.

TEST HELPER   LOOKING AT GEOGRAPHY

THE FIVE THEMES OF GEOGRAPHY

Teachers of geography, in an effort to organize knowledge, have identified five major themes:

1. LOCATION. This theme deals with where something is located in relation to other things. To help us find any fixed point on the earth, geographers pretend there are imaginary lines running up and down and across the earth's surface.

• **Longitude** is the name given to imaginary lines running up and down. The middle line is zero degrees (0) and is called the **Prime Meridian**. From that point, each longitude line is assigned a number to help us measure distances east and west. The Prime Meridian divides the earth into the Western Hemisphere (North, Central and South America) and the Eastern Hemisphere (Europe, Africa, Asia and Australia).

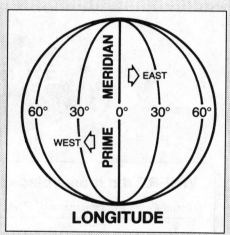

• **Latitude** is the name given to imaginary horizontal lines running across the earth. The middle line is also zero degrees (0). You may know it better as the **equator**. The equator divides the earth into the Northern Hemisphere and the Southern Hemisphere. Each latitude line is assigned a number to help us measure distances north and south from the equator.

2. PLACE tells us something about a location's special features that distinguish it from other places. Geographers use certain terms to describe the physical characteristics of a place. They look at its **topography** (*land surface features*) and its **climate** (*weather conditions over a long period*). Each place also has its own particular natural resources such as minerals, fertile soil, and plentiful fresh water. Besides using general terms to describe items associated with geography — mountains, rivers, plateaus, etc. — geographers have created special terms to use when describing certain unique features:

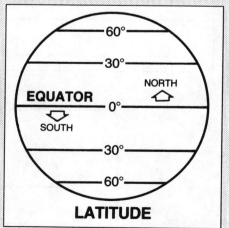

SPECIAL TERMS USED IN GEOGRAPHY

Monsoons. Seasonal winds that blow across Asia. In summer, they bring heavy rains, while in winter they bring hot, dry weather.

Plateau. A high, flat land surface surrounded by mountain ridges.

Tundra. Marshy, treeless plains near the North Pole that are frozen in winter but thaw in the spring.

3. REGIONS. Certain large land masses of the world are called continents. There are seven continents — Asia, Africa, North America, South America, Europe, Australia, and Antarctica. **Regions**, on the other hand, are any areas of the earth that share certain features and have greater contact with other places within the region than with the outside.

Example: Africa is a continent because it is a large land mass. However, many geographers divide Africa into two *regions*: North Africa and sub-Saharan Africa. These geographers place North Africa with the Middle East because it shares the same climate and topography, and its peoples have similar lifestyles. They see Africa south of the Sahara Desert, with its different climate, topography and lifestyles, as forming a separate and distinct region.

In studying the regions presented in Global Studies, ask yourself: What makes this area a region? What are its common features?

4. HUMAN-ENVIRONMENT INTERACTIONS. These describe the many ways in which people affect the environment: cutting down forests, building roads and cities, turning the countryside into farmland, and creating pollution. You should also think about how the environment shapes what people can do. How is life in a desert different from life in a big city like New York?

5. MOVEMENT. Certain areas have a surplus (*more of something than they can use*) of some goods, while other areas experience a shortage of these same goods. To get what people need they must interact with each other (trade, travel, and communicate). Understanding the movement of goods, services, ideas and peoples from one place to another is another important theme of geography.

ANSWERING GEOGRAPHY QUESTIONS

Questions on geography generally focus on how the physical setting of a country or region has affected the development of its people. The question might ask how geographical factors have influenced an area's economic development. To help you answer any type of geography question, each content area in this book contains a section discussing the physical setting. Here you will find information about:

- the size and location of the region
- a map and a description of the principal geographical features
- the effects of the geographical features on the area's development

To help you summarize your understanding, you will be asked to complete a chart at the end of each chapter which lists geographical features and their effects. These charts will help you in reviewing the material. Keep in mind that:

- location often determines the degree of interaction with people of other areas.
- the topography (land features), climate, and resources of a place usually determine the number of people who live in the area, where they live, and how they make a living.
- population density is usually greatest along coasts, in river valleys and fertile plains because these places allow people to raise enough food to feed themselves.

TESTING YOUR UNDERSTANDING

Base your answers to questions 1 through 4 on the following map and on your knowledge of Global Studies.

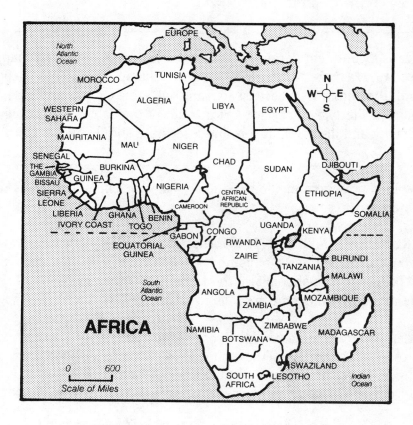

1 This map shows Africa's
  1 annual rainfall   3 mountain areas
  2 political boundaries 4 population

2 The large island off Africa's east coast is
  1 Lesotho   3 Swaziland
  2 Burundi   4 Madagascar

3 At its narrowest point, the continent of Africa is
  1 6 miles wide
  2 600 miles wide
  3 6,000 miles wide
  4 60,000 miles wide

4 Which country is located in North Africa rather than sub-Saharan Africa?
  1 Angola   3 Kenya
  2 Zambia   4 Libya

5 Which statement is most accurate about Africa's geography?
  1 It is a land surrounded by large mountains.
  2 Africa has large deposits of coal.
  3 It has created obstacles to political and cultural unity.
  4 Africa has few deserts and no rain forests.

6 The Atlantic slave trade resulted in
  1 greater unity among Africa's tribes
  2 immense suffering and loss of life
  3 an increase in African power and prestige
  4 a decrease in the birth rate

7 One barrier to economic progress in African nations has been a
  1 shortage of raw materials
  2 small pool of unskilled workers
  3 low birth rate
  4 lack of money for investment

8 "All men are created equal." A person who believes this would oppose
  1 cultural diffusion   3 apartheid
  2 nationalism   4 universal voting

9 The introduction of African music into American culture is an example of
  1 apartheid
  2 economic interdependence
  3 cultural diffusion
  4 animism

10 During the 1950s and 1960s the African continent was characterized by
  1 imperialism by European nations
  2 a sharp decrease in the birth rate
  3 the achievement of political independence by most African nations
  4 the elimination of hunger and poverty

ESSAYS

In addition to answering multiple choice questions, global studies examinations usually require you to write essays. These essay questions often follow a similar pattern. For example:

The policy of apartheid has influenced life in South Africa.

Part A

List two features of apartheid as it was practiced in South Africa.

1._____   2. _____

Part B
In your Part B answer, you should use information you gave in Part A. However, you may also include different or additional information in your Part B answer.

Write an essay explaining how life in South Africa has been influenced by the government's policy of apartheid.

Notice that this essay question has three parts:

➤ It begins with a general statement: "The policy of apartheid has influenced life in South Africa."

➤ Next, Part A asks that you give some information about the general statement: "List two features of apartheid as it was practiced in South Africa."

➤ Lastly, Part B asks you to use the information you gave in your Part A answer to write an essay about the general statement. In this chapter you will concentrate *only* on answering Part A.

STRATEGIES FOR ANSWERING PART A

The purpose of Part A in this kind of question is for you to "outline" the important facts about the topic. You will later use this information to write your essay in Part B. There are four main "action" words used in Part A. They are: **give**, **state**, **identify** and **list**.

➤ **identify** means "to name something." It is generally used when you are asked to name one or more causes, features, or changes. For example,

> • identify a group that has suffered discrimination in South Africa: *black South Africans*
>
> • identify a major problem facing Africa today: *hunger*

➤ **list** is a term used for naming *more* than one thing. For example,

> • list two groups that suffered discrimination in South Africa: *blacks, coloreds*
>
> • list two major problems facing Africa today: *hunger, tribalism*

➤ **state** means writing a sentence about something. It calls for more than just naming. For example,

> • state one way a group in South Africa has suffered discrimination: *Blacks in South Africa could not vote.*
>
> • state one way this problem is affecting Africa today: *There have been many protests in South Africa over discrimination against blacks.*

➤ **give** is like "identify," in that it asks you to name something. However, it is generally used when asking for an example or for supplying a reason. For example,

> • give one example of apartheid: *Blacks in South Africa were not permitted to live in white areas.*
>
> • give two reasons for hunger in Africa: *One reason for hunger in Africa is that frequent civil wars have hurt farming. A second reason is that the Sahara Desert is spreading southward.*

Looking at these "action" words, you can see that Part A concentrates on *key terms and concepts* and their problems, causes, effects and features. Therefore, pay special attention to the words that are printed in **boldface** in every chapter.

Now let's test your understanding of the Part A section of this kind of essay question:

Identify one feature of apartheid as practiced in South Africa.

> 1. _____

List two problems facing Africa today.

> 1. _____
>
> 2. _____

State one way in which geography has affected Africa's development.

1. _____

Give two examples of how European imperialism affected Africa.

1. _____

2. _____

Note that even if your essay question does not contain a Part A section, it is still a good idea to jot down the main information asked for, to serve as an outline of the basic facts you need.

GLOBAL CHECKLIST

SUB-SAHARAN AFRICA

Directions: Before going on to the next chapter, you should check your understanding of the important people, terms and concepts covered in this chapter. Place a check mark (✔) next to those that you are able to explain. If you have trouble remembering a term, refer to the page listed next to the item.

A traditional African village

❑ Sub-Saharan Africa (10)	❑ Nationalism (19)	❑ Jomo Kenyatta (27)
❑ Nile River (12)	❑ Organization of African Unity (20)	❑ Desmond Tutu (27)
❑ Sahara Desert (12)	❑ Extended Family (23)	❑ F.W. de Klerk (27)
❑ Savanna (12)	❑ Tribe (23)	❑ Nelson Mandela (27)
❑ Early African Kingdoms (16)	❑ Subsistence Farming (23)	❑ Apartheid (29)
❑ Atlantic Slave Trade (16)	❑ Nationalized (23)	❑ A.N.C. (30)
❑ Cultural Diffusion (17)	❑ Urbanization (23)	❑ Tribalism (30)
❑ Imperialism (18)	❑ Animism (24)	❑ Desertification (31)

1

GEOGRAPHY
- Size and Location
- Geographic Features and Their Effects

2

HISTORY
- Pre-Columbian Heritage
- European Explorations
- Colonial Period
- Independence Movements

5

CONCERNS
- US-Latin American Relations
- The War on Drugs
- Economic Development
- Deforestation
- NAFTA

CHAPTER 3

LATIN AMERICA

4

IMPORTANT PEOPLE
- Christopher Columbus
- Simon Bolivar
- Fidel Castro
- Javier Perez de Cuellar

3

SYSTEMS
- Government
- Economy
- Society
- Religion
- The Arts

What do these pictures show you about Latin America? _____

_____

_____

_____

1 GEOGRAPHY

In this section you will read about the major geographic features of Latin America, and how these features have affected its people and their history.

THINK ABOUT IT

Look at the map of Latin America below. What do you think are Latin America's major

geographic features? _____

_____

Important Terms: As you read this section, look for the following terms:

◆ **Latin America**
◆ **Andes Mountains**

◆ **Population Density**
◆ **Single Cash Crop**

SIZE AND LOCATION

◆ The name **Latin America** describes the lands in the Western Hemisphere south of the United States. These countries, stretching over 7,000 miles from north to south, cover a large area between the Atlantic and Pacific Oceans. Latin America is made up of four regions:

1. **Mexico**, the country just south of the United States.

2. **Central America**, the countries which lie between Mexico and Colombia.

3. **West Indies** (or *Caribbean*), the islands located in the Caribbean Sea. They were called the West Indies by European explorers because they thought the islands were part of India.

4. **South America**, the continent south of Central America, made up of many nations.

MAJOR GEOGRAPHIC FEATURES AND THEIR EFFECTS

MOUNTAINS
The **Andes Mountains**, stretching over 4,500 miles in the western part of South America, are among ◆ the highest in the world. The Andes have separated people in different parts of South America from each other. This has resulted in the development of many different cultures.

GRASSLAND PLAINS (PAMPAS)
Mountains and poor soils make much of Latin America's land unproductive. There are a few exceptions, such as the **pampas** of Argentina and Uruguay and the **llanos** of Venezuela.. Like the African savannas, the pampas provide much of the fertile soil in Latin America. The rest of the land cannot produce enough to feed the people of the region. Despite this, most people in Latin America work in agriculture.

RAIN FORESTS
Rain forests are located on the east coast of Central America and the northern part of South America. They have warm, humid climates and receive a great deal of rainfall. Rain forests have made transportation and communication difficult among the peoples of Latin America.

RIVERS
The **Amazon River**, flowing 2,300 miles, is the second longest river in the world. Two other important rivers are the Orinoco and the Rio de la Plata. A large percentage of the Latin America's population lives near these river systems. They provide an important link in the area's transportation system.

CLIMATE
Much of Latin America is warm because it lies near the **equator**. However, because of the mountains and the winds from the oceans, many places in Latin America have a moderate climate. As a result, **population density** (*the average number of people living in an area*) is greatest in the higher elevations ◆ where temperatures are comfortably cool. In areas of dense population, food shortages occur, and there is inadequate housing, health and educational services.

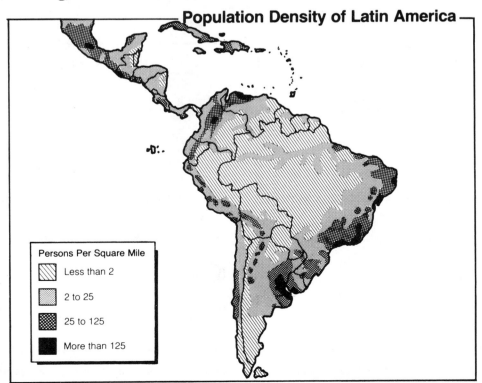

Population Density of Latin America

Persons Per Square Mile
- Less than 2
- 2 to 25
- 25 to 125
- More than 125

RESOURCES

Some countries like Mexico and Venezuela have large amounts of oil. But other countries lack oil and other resources like coal and iron. This hurts their industrial development. The major crops grown in Latin America are coffee, bananas, sugar and cocoa. Most nations rely on these **single cash crops** (*crops raised for a profit*), making them dependent on changes in world prices. For example, if the world price for cocoa drops sharply, Ecuador—a large exporter of cocoa—will suffer economically.

SUMMING UP: PHYSICAL SETTING

Latin America makes up the largest group of nations in the Western Hemisphere. Its geography and climate explain some of the differences in the way the peoples of Latin America live.

CHECKING YOUR UNDERSTANDING

THINKING IT OVER

Now that you have read the material, were you correct in identifying some major geographic features? (Yes____ No ____) What features should you add? _____

_____

Directions: Complete each of the following cards. Then answer the multiple choice questions that follow.

LATIN AMERICA

Describe it: _____

Which regions make it up? _____

_____

ANDES

Define it: _____

Major effect on the area: _____

_____

POPULATION DENSITY

Define it: _____

Name a country where it is high: _____

_____

SINGLE CASH CROP

Define it: _____

Importance: _____

_____

1 The Orinoco, Amazon, and Nile are names of
   1 mountains   3 lakes
   2 rivers   4 deserts

2 Brazil is a part of which continent?
   1 Europe   3 South America
   2 North America   4 Australia

3 Latin America includes the areas of
   1 South America, Central America and Canada
   2 Central America, South America, and the West
     Indies
   3 South America and Africa
   4 Only South America

4 The pampas of South America and the savannas of
   Africa are examples of
   1 river systems   3 rain forests
   2 grassy plains   4 mountain ranges

5 The greatest population density in Latin America is
   found in the
   1 higher altitudes 3 deserts
   2 lowlands   4 rain forests

6 Which best describes South America's geography?
   1 climatic conditions led to an abundance of food
   2 there are no major mountains in South America
   3 most South American countries have large re-
     serves of coal and iron
   4 much of South America is unsuitable for agricul-
     ture

2 HISTORY

In this section you will read about the major historical developments in Latin America, from its earliest native civilizations to its present role in the world community.

THINK ABOUT IT

Complete the first two columns of the chart:

THE HISTORY OF LATIN AMERICA

What I Know	What I Want to Learn	What I Have Learned

Important Terms: As you read this section, look for the following terms:

◆ **Native American Civilizations**
◆ **Encomienda System**
◆ **Mercantilism**
◆ **European Explorations**

Sometimes tests have questions about *outlines* and how to organize items. Before you start to read the history of Latin America, the following **Skill Builder** will help you to better understand outlines.

SKILL BUILDER: UNDERSTANDING OUTLINES

What Is an Outline?

An outline is a brief plan in which a topic (or major idea) is broken down into smaller units called sub-topics. The main purpose of an outline is to show the relationships between a topic and its sub-topics. An outline also helps to guide the thinking of the writer.

Keys to Understanding an Outline

To understand an outline, look at its major parts:

Title. The title always tells you the main topic.

Format. Outlines follow a specific format so you can understand how the topic is broken down. Usually, the first sub-topics are given Roman numerals (I, II, III). When these sub-topics are further divided, they are given capital letters (A, B, C). If the sub-topics are divided again, they are given Arabic numbers (1, 2, 3). As an example, let's see how the first part of the history section in this chapter is organized:

LATIN AMERICA'S HISTORY

We could write about its early history or its modern history. To narrow down the things we wish to cover, we use sub-topics like this one:

I. Pre-Columbian Heritage

The outline now tells you that Latin American history before Columbus will be covered. But what will be written about this early history?

I. Pre-Columbian Heritage
　A. Mayan Civilization
　B. Aztec Empire
　C. Inca Empire

The outline now shows what empires existed before Columbus landed. To tell more about any of these empires, the outline would include additional sub-topics:

I. Pre-Columbian Heritage
　A. Mayan Civilization
　　1. Government
　　2. Economy
　　3. Social Life

Notice how outlining shows you what details help explain or support the "big" ideas or facts.

Interpreting an Outline

Remember that in an outline you start with a large idea and break it down into smaller and smaller units. In our example, each smaller unit also develops the larger concept. Understanding outlines helps you to answer data-based questions on tests, and provides a useful tool to organize your thoughts when writing an essay.

Outline-type questions may appear as follows:

In an outline, one of these is a main topic and the others are sub-topics. Which is the main topic?

1 Trade Routes Changed　3 Slavery
2 Effects of Explorations　4 New Inventions

Remember that the main topic is the broadest one covering all the smaller ones. In the question above, the main topic is the "Effects of Explorations" because the three other choices are various effects of explorations. Now that you have learned about outlines, it will be easier to follow how this section is organized. After you have read the history section, fill in the blank outline at the end of the section, on page 55.

TIMELINE OF HISTORICAL EVENTS							
1492	**1823**	**1846**	**1898**	**1914**	**1933**	**1959**	**1990**
Columbus lands in the "New World"	Monroe Doctrine issued	Mexican-American War begins	Spanish-American War begins	Panama Canal opens	U. S. announces Good Neighbor Policy	FidelCastro comes to power in Cuba	U. S. arrests General Manuel Noriega

PRE-COLUMBIAN HERITAGE

For thousand of years before Christopher Columbus arrived in the Western Hemisphere in 1492, **native** ◆ **American civilizations** existed there. These civilizations had many important achievements.

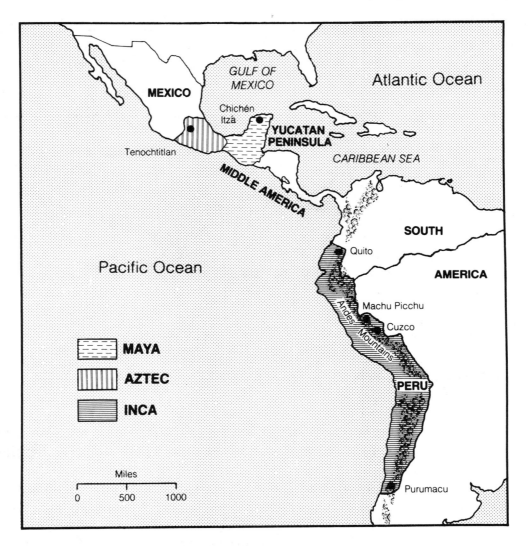

MAYAN CIVILIZATION (1500 B.C.-1200 A.D.)

Located in southern Mexico and parts of Central America, the Mayans made contributions in science, astronomy (*study of the stars*), mathematics, sculpture and painting. For example, their calendar was extremely accurate, and had 365 days

AZTEC EMPIRE 1400-1520

An **empire** is a group of nations or territories controlled by one ruler or country. In Central America and Mexico, the Aztecs conquered other native peoples. The capital of their empire had a population of over 300,000 in the mid-1400s. Religion was an important part of Aztec life. They built great pyramids that still stand in Mexico City.

INCAN EMPIRE (1000-1530)

The Incas, who lived in the mountains of western South America, controlled a large amount of land. In order to connect the different parts of their empire, the Incas built roads which stretched for thousands of miles. They also constructed great stone buildings, high in the Andes Mountains.

◆ EUROPEAN EXPLORATIONS (1492-1542)

European explorers first came to Latin America, which they called the "New World," while looking for a shorter all-water route to India (in Asia). In time, European nations—mainly Spain and Portugal—took over most of what is now Latin America, and established **colonies** in those lands. There were many reasons for the European exploration of Latin America.

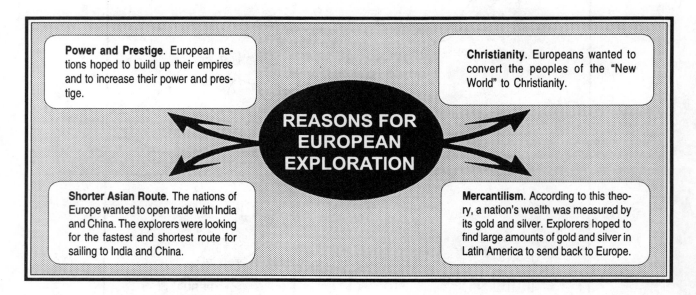

Power and Prestige. European nations hoped to build up their empires and to increase their power and prestige.

Christianity. Europeans wanted to convert the peoples of the "New World" to Christianity.

REASONS FOR EUROPEAN EXPLORATION

Shorter Asian Route. The nations of Europe wanted to open trade with India and China. The explorers were looking for the fastest and shortest route for sailing to India and China.

Mercantilism. According to this theory, a nation's wealth was measured by its gold and silver. Explorers hoped to find large amounts of gold and silver in Latin America to send back to Europe.

FAMOUS EXPLORERS

European explorers were adventurous and daring; the dangers of sailing into the unknown were great, but so were the rewards—excitement, adventure and riches. Some of the important explorers were:

➤ **Christopher Columbus (1492)**. Columbus is credited with being the first European to come to the Americas.

➤ **Vasco De Balboa (1513)**. Balboa was a Spanish explorer who became the first European to discover the Pacific Ocean (while he was exploring near Panama).

➤ **Ferdinand Magellan (1519)**. Magellan, sailing for Spain, organized the first expedition to sail around the world. His voyage proved to many that the world was round.

*Columbus at the court of King Ferdinand and Queen Isabella of Spain,
who financed his voyages of exploration*

EFFECTS OF EXPLORATION

The European explorations of Latin America had some important results:

➤ **New inventions.** Improvements were made in map-making, shipbuilding and sailing.

➤ **Cultural diffusion.** The native peoples and the Europeans exchanged ideas and products. For example, the Spaniards introduced new foods to the Americas—coffee and sugar—and brought back to Europe such foods as potatoes and corn.

➤ **Slavery.** The Europeans enslaved a large number of native peoples, and also brought enslaved Africans to Latin America.

➤ **Trade Routes Changed.** More trade took place over the Atlantic Ocean, and less over the Mediterranean Sea. Nations on the Atlantic coast of Europe, such as Spain, Portugal, France and England, became very powerful.

THE COLONIAL PERIOD (1520-1808)

To explore the "New World," Spain used soldiers called **conquistadors**. These conquistadors, with their horses and cannons, proved too powerful for the native peoples of the area. The Aztec Empire was defeated in 1519, the Incas in 1530 and the Mayans in 1546. Once the native peoples were conquered, most of the lands were claimed by Spain and Portugal.

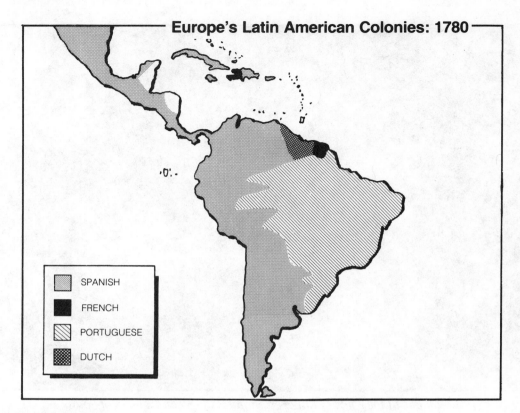

Europe's Latin American Colonies: 1780

Legend:
- SPANISH
- FRENCH
- PORTUGUESE
- DUTCH

ECONOMIC POLICY

Spain and Portugal treated the lands of Latin America as colonies (*a colony is a weak nation controlled by a more powerful one*). According to the theory of **mercantilism**, colonies existed only for the benefit of the "mother country" (the imperialist power). This meant that Spain and Portugal took everything they wanted from Latin America, such as gold and other resources. Wealthy landowners and military rulers held political and economic power in Latin America, because they were given large tracts of land and the native peoples living on the land, as a reward for their loyal service to Spain. This was called the **encomienda system**. Today these large estates are known as haciendas.

SOCIAL CLASSES

Mercantilism and the hacienda system resulted in the people in the colonies being grouped into social classes. The Europeans and **Creoles** (*people born in Latin America of European parents*) had the greatest power and wealth. The people of other social classes (people of mixed European, Indian or African ancestry) had the least power and did most of the hard work.

THE ROLE OF THE CHURCH

The **Catholic Church** was a powerful force in the Latin American colonies. Priests tried to convert the native peoples to Catholicism, taught them skills and protected them from slavery. The Church also became a great landowner and supported the power of the local ruling elites.

INDEPENDENCE MOVEMENTS

REASONS FOR SEEKING INDEPENDENCE

Between 1803 and 1825, many Latin American colonies revolted against Spain and Portugal and won their independence.

Unfair Treatment. The people in the colonies were treated unfairly. Most had to pay high taxes, and few had any voice in government.

Influence of Other Revolutions. The American and French Revolutions spread ideas of freedom in Latin America, helping to justify revolutions against unfair government.

WHY LATIN AMERICANS FOUGHT FOR INDEPENDENCE

Weakened Spain and Portugal. Spain and Portugal were weakened because of years of fighting in Europe against the French leader Napoleon.

Monroe Doctrine. In 1823 the U.S. issued the Monroe Doctrine, prohibiting further European colonization in Latin America. This helped protect nations seeking their independence.

LEADERS IN THE STRUGGLE FOR INDEPENDENCE

Among the most important leaders who participated in the struggle to achieve independence were:

➤ **Toussaint L'Ouverture.** He led a rebellion (1803-1804) of enslaved people that overthrew the French in Haiti.

➤ **Simon Bolivar.** Between 1819 and 1825, he helped bring about independence in Venezuela, Colombia, Ecuador, Peru and Bolivia.

➤ **Jose de San Martin**. He helped liberate Argentina and Chile in the years 1816-1818.

Statue of Simon Bolivar in Caracas, Venezuela

CHANGES IN GOVERNMENT SINCE INDEPENDENCE

After independence, few democratic governments were established in Latin America. Many of the governments were run by military leaders, acting as dictators. These leaders stayed in power only as long as the army supported them. In the 20th century, some major revolutions occurred against these dictators. They included:

➤ **Mexico.** In 1910 a civil war broke out against the military dictator, and he was overthrown. By the 1930s a number of changes had improved people's lives—new health and social services, the right to strike, and the encouragement of land reform.

➤ **Cuba.** In 1959 **Fidel Castro** led a revolution overthrowing Cuba's dictator. Castro then declared Cuba a Communist nation, and received support from the Soviet Union. (Further details on Castro and Cuba are on page 61.)

Mexican rebel Pancho Villa

LATIN AMERICA TODAY

In the 1980s and 1990s, many Latin American countries have been promoting social reform and economic modernization. People are migrating to cities in search of work. Many of the governments have been changing from one-man, military dictatorships to democracies with free market economies. You will read more about these developments in the sections on Systems and Concerns.

SUMMING UP: LATIN AMERICA'S HISTORY

Advanced civilizations existed in the Americas long before European explorers came to the continent. Like Africa, the Americas became a prime area for European imperialism. By the 19th century, much of Latin America revolted against European control and achieved independence.

CHECKING YOUR UNDERSTANDING

THINKING IT OVER

Now that you have read the History section, fill in the blanks in the outline on the next page. We have started it for you. (If you need to refresh your memory about outlines, you can re-read the Skill Builder on page 48.)

HISTORY OF LATIN AMERICA

I. Pre-Columbian Heritage
    A. Mayan Civilization
    B. _____
    C. _____

II. _____
    A. Reasons for European Exploration
        1. _____
        2. _____
        3. _____
        4. _____

    B. _____
        1. _____
        2. _____
        3. _____
        4. Trade Routes Changed

III. _____
    A. _____
    B. Social Classes
    C. The Role of the Church

IV. _____
    A. Leaders in the Struggle for Independence
        1. _____
        2. _____
        3. Jose de San Martin

    B. Changes in Government Since Independence
        1. _____
        2. _____

    C. _____

THINKING IT OVER

Return to page 47, where you completed the first two columns of the chart. Now that you have read about Latin American history, complete the third column of that chart, indicating what you have just learned.

Directions: Complete the following cards. Then answer the multiple choice questions that follow.

NATIVE AMERICAN CIVILIZATIONS

Name two: _____

Achievements: _____

_____

EUROPEAN EXPLORATIONS

Describe: _____

Reasons: _____

Effects: _____

MERCANTILISM

Definition: _____

Example: _____

_____

ENCOMIENDA SYSTEM

Describe it: _____

Effect: _____

_____

---

1   The Mayans, Aztecs and Mali are
   1 past civilizations   3 river systems
   2 mountain ranges   4 capital cities

2   Which event occurred last?
   1 The Inca civilization was defeated by Europeans.
   2 Columbus set sail for the "New World."
   3 Magellan sailed around the world.
   4 Castro took control of Cuba.

3   Which statement best describes the role of Fidel Castro?
   1 He introduced democracy into Cuba.
   2 He sought a greater role for American investors in Cuba.
   3 He introduced Communism into Cuba.
   4 He is a friend of the United States.

4   A term paper about Simon Bolivar, Jose de San Martin and Jomo Kenyatta would probably be about
   1 assassinated leaders
   2 national independence fighters
   3 presidents of Argentina
   4 religious leaders

5   Balboa, Magellan and da Gama made contributions in the field of
   1 religion   3 exploration
   2 science   4 politics

6   At first, European explorers coming to the Americas were primarily interested in
   1 finding gold and silver
   2 buying industrial products
   3 copying technology
   4 establishing schools

7   The term "mercantilism" refers to the
   1 division of a nation into smaller states
   2 unification of a people under a central government
   3 use of colonies for the benefit of the mother country
   4 use of department stores to market goods

8   Which nations played the greatest role in colonizing what is now Latin America?
   1 Italy and Russia
   2 Great Britain and Austria
   3 Spain and Portugal
   4 Germany and Greece

3 SYSTEMS

In this section you will read about Latin America's major political institutions, economic development, social structure, major religions and cultural achievements.

THINK ABOUT IT

Democracy and *machismo* are two important terms in this section. Find the meaning of these terms in this section or in the glossary (at the back of the book). They will play an important part in helping you to understand this section.

Democracy: _____

Machismo: _____

Important Terms: As you read this section, look for the following terms:

◆ **Capitalism**   ◆ **Catholic Church**

GOVERNMENT

Traditionally, political power in Latin America was held by a small group of wealthy landowners. However, in the 1980s and 1990s more and more Latin American nations have been introducing democratic governments. In a **democracy**, people have a voice in their government, and power is shared among all citizens. The government protects individual rights. An example of democracy in action is when people vote to elect their government officials. However, a few Latin American countries are still ruled by **dictators** (*rule by one person with absolute power*), and people's rights are limited. Cuba is an example of a military **dictatorship**. Fidel Castro, a Communist, controls what the government does. In other countries, corruption among public officials is a key problem.

Although it is not a state, Puerto Rico is a part of the United States. It receives many benefits granted to citizens of the United States, but the people are not permitted to vote in presidential elections. Puerto Rico calls itself a **commonwealth** (*special status under the U.S. Government*).

ECONOMY

Most Latin American nations today have an economic system known as **capitalism**, or the **free enterprise system**, where businesses are owned privately and run for profit. However, only a few people own businesses or land. The majority are very poor peasant farmers. Others are workers in the growing cities. Over the years, many Latin American governments followed a policy called **nationalization** (*taking property away from private owners and foreign-owned businesses, and placing it under government control*). Cuba under Castro in 1959, Venezuela in 1976 and Nicaragua in 1979 all nationalized many of their countries' foreign-owned businesses and private lands. However, some Latin American countries are now reversing nationalization and allowing greater private enterprise.

SOCIETY

Traditionally, the family is the center of life in Latin America. Many live together in **extended families**, where children, parents and grandparents share one house. In Latin American society **machismo** is an important concept. Machismo places great emphasis on male pride and honor, and physical and moral strength. Women are sometimes seen as objects to be dominated. In Latin American families, machismo often means the male is the chief provider and makes all the important decisions.

Latin America was traditionally marked by a sharp division between social classes. There was a small, highly-educated, wealthy elite and a large number of poor farmers and workers. It was extremely difficult for a person to move from one social class to the other. Today there are several forces bringing about changes in the social system. This is leading to greater opportunities for members of all social classes. Among the forces for change are the movement of people to the cities (**urbanization**) resulting in new employment opportunities, the chance for more education, the influence of television, and the desire of the Catholic Church to encourage change.

RELIGION

Today, most people in Latin America are Catholic, a religion first introduced there by the Spanish and Portuguese. The **Catholic Church** has acted as a unifying force throughout Latin America's history. It has had a great influence on family life. For example, high birth rates can be partly explained by the Church's opposition to birth control devices and to abortion. Recently, many Latin American church leaders have taken an active role in working for greater individual rights, more democracy, and improving the conditions of the poor.

THE ARTS

The art of Latin America can be grouped into two time periods: before and after the arrival of Christopher Columbus. Art in the pre-Columbian era (*the time before Columbus*) served a religious purpose. This type of art can be seen in Mayan temples, which compare in beauty and architectural achievement with the work of the ancient Egyptians.

Post-Columbian art is a blend of European, African and native American traditions. For example, Latin Americans built huge cathedrals similar to those found in Europe. You can also see this diverse blend of traditions in such Latin American dances as the tango and rumba.

Pictured at right: Aztec statue carved in basalt.

SUMMING UP: LATIN AMERICA'S SYSTEMS

GOVERNMENT: Many Latin American nations have had little experience with democratic government. However, in recent years, there has been a trend toward democracy.

ECONOMY. Most wealth in Latin America is controlled by a small group of people, while the majority are poor. However, in recent years Latin America has experienced economic growth.

SOCIETY. Traditional life in Latin America was centered in the family. Changes are coming about as a result of people moving to cities, modern communications and the influence of the Church.

RELIGION. The Catholic Church, first introduced by Europeans, has been a unifying force and influence in Latin America.

THE ARTS: Pre-Columbian art served religious purposes; post-Columbian art reflects the blending of native American, European and African traditions.

CHECKING YOUR UNDERSTANDING

THINKING IT OVER

After reading this section about Latin America's systems, are there any other important terms you think should be included? What are they? _____

_____

_____

Directions: Complete each of the following cards. Then answer the multiple choice questions that follow.

DEMOCRACY

Definition: _____

Example: _____

_____

CAPITALISM

Definition: _____

Example: _____

_____

MACHISMO

Definition: _____

Characteristics: _____

_____

CATHOLIC CHURCH

What is it? _____

Importance: _____

_____

1 Which statement is true about a democracy?
  1 It can only exist in a highly industrialized society.
  2 It exists only in the United States.
  3 Democratic governments protect people's basic rights.
  4 A democracy has only one political party.

2 In Latin America, political power has traditionally been in the hands of
  1 farmers and hunters
  2 factory workers and artists
  3 landowners and military leaders
  4 scientists and religious leaders

3 The major occupation for most workers in Latin America today is
  1 skilled factory work   3 computer repairs
  2 agricultural work   4 government service

4 Which group in Latin America would benefit the most from land reform?
  1 wealthy landowners   3 peasant farmers
  2 church officials   4 government workers

5 The spread of the Catholic religion throughout Latin America is an example of
  1 national security   3 cultural diffusion
  2 socialism   4 machismo

6 The role of the Catholic Church in Latin America can best be described as
  1 having much influence on daily life
  2 becoming active in trade talks
  3 being confined only to religious activities
  4 being controlled by national governments

7 In Latin America, military governments and the importance of the Catholic Church can trace their roots to
  1 early native American civilizations
  2 English military traditions
  3 Spanish colonial rule
  4 African influence

8 The main source of unity in Latin American nations has traditionally been
  1 the Catholic Church   3 the hacienda system
  2 the influence of Islam 4 economic prosperity

**4
IMPORTANT
PEOPLE**

In this section you will read about some people who have played a key role in shaping Latin America's history.

THINK ABOUT IT

How many famous people from Latin America can you name? _____

Who are they? _____

THE LATIN AMERICAN TIMES

Volume 7   **Number 21**

CHRISTOPHER COLUMBUS

Until 1492, Europeans had no knowledge of the Americas, and Native Americans had no knowledge of Europe, Asia or Africa. Christopher Columbus brought the Western and Eastern Hemi-

spheres into contact with each other, giving birth to our modern world. In 1492, Columbus set out in search of a new sailing route to the East Indies. Believing he had reached India, he called the native peoples Indians. His "discovery" brought about great changes in the world — opening the Americas to Europeans, introducing them to new foods and knowledge about other peoples, and making Europeans rich. But the meeting also sadly led to the conquest and destruction of Native American civilizations.

SIMON BOLIVAR

Simon Bolivar is one of Latin America's best known fighters for independence. He is honored with the title "The Liberator," and statues of Bolivar are found throughout the northern regions of Latin America. As a young man, he fought for Venezuelan independence from Spain. Next, Bolivar led an army across the Andes Mountains and defeated the Spanish army in Colombia. In 1822, he helped Jose de San Martin defeat the Spanish forces in Peru and Bolivia. He died in 1830, never fully achieving his dream of a union between Colombia, Venezuela and Ecuador, similar to that of the United States. Although his "Gran Colombia" dream did become a reality for eight years, it was unable to hold together.

FIDEL CASTRO

In the **Cuban Revolution of 1959**, Fidel Castro and his guerrilla forces overthrew Cuba's military dictator. Once in power, he **nationalized** (*took control of*) the banks and other foreign-owned businesses, turning Cuba into the Western Hemisphere's first Communist nation. The

Soviet Union had helped to support the Cuban economy, but cut its aid in 1990. As a result, after 30 years of Communism, the Cuban economy is on

the brink of collapse. Food and basic consumer goods are rationed. Castro is determined to keep the Communist system in Cuba, whatever the costs. Some Cubans side with Castro, whom they see as a symbol of national independence, while others oppose his policies.

JAVIER PEREZ DE CUELLAR

Perez de Cuellar was a member of Peru's diplomatic service, and rose to become the Secretary-General of the United Nations in 1982. He worked

tirelessly on missions around the world to prevent ethnic, religious and border conflicts from developing into full-fledged wars. De Cuellar played an important role in attempting to avoid war in the Persian Gulf, and was a key supporter of U.S. actions. He also helped obtain the release of Western hostages in the Middle East.

His term as Secretary-General of the U.N. ended in 1991.

SUMMING UP: IMPORTANT PEOPLE

Latin American leaders, such as Simon Bolivar in the past and Fidel Castro today, have greatly influenced events in Latin America and the world.

CHECKING YOUR UNDERSTANDING

THINKING IT OVER

Which famous people connected with Latin America can you now add to your list?

_____   _____   _____

Directions: Complete the following cards. Then answer the multiple choice questions that follow.

CHRISTOPHER COLUMBUS

Time Period: _____

Achievements: _____

Impact: _____

SIMON BOLIVAR

Time Period: _____

Achievements: _____

Impact: _____

FIDEL CASTRO

Time Period: _____

Achievements: _____

Impact: _____

JAVIER PEREZ DE CUELLAR

Time Period: _____

Achievements: _____

Importance: _____

1 Simon Bolivar and Nelson Mandela are similar in that they
   1 fought for their people's freedom
   2 ran for political office
   3 put an end to the policy of apartheid
   4 achieved independence for their countries from Spain

2 Jomo Kenyatta, Simon Bolivar and Toussaint L'Ouverture are best known as
   1 economic theorists   3 political leaders
   2 military geniuses   4 guerrilla fighters

3 Which has been a characteristic of Cuba under Fidel Castro?
   1 an official foreign policy of friendship with the United States
   2 many different political parties
   3 public ownership of businesses and industries
   4 the absence of a written constitution

4 Which economic system was introduced into Cuba by Fidel Castro?
   1 Communism   3 interdependence
   2 mercantilism   4 feudalism

In this section you will read about some of the important events between the United States and Latin America. In addition, you will learn about some major problems and concerns facing Latin America today.

THINK ABOUT IT

Below are some statements about U.S.-Latin American relations. Read each statement and then indicate whether you think the statement is true (T) or false (F):

_____ The Monroe Doctrine was issued to protect the Panama Canal.

_____ President Wilson created the "Big Stick Policy" to protect American sailors.

_____ Under the Good Neighbor Policy, the U.S. agreed not to interfere in Latin America's internal affairs.

_____ The Bay of Pigs Invasion happened in Panama.

Important Terms: As you read this section, look for the following terms:

- ◆ **Monroe Doctrine**
- ◆ **Good Neighbor Policy**
- ◆ **Organization of American States**
- ◆ **Cuban Revolution**
- ◆ **Deforestation**
- ◆ **NAFTA**

U.S.- LATIN AMERICAN RELATIONS

Since the establishment of the United States, relations between the United States and Latin America have been of major importance. There are many reasons for this ongoing interest.

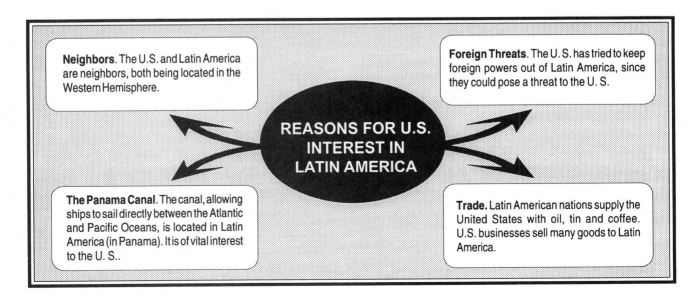

CONFLICT AND COOPERATION WITH THE U. S.

Relations between the U.S. and its Latin American neighbors have been marked by periods of conflict and periods of cooperation.

◆ ➤ **The Monroe Doctrine.** In 1823, the United States issued the Monroe Doctrine, warning European nations against establishing new colonies in North and South America. It established the U. S. as the major power in the Western Hemisphere, and helped Latin American countries to keep their independence. The Monroe Doctrine has been the basis for most of U.S. policy in Latin America. Many Latin American leaders opposed the Monroe Doctrine, believing that the United States should stay out of Latin America's affairs and mind its own business.

➤ **The Mexican-American War** (1846-1848). This war started as a border dispute. By winning, the U.S. acquired a large part of Mexican land that eventually became the states of California, New Mexico, Arizona, Utah and Nevada. The war caused much ill will towards the U.S. in Latin America.

➤ **The Spanish-American War** (1898). This war began when the U.S. battleship *Maine*, on a visit to Havana harbor in Cuba, was blown up. Although it was never determined who set the blast, it led to a war between the United States and Spain. The United States claimed to enter the war to free Cuba from harsh Spanish rule. The war ended with a U.S. victory, resulting in the U.S. assuming informal control over Cuba and taking over Puerto Rico.

➤ **The "Big Stick" Policy** (early 1900s). The U.S. under President Theodore Roosevelt was often involved in the affairs of Latin America. As an extension of the Monroe Doctrine, he sent troops to countries that had debts or had trouble keeping order. He also built the **Panama Canal**, so that ships could sail quickly from the Atlantic Ocean to the Pacific.

◆ ➤ **Good Neighbor Policy** (1933-1945). Relations improved when President Franklin Roosevelt established a policy in which the United States agreed not to interfere in Latin American affairs.

➤ **Organization of American States** (1948). This organization, known as the **O.A.S.**, was created to solve disputes between countries in the Americas. It continues to be a place where nations in the Americas can peacefully settle disagreements and discuss their mutual problems.

➤ **Relations after World War II** (1960-present). Later U.S. relations with Latin America were focused on attempts to stop the spread of Communism from Cuba (see following paragraph). The United States sent military forces or military aid to several Latin American countries, including the Dominican Republic, Chile, Nicaragua, El Salvador and Grenada, to fight Communist rebels. The United States also gave economic assistance to many countries.

COMMUNISM IN CUBA

The **Cuban Revolution of 1959** was a major concern for the Latin American countries and for the United States. **Fidel Castro** overthrew the dictator of Cuba and established a Communist government under his leadership. Once in power, Castro nationalized foreign-owned banks and industries. In 1961 the United States attempted to overthrow Castro by supporting an invasion by Cuban refugees. After the invasion failed, it was discovered that Soviet nuclear missiles were being secretly placed in Cuba, aimed at U.S. cities. This caused the **Cuban Missile Crisis**. Under an imposed U.S. blockade, the missiles were withdrawn. However, relations between Cuba and its North and South American neighbors have remained unfriendly.

CARIBBEAN AREA

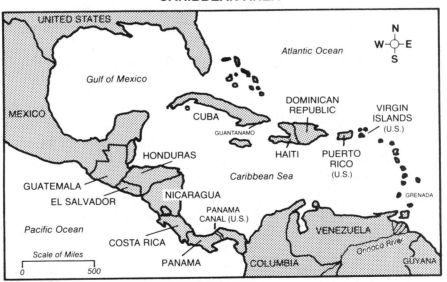

THE WAR ON DRUGS

Latin American countries such as Mexico, Colombia and Peru are producers and distributors of cocaine and marijuana, which are illegally brought to the U.S. The U.S. has taken active steps in Latin America to curb drug production. These include giving military aid to Colombia, and the invasion of Panama to oust military dictator **Manuel Noriega**, who may have been helping the drug trade. However, it is difficult to stop these illegal activities because the drug suppliers in Latin America are very powerful and many Latin Americans depend on the sale of drugs for their income. Most experts believe the key to drug control is to cut the use of drugs in the United States.

PROBLEMS OF ECONOMIC DEVELOPMENT

Three major economic problems facing Latin America are:

OVERBORROWING

Many Latin American countries, needing capital for investment, borrowed heavily from other countries, which resulted in large debts. Many of the countries are unable repay their loans, creating a serious problem. Recently, indebted nations like Mexico, Argentine, and Brazil have agreed to a series of requirements such as reducing inflation and opening their economies to foreign investment, in return for lower interest rates and new long-term loans from major banks.

OVERPOPULATION

The population is growing so rapidly in some parts of Latin America that every 30 years the number of people doubles. This growth has created many new problems. It uses up any gains Latin Americans make in productivity. It is driving people from rural areas to cities looking for jobs and a better way of life, and leads to severe overcrowding in the cities.

DEFORESTATION

◆ Deforestation is caused by clearing the lands of the rain forest to increase the amount of land available to grow crops. Unfortunately, this has resulted in the opposite effect. After the trees are cut down and crops are planted and harvested for a year or two, the soil becomes dry and barren. Since it cannot be used again for planting, the farmers have to move to a new location and cut down more trees. Deforestation has had global effects, since these forests produce a large portion of the world's oxygen supply.

MEXICO AND FREE TRADE IN NORTH AMERICA

Free trade means eliminating **tariffs** (*taxes on goods sold from one country to another*). Mexico has
◆ reached an agreement — known as **NAFTA** (North American Free Trade Agreement) — to create a free trade area with the U.S. and Canada. To take effect, this treaty must be approved by the U.S. Congress. If NAFTA goes into effect, many tariffs between Mexico and the U.S. will be reduced or eliminated. Additional agreements will set up special rules to protect workers and the environment in Mexico. Supporters of NAFTA say it will allow Americans to export more goods to Mexico. Opponents say that because labor costs are lower in Mexico, U.S. companies will move their manufacturing operations there, leading to a loss of American jobs.

◆ **ANALYSIS**

If you were a member of the U.S. Congress, would you support or oppose NAFTA?
❑ Yes ❑ No. Explain your answer:

_____

_____

SUMMING UP: CONCERNS

Latin American nations have been greatly affected by U.S. policies. Among the most serious concerns facing many Latin Americans today are economic development, overpopulation, the growing and sale of illegal drugs, a low standard of living, and NAFTA.

CHECKING YOUR UNDERSTANDING

THINKING IT OVER

Which statements were you correct on, and which ones did you get wrong?

❑ The Monroe Doctrine was issued to protect the Panama Canal.

❑ President Wilson created the "Big Stick Policy" to protect American sailors.

❑ Under the Good Neighbor Policy, the U.S. agreed not to interfere in Latin America's internal affairs.

❑ The Bay of Pigs Invasion happened in Panama.

Directions: Complete each of the following cards. Then answer the multiple choice questions.

MONROE DOCTRINE

What was it? _____

Main purpose: _____

Importance: _____

GOOD NEIGHBOR POLICY

What was it? _____

Main purpose: _____

_____

ORGANIZATION OF AMERICAN STATES (O.A.S.)

What is it? _____

Purpose: _____

CUBAN REVOLUTION

Describe it: _____

Result: _____

DEFORESTATION

What is it? _____

Result: _____

_____

NAFTA

What is it? _____

Possible effects: _____

_____

1 The United States sees Cuba as a threat because Cuba
   1 refuses to sell sugar to industrialized nations
   2 maintains a Communist government
   3 supports the foreign policy of Canada
   4 prevents trade among countries in Latin America

2 Which is a major problem facing many Latin American nations today?
   1 the threat of an invasion by the United States
   2 illegal immigrants moving into Latin American nations
   3 a decline in the birth rate throughout Latin America
   4 inability to repay foreign debts

3 Which U.S. policy refused to allow European nations to establish new colonies in Latin America?
   1 Good Neighbor Policy   3 creation of the O.A.S.
   2 "Big Stick" policy   4 Monroe Doctrine

4 The U.S. "Good Neighbor" policy sought to
   1 improve U.S.-Canadian relations
   2 expand the Monroe Doctrine
   3 encourage better U.S.-Latin American relations
   4 limit illegal drugs coming into the U.S.

5 A major goal of the Organization of American States (OAS) is to
   1 provide a place to discuss mutual problems in Latin America
   2 preserve democracy in Cuba
   3 promote Communism in developing nations
   4 prevent U.S. investments in Latin America

6 In an outline, one of these is the main topic; the other three are subtopics. Which is the main topic?
   1 Problems of Economic Development
   2 Overpopulation
   3 Deforestation
   4 Overborrowing

SUMMARIZING YOUR UNDERSTANDING

Complete the following paragraphs by writing in the proper words from the Word Game box.

Word Game			
	AMAZON	CHRISTOPHER COLUMBUS	MAYANS
	AZTECS	COMMUNISM	MERCANTILISM
	SIMON BOLIVAR	EQUATOR	MONROE DOCTRINE
	FIDEL CASTRO	THE WEST INDIES	PORTUGAL

   The lands of Mexico, Central America, [   ] and South America make up an area known as Latin America. This area has several important rivers; the longest is the [   ] river. The climate is quite hot, because much of the region lies near the [   ].
   Before the arrival of [   ] in 1492, several great native civilizations existed in the area: [   ] , [   ] and Incas. However, European explorations changed the region forever. A major reason for European interest in Latin America was its belief in the economic system known as [   ] , in which colonies exist for the benefit of the mother country. Much of Latin America's language and cultural heritage came from Spain and [   ] . These two nations established the largest number of colonies in the area. By the 1800s, people like [   ] led uprisings against European control, and successfully gained independence for Latin American countries.
   In 1823, the United States issued the [   ] to protect its interests in the region, warning European nations against establishing new colonies in Latin America. Since that time, the United States has continued to show a great interest in the area, fearing other nations like Cuba under the leadership of [   ] might also turn to [   ] .

Directions: Fill in the blanks in the two visual organizers below, based on the information you have learned in this chapter.

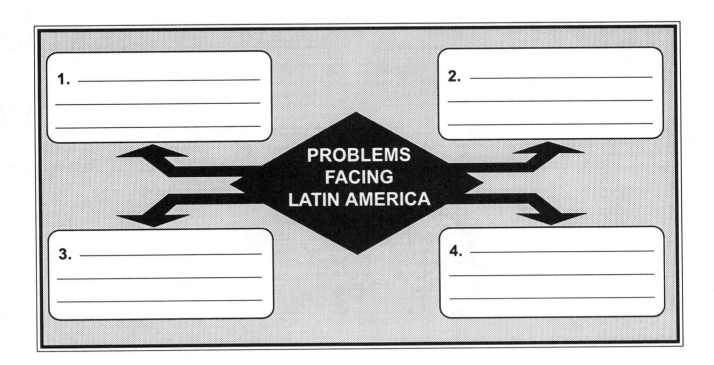

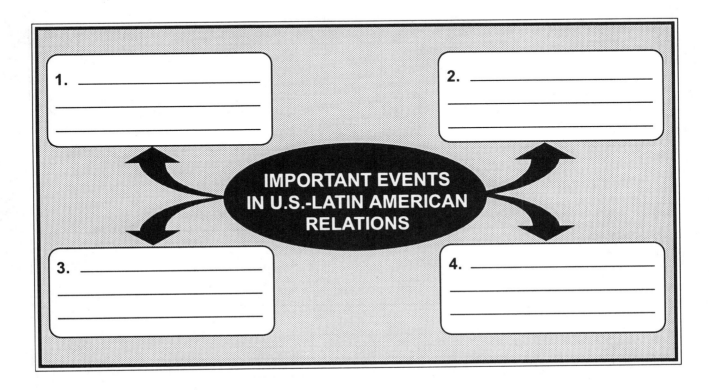

DESCRIBING HISTORICAL EVENTS

Directions: Describe fully an important historical event you learned about in this chapter. Complete the chart by filling in the information called for in each box.

WHO issued it?

_____

_____

_____

WHEN was it issued?

_____

_____

_____

THE MONROE DOCTRINE

WHAT was its main purpose?

_____

_____

_____

WHY was it issued?

_____

_____

_____

RESULTS:

1. _____

2. _____

3. _____

4. _____

THE PROBLEMS OF DEVELOPING NATIONS

TEST HELPER

The information in this Test-Helper section will help prepare you to answer questions dealing with the problems faced by developing nations.

WHAT IS A "DEVELOPING NATION"?

One way to look at a country is to measure either what its total economy produces, or its income per person. Countries having a high level are called **developed nations,** while those trying to make more effective use of their resources are called **developing nations.** You can better understand the difference between a developed and a developing country by examining the following chart.

COMPARING THE U.S. WITH SOME DEVELOPING NATIONS (1991)

	U.S. No. America	Zaire Africa	Haiti Latin Am.	Bangladesh South Asia	S. Yemen Middle East
Per Capita Income	$16,441	$275	$300	$113	$310
Autos	139,000,000	24,000	34,000	41,000	150,000
Telephones	134,000,000	245,000	38,000	143,000	63,000
Life Expectancy	75.5	55.5	55.5	53.5	48
Doctors	528,000	705	803	12,306	406
Literacy Rate	99%	55%	23%	29%	25%
Imports	$492 billion	$0.756 bil.	$0.344 bil.	$3.6 bil.	$7.1 bil.
Exports	$363 billion	$1.1. bil.	$0.183 bil.	$1.3 bil.	$.38 bil.

Sometimes developing countries are referred to as **Third World Nations.** Most of these nations are located in Africa, Asia, and Latin America.

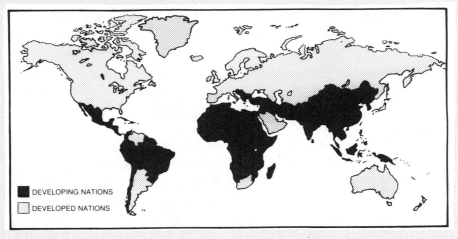

DEVELOPING NATIONS
DEVELOPED NATIONS

MAJOR PROBLEMS OF DEVELOPING NATIONS

LOW AGRICULTURAL PRODUCTION

In most of these countries, the majority of the people are peasant farmers, working by hand. For example, in Bangladesh about 74% of the people are farmers, while in the U.S. only 4% are. Because of machinery and fertilizers, one U.S. farmer can grow much more food than a Bangladesh farmer.

LACK OF A SKILLED WORKFORCE

Most developing nations lack skilled workers because many of their people cannot read and write. To become skilled workers, peasants would have to go to school instead of working. Then there might be even less food to go around. There is also a shortage of schools and teachers.

LACK OF CAPITAL FOR INVESTMENT

Most developing countries lack the money to buy modern machinery and build needed roads, bridges and communications systems to make their workers more productive.

POPULATION GROWTH

Advances in medicine have greatly reduced the death rate in the Third World, but birth rates are still high. Families traditionally have many children to help with farm and housework. Birth rates are also high because many couples do not know about modern birth control methods. Agricultural gains are used up by the increased population. As a result, living standards do not rise.

SOCIAL AND POLITICAL INSTABILITY

Developing countries often suffer from ethnic, religious and class tensions. In Africa, different tribal groups clash. In many Latin American countries, a small group is wealthy and the rest of the people are very poor. In the Middle East and Southeast Asia, religious differences cause constant unrest.

STRATEGIES USED TO OVERCOME THESE PROBLEMS

THE GREEN REVOLUTION

Many developing countries tried to improve farm production by using modern science and technology. New fertilizers, pesticides, and better irrigation were introduced; this is called the **Green Revolution.** Some spectacular results were achieved. However, many Third World farmers could not afford to buy the fertilizers and machinery, and they lacked training in how to use them.

POPULATION CONTROL

Many developing nations have created programs to limit birth rates. The Chinese government encourages people to have only one child. In Latin America and other parts of the world, population control programs meet with great problems because of traditions, religion and lack of education.

THE FREE-MARKET APPROACH TO ECONOMIC DEVELOPMENT

In the late 1980s and early 1990s, the free market became the most popular approach to economic development. With free markets, foreign goods and investments enter a developing country with little interference by the home government. Foreign money is attracted to developing countries because labor costs are low, giving them an advantage over manufacturers in the developed world.

TESTING YOUR UNDERSTANDING

Directions: Answer all of the multiple choice questions in this part by circling the number of the word or expression that best completes the statement or answers the question. Then answer the essay questions.

Three items have been omitted from the following outline. For each blank space, select the item which best completes that blank.

1 Climate	3 Physical Features
2 Natural Resources	4 Central America

Latin America's Physical Setting

1 I   Regions
           A South America
           B _____
           C West Indies
           D Mexico

2 II _____
           A Mountains
           B Rain Forest
           C Rivers

3 III _____
           A Fertile Grasslands
           B Minerals

_____

4 An important effect of geography on Latin American nations has been the development of
   1 Communism as the best economic system
   2 strong anti-democratic feelings
   3 isolation from one another
   4 hostile treatment by other nations of the world

5 Which U.S. policy sought to end foreign interference in Latin America's affairs?
   1 "Big Stick" Policy
   2 Good Neighbor Policy
   3 Cuban blockade
   4 Monroe Doctrine

6 Which person is correctly paired with his country?
   1 Desmond Tutu - United States
   2 Fidel Castro - Cuba
   3 Nelson Mandela - Brazil
   4 Simon Bolivar - Mexico

7 Which statement best illustrates the concept of machismo?
   1 A husband stays home to help care for the children.
   2 A wife decides how to spend the family earnings.
   3 The father is the only family decision-maker.
   4 A father and son work together.

8 Which statement best illustrates the existence of cultural diffusion?
   1 Most Latin Americans speak Spanish.
   2 Latin Americans enjoy sports.
   3 The Aztecs built large pyramids.
   4 There are frequent military takeovers in Latin America.

9 The economic system found in most Latin American nations today is
   1 communism   3 socialism
   2 capitalism   4 imperialism

10 References to debt payments, human rights violations, and deforestation are most closely associated with
   1 the ancient civilizations of Latin America
   2 the policies introduced by Fidel Castro
   3 the civil war that took place in Nicaragua
   4 current problems in Latin America

ESSAYS

In the chapter on Africa, you learned how to answer **Part A** of one kind of essay question. You are now ready to learn how to answer **Part B** of this kind of question. The **Part B** section requires that you write an essay based on the information you have already provided in your **Part A** answer. **Part B** asks you to prove your understanding of the opening statement by giving information that supports it. Often, students who know the necessary information to support the general statement do poorly on the essay section because they do not know how to *organize* their essays.

To help you organize your Part B answer, try to imagine your answer as a cheeseburger consisting of a top bun, slices of cheese, patties of meat, and a bottom bun.

- The "top bun" is the *topic sentence* (the first sentence you write). You just restate the opening statement that introduced the Part B question.

- The "cheese slice" is the *bridge sentence*. It helps the reader to go from the first section of your essay to the next.

- Then come the "patties of meat." These meat patties are *the information you used in Part A*.

- The bottom "bun" comes last. It is a *restating of the opening statement*. The one difference is that it is introduced with such words as "therefore" or "in conclusion, one can see that..."

Let's answer a sample essay question to show how this approach works:

Developing nations share similar problems that hinder their economic growth and development.

Problems

High birth rate	Lack of investment capital
Unskilled labor force	Unstable social conditions

Part A

Choose *one* problem listed above:_____

State how this is a problem for many Latin American countries. _____

Choose *another* problem listed above: _____

State how this is a problem for many Latin American countries. _____

Part B

In your part B answer, you should use information you gave in Part A. However, you may also include different or additional information in your Part B answer.

Write an essay explaining how Latin America nations share common problems that hinder their economic growth and development.

Your **Part A** answer should look something like this:

Choose *one* problem listed above: *High birth rate*
_____

State how this is a problem for many Latin American countries. *It means more people have to be fed.*
_____

Choose *another* problem listed above: *Lack of investment capital.*
_____

State how this is a problem for many Latin American countries. *If a country does not have money it cannot buy modern machinery.*
_____

You are now ready to write your **Part B** essay answer. Using the "cheeseburger" method, it should look something like this:

T o p   B u n

Topic Sentence: *Many developing nations share similar problems that hinder their economic growth and development.*

Notice that this topic sentence is *identical to the opening statement* in the question. All you have done is restate the introduction to the question. The opening statement is easy to recognize, since it is always in **bold print**.

C h e e s e

Bridge Sentence: *This can be shown by looking at the problem of high birth rates and a lack of investment capital.*

The bridge sentence connects the main idea in the topic sentence with specific information you are going to use. It helps the reader follow your thoughts by pointing out the connection. There are other bridge sentences that you can use, such as *The following examples support this statement* -or- *First, I will look at the problem of.......... Second, I will look at the problem of ....*

M e a t   P a t t i e s

Main Essay Sentences:

One problem for many Latin American countries is the high birth rate, which adds to the population. This increase means more people have to be fed, more homes have to be built, and more resources have to be used.

Another problem for many Latin American countries is the lack of investment capital. If a country does not have money, it cannot buy modern machinery nor can it build roads, bridges, and communications systems.

Notice that the meat patties are a *restatement of the information you have given in Part A.* They explain the topic sentence with examples and facts. You may also add extra information to give a fuller explanation.

B o t t o m   B u n

Ending Sentence: *In conclusion, we can see that many developing nations share similar problems that hinder their economic growth and development.*

Notice that this ending sentence is identical to the opening statement, except that it is expressed as a conclusion. It reminds the reader of what you have just explained. There are other ways of writing this. For example: *Therefore, we can see that .... -or- Thus, we can see that ....*

Let's test your understanding of the "cheeseburger" method. Here is another sample essay question:

The way people live in an area is often greatly influenced by its geographic features.

Geographic Features

Mountains   Rivers
Rain Forests   Coastline
Resources   Climate

Part A

Select *two* features from the list For *each* feature you selected, identify one geographic effect of this feature on the way people live in **Africa** or **Latin America**.

FEATURE   EFFECT

1. _____   1. _____

2. _____   2. _____

PartB

In your part B answer, you should use information you gave in Part A. However, you may also include different or additional information in your Part B answer.

Write an essay explaining how the way in which people live in Africa or Latin America is often influenced by that region's geographic features.

(While you are writing in your answers to **Part A** of the question, use those same answers to fill in various parts of the "cheeseburger" — the Topic Sentence, the Bridge Sentence, etc.)

Top Bun

Cheese

Meat

Bottom Bun

GLOBAL CHECKLIST

LATIN AMERICA

Directions: Before going on to the next chapter, you should check your understanding of the important people, terms and concepts covered in this chapter. Place a check mark (✔) next to those that you are able to explain. If you have trouble remembering a term, refer to the page listed next to the item.

CORTEZ FACES THE TLASCALANS.

Conquistador Hernando Cortez
fighting the Tlascalans in Mexico

❑ Latin America (44)
❑ Andes Mountains (45)
❑ Population Density (45)
❑ Single Cash Crops (46)
❑ Native American civilizations (49)
❑ European Exploration (50)
❑ Encomienda System (52)

❑ Mercantilism (52)
❑ Democracy (57)
❑ Capitalism (57)
❑ Machismo (58)
❑ Catholic Church (58)
❑ Christopher Columbus (61)
❑ Simon Bolivar (61)

❑ Fidel Castro (61)
❑ Monroe Doctrine (64)
❑ Good Neighbor Policy (64)
❑ Cuban Revolution (65)
❑ O.A.S. (65)
❑ Deforestation (66)
❑ NAFTA (66)

GEOGRAPHY

- Size and Location
- Geographic Features and Their Effects

HISTORY

- Early Civilizations
- The Rise of Islam
- Invasions
- European Imperialism
- The Rise of Nationalism

CONCERNS

- Israel/Palestinians
- Mideast Oil and the West
- Islamic Fundamentalism
- The Gulf War

CHAPTER 4

THE MIDDLE EAST

IMPORTANT PEOPLE

- Anwar Sadat
- Ayatollah Khomeini
- Golda Meir
- Saddam Hussein

SYSTEMS

- Government
- Economy
- Society
- Religion
- The Arts

What do these pictures show you about the Middle East? _____

_____

_____

_____

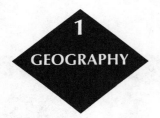

1 GEOGRAPHY

In this section you will read about the Middle East's major geographic features and how these features affect its people.

THINK ABOUT IT

The Middle East has always been of great importance to world trade. What could be some of the

reasons? _____

_____

_____

Important Terms: As you read this section, look for the following terms:

◆ **Middle East**
◆ **Suez Canal**
◆ **Tigris and Euphrates Rivers**
◆ **Oil reserves**

SIZE AND LOCATION

◆ The **Middle East** got its name because the area lies at the "crossroads" of three continents, connecting
◆ Africa, Asia and Europe. It contains one of the world's most important waterways, the **Suez Canal**, which shortens the traveling distance by sea between Europe and Asia.

MAJOR GEOGRAPHIC FEATURES AND THEIR EFFECTS

DESERTS
Much of the Middle East is desert, where rainfall is rare and few people live. The world's largest desert, the **Sahara** in north Africa, extends from the Atlantic Ocean in the west to the Nile River in the east. In addition, most of the Arabian Peninsula is desert.

RIVERS AND RIVER VALLEYS
There are three important rivers in the Middle East: the **Nile** (the world's longest river), the **Tigris** and
◆ the **Euphrates**. The mild climate and good soil alongside these rivers, good for growing crops, made these river valleys centers of early Egyptian and Mesopotamian civilizations.

CLIMATE
The countries of the Middle East are near or within the tropical zone. This explains why the area has warm winters and hot, dry summers.

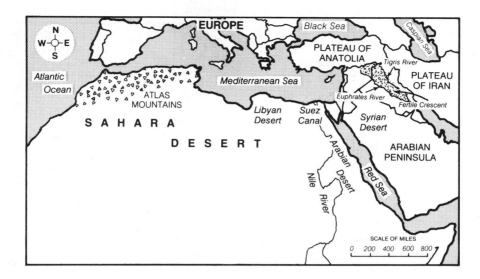

RESOURCES

The Middle East lacks many natural resources, especially water. The lack of rainfall makes it difficult to grow crops. As a result, the greatest population density is found near rivers, where water supplies are plentiful.

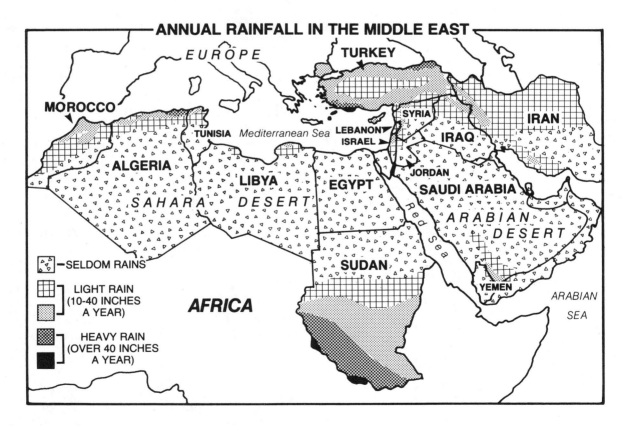

While lacking adequate water, the Middle East is rich in oil, producing about half of the world's supply. Although estimates differ, the Middle East contains at least 60% of the world's known **oil reserves** ◆ (*amount of oil still in the ground*). Many people have commented about this fact. Often the commentary takes the form of a *political cartoon*. In the following section you will see such a cartoon; since many cartoons appear in this book and on tests, it will be helpful to know how to interpret them.

SKILL BUILDER: INTERPRETING CARTOONS

A political cartoon is a drawing that expresses an opinion about a topic or issue. Political cartoons are humorous, but the point they make is usually serious.

Keys to Understanding a Cartoon
First, look at its major parts:

The Medium. Cartoons are visual representations. Cartoonists will use the size and type of objects, facial expressions, exaggerations, or words spoken by the characters to persuade you to their point of view.

Symbols. Cartoonists use symbols (*any object that stands for something else*) to get across their point of view. Animals are often used to represent countries—a bear representing the former Soviet Union, or an eagle representing the United States. Can you think of any other symbols used by cartoonists?

People. Cartoonists depict certain individuals who are closely associated with an issue or a country. For example, Saddam Hussein of Iraq is often shown in political cartoons with a thick mustache and a military uniform. Therefore it will be helpful to recognize him, as well as key people who are associated with other areas:

Top, left to right: Adolf Hitler, Mikhail Gorbachev, Fidel Castro

Bottom, left to right: Saddam Hussein, Josef Stalin, Mao Zedong

Interpreting a Cartoon
Let's see if you can interpret the cartoon below.

Here are the kinds of questions to ask yourself about any cartoon you must interpret:

■ *What objects, people, or symbols are used*? This cartoon depicts an Arab (note the clothing) and the U.S. (the person dressed as Uncle Sam). The barrel represents Middle Eastern oil.

■ *What is the situation*? The Arab is standing by, while the U. S. is tied to oil barrels.

■ *Which items are exaggerated or highlighted*? The Arab is laughing at the United States (Uncle Sam figure), showing that the cartoonist believes the oil-producing countries of the Middle East are in control.

■ *What is the main idea of the cartoon*? The Arab, representing Arab oil-producing countries, has the U.S. "over a barrel." Since the barrels represent the supply of oil, the cartoonist is implying that the U.S. is at the mercy of these oil-producing nations.

SUMMING UP: GEOGRAPHY

At the crossroads of three continents, connecting Africa, Asia and Europe, the Middle East has been considered an important trading location throughout history. More recently, the Middle East has attracted much world attention because it has most of the world's oil reserves.

THINKING IT OVER

Now that you have read this section, what other reasons can you add as to why the Middle East

is of such global importance? _____

_____

CHECKING YOUR UNDERSTANDING

Directions: Complete the following cards. Then answer the multiple choice questions that follow.

MIDDLE EAST

Location: _____

Importance: _____

_____

SUEZ CANAL

Location: _____

Importance: _____

_____

OIL RESERVES

What are they? _____

Location: _____

Importance: _____

TIGRIS AND EUPHRATES

What are they? _____

Importance: _____

_____

---

1 The most valuable natural resource in the Middle East is its reserves of
1 uranium   3 oil
2 cotton   4 gold

2 Early civilizations developed mainly near
1 river valleys   3 mountains
2 tropical rain forests   4 savannas

3 The Suez Canal is an important link between
1 Asia and Europe
2 Europe and South America
3 Asia and North America
4 Europe and the United States

4 Which feature has had the most effect on the population density in the Middle East?
1 coal deposits   3 location of water
2 natural harbors   4 presence of rain forests

5 Which resource is scarce in most Middle East nations?
1 unskilled laborers   3 water
2 crude oil   4 tobacco

6 The Middle East is a "crossroads" for
1 Asia, Antarctica, and Europe
2 Australia, Asia, and Europe
3 South America, Asia, and Africa
4 Africa, Europe, and Asia

2 HISTORY

In this section you will learn about the history of the Middle East, from its ancient civilizations to its independence from European imperialism.

THINK ABOUT IT

Look at the map on page 86 of the Muslim world during the 9th century. What does this map tell us about Islam (the religion of the Muslims) and its impact on the Middle East?

_____

_____

Important Terms: As you read this section, look for the following terms:

- ◆ **hieroglyphic / cuneiform**
- ◆ **Crusades**
- ◆ **Code of Hammurabi**
- ◆ **Mesopotamia**
- ◆ **monotheism**
- ◆ **nationalism**

TIMELINE OF HISTORICAL EVENTS							
622	**1099**	**1869**	**1948**	**1967**	**1979**	**1981**	**1990**
Islam founded	Crusaders conquer the Holy Land	Suez Canal completed	State of Israel established	Six Day War	Camp David Peace Accords	Anwar Sadat assassinated	Gulf War begins

EARLY CIVILIZATIONS

EGYPT (3100 B. C.- 332 B. C.)
Egypt, one of the world's first civilizations, developed in North Africa along the Nile River. The ancient Egyptians developed **hieroglyphics** (*one of the first kinds of writing, using pictures instead of* ◆ *letters*). They were also known for their skill in mathematics, building monuments, and creating paintings and statues. Egyptians built huge **pyramids** as tombs for their rulers, the Pharaohs. It was believed that the Pharaohs would live an eternal life after death.

At right: One of the great Egyptian pyramids at Giza.

OTHER ANCIENT CIVILIZATIONS AND THEIR CONTRIBUTIONS

There were other important Middle Eastern peoples who supplied humankind with important new ideas:

➤ **Writing. Mesopotamia** was one of the earliest civilizations that developed in the land between ◆ the Tigris and Euphrates Rivers, in what is today Iraq. The Mesopotamian people invented **cu-** ◆ **neiform**, a form of symbol writing on clay.

➤ **Transportation**. The Mesopotamians invented the wheel and the sailboat.

➤ **Law**. In Mesopotamia, the **Code of Hammurabi** was developed. It was the first written legal ◆ code and had very harsh punishments for criminals. It stressed the idea of an "eye for an eye, and a tooth for a tooth" as a concept of justice.

➤ **Religion**. The Hebrews were the first group to develop a religion based on **monotheism**, the ◆ belief in one God. This is also a key belief of the Christian and Islamic faiths.

THE SPREAD OF MIDDLE EAST CULTURE
At a later time, 336 B.C. - 476 A.D., the Greeks and then the Romans conquered parts of the Middle East. They brought back to Europe much of the learning and culture of the ancient Middle East.

THE RISE OF ISLAM

Islam, the religion of Muslims (or Moslems), first developed in the Middle East in the 7th century. It stressed the belief in one God, Allah.

THE GROWTH OF ISLAM
Islam spread throughout the Arabian Peninsula as a result of the teachings and leadership of **Moham-med**. Muslims in Arabia fought holy wars to convert non-Muslims. After Mohammed's death, the Islamic Empire spread to include a large part of the Middle East, North Africa and Spain.

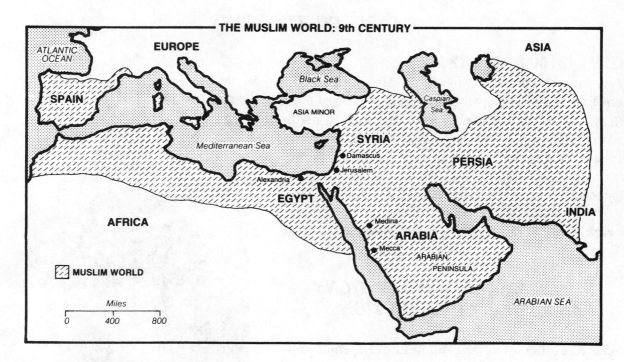

THE GOLDEN AGE OF MUSLIM CULTURE

From the 9th to the 14th centuries, Muslims made important scientific and cultural contributions to civilization. They include the invention of Arabic numbers, new scholarship in medicine (using anesthetics) and furthering the study of algebra, geometry and trigonometry.

INVASIONS

Because of its location at the crossroads of three continents, the Middle East was frequently invaded.

◆ THE CRUSADES

Between the years 1095-1291 European armies, in the name of Christianity, invaded the Middle East in hopes of taking it back from the Muslim peoples who controlled it. One of the results of the Crusades was that many Middle Eastern ideas and products spread to Europe (**cultural diffusion**). For example, foods like lemons and melons found their way from the Middle East to Europe.

OTTOMAN TURKS

By the 16th century, the Ottoman Turks gained control over all of the Middle East and parts of Europe. However, by the middle of the 20th century, after a series of wars, the Turks lost most of their lands in the Middle East, outside of present-day Turkey.

EUROPEAN IMPERIALISM

In the late 1800s, Britain, France and Italy came to believe that controlling the Middle East would make their nations more powerful for the following reasons:

➤ **Importance of its Location.** The Suez Canal in the Middle East connected European nations by water with the Asian countries with whom they traded, such as India and China.

➤ **Economic Reasons.** Europeans could sell their manufactured goods in the Middle East, as well as obtain important raw materials such as Egyptian cotton.

Most of the Middle East was eventually colonized and controlled by Britain, France and Italy.

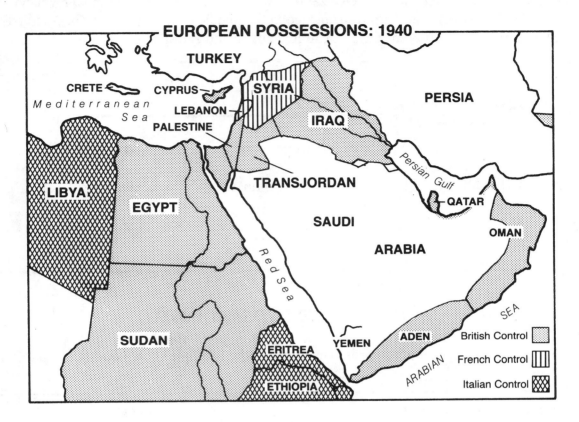

THE RISE OF NATIONALISM

Nationalism is the desire of a people to control their own government, free from foreign rule. Nationalism swept through the Middle East following World War I, and brought about many important changes. ◆

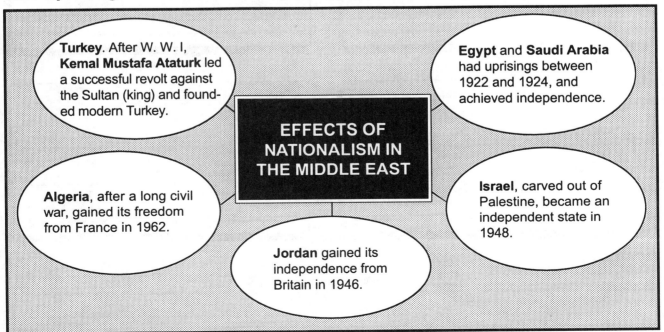

SUMMING UP: HISTORY

Two of the world's early centers of civilization, Ancient Egypt (in the Nile River Valley) and Mesopotamia (in present-day Iraq) were located in the Middle East. Since then the Middle East has been controlled, at different times, by Arabs, Turks, and Europeans.

THINKING IT OVER

Now that you have read the material in this section, was your answer accurate about Islam and

its impact on the Middle East? (Yes ___ No ___) If no, what did you leave out? _____

_____

CHECKING YOUR UNDERSTANDING

Directions: Complete the following cards. Then answer the multiple choice questions that follow.

HIEROGLYPHIC / CUNEIFORM

What are they? _____

Importance: _____

_____

CRUSADES

What were they? _____

Major effect on the area: _____

_____

CODE OF HAMMURABI

Describe it: _____

Characteristics: _____

_____

MESOPOTAMIA

Describe it: _____

Contributions: _____

_____

MONOTHEISM

Define it: _____

Example: _____

_____

NATIONALISM

Define it: _____

Example: _____

_____

1 Cuneiform and hieroglyphic are forms of
   1 dance   3 architecture
   2 sculpture   4 writing

2 The Golden Age of Muslim culture was marked by
   1 the discovery of gold in the Middle East
   2 scientific and cultural advances
   3 increased European imperialism
   4 the participation of women in government

3 Which event occurred last?
   1 birth of the Islamic religion
   2 Castro's takeover of power in Cuba
   3 end of the Crusades
   4 start of the Mesopotamian civilization

4 An effect of the Crusades was that it
   1 strengthened the feudal system
   2 led to cultural diffusion between Europe and the Middle East
   3 ended European interest in the Middle East
   4 increased European isolation

3 SYSTEMS

In this section you will read about the political, economic, social, religious and cultural systems of the Middle East.

THINK ABOUT IT

How much do you know about the three major religions of the world?

	Judaism	Christianity	Islam
Beliefs:	1	1	1
	2	2	2
Key People:			

Important Terms: As you read this section, look for the following terms:

◆ Judaism   ◆ Islam
◆ Christianity ◆ Koran / Torah / Bible

GOVERNMENT

There are different kinds of governments among the nations of the Middle East.

TRADITIONAL GOVERNMENTS
Some countries, like Saudi Arabia and Jordan, are ruled by kings and a small group of powerful, wealthy people.

SINGLE PARTY GOVERNMENTS
In some countries like Libya and Iraq, a single political party controls the government, and is often led by a dictator like Qadafi in Libya or Saddam Hussein in Iraq. Opposition parties are not allowed, and the people's freedoms are limited.

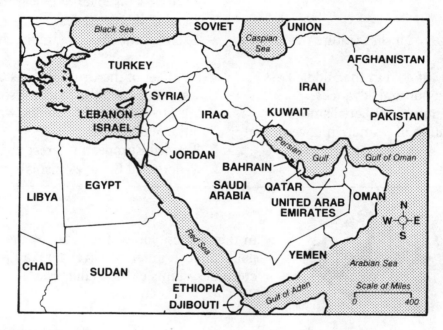

MULTI-PARTY DEMOCRACIES
Examples of multi-party democracies are found in the governments of Israel and Turkey.

ISLAMIC FUNDAMENTALISM
Under this type of government, real power is held by Islamic religious leaders. They strictly follow Islamic law, and reject all western ways. Iran has such a government.

THE PAN-ARAB MOVEMENT
The goal of the Pan-Arab Movement was to unite all Arabs into a single nation. However, nationalism and differences among Arab countries today stand in the way of Pan-Arab unity.

ECONOMY

TRADITIONAL ECONOMY
More than 75% of the people in the Middle East are farmers. Many follow a way of life similar to their fathers and ancestors. They work on small plots of land, using simple primitive tools, and food production is quite low. Many others follow a life of herding goats, sheep or camels.

In the 1970s, the world price of oil tripled. This brought newfound wealth to the oil-rich nations in the Middle East, resulting in important economic changes.

MIXED ECONOMY

Many countries of the Middle East have economies in which the government owns and controls certain parts and private individuals own and control the rest. Israel is an example of a country with a mixed economy.

SOCIETY

THE FAMILY

In the Middle East, traditionally, the extended family is the central point of life. Such a family has the eldest male as its head, and women spend their time at home. Male children are expected to follow their father's occupation. Marriages are arranged by parents.

THE MUSLIM WAY OF LIFE

The majority of people in the Middle East are Muslims. This is not only a religion, but a way of life as well. Muslims are forbidden to eat pork, lend money for profit, or gamble. Muslims pray in a house of worship called a **mosque**. In strict Muslim countries, women are not allowed in public without wearing the traditional cape-like **chador**, with their bodies completely covered and a veil hiding their faces. There is a growing conflict in the Middle East between the forces for modernization and the values of traditional Islamic culture. This conflict is leading to many changes in the Middle East.

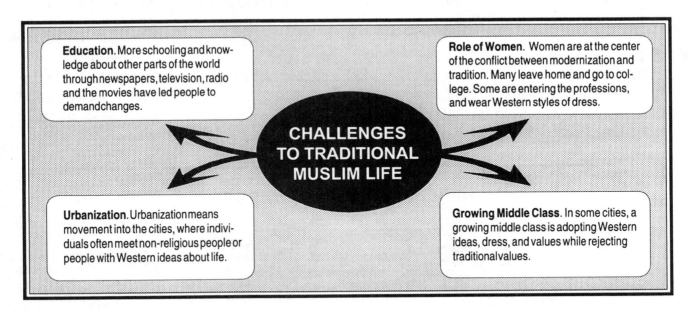

RELIGION

The Middle East is the birthplace of three of the world's great religions: Judaism, Christianity and Islam.

JUDAISM

Judaism is the oldest of the three religions. According to tradition, Jews first settled in the Middle East about 6,000 years ago. Many years later, the Romans drove the Jews from their homeland in Israel to all parts of Europe, Africa and Asia. Their early history and relationship with God is written about in

◆ the **Torah**. One of the holiest places to Jews is the **Wailing Wall** in Jerusalem — all that remains of their temple after it was destroyed by Roman soldiers in biblical times. Judaism is based on:

➤ **Monotheism**. Unlike other people at the time, the Jews were the first to believe in the existence of a single God.

➤ **The Ten Commandments**. According to the Bible, Jews must follow many rules. Among the most famous of these rules are the Ten Commandments. Jews (and Christians) believe that their laws were given to **Moses** by God. The Ten Commandments order Jews to obey the Sabbath, honor their parents, and forbid stealing and murder.

◆ **CHRISTIANITY**

Christianity, founded on the beliefs of **Jesus** of Nazareth, began in the Middle East about 2000 years ago. After his death, his followers spread the new Christian religion. The story of Jesus is told in the ◆ New Testament in the **Bible**. One of the holiest Christian places is the **Church of the Holy Sepulcher** in Jerusalem, believed to have been built on the site were Jesus was crucified. Some of Christianity's major beliefs are:

➤ **The Role of Jesus**. Christians believe that Jesus, although the son of God, allowed himself to be killed by the Romans to save humankind from punishment for its sins. After his death, he rose to heaven.

➤ **Christian Conduct**. Jesus taught brotherhood, peace and charity, and the importance of treating others with love and respect.

◆ **ISLAM**

Islam, the major religion in the Middle East, is based on the teachings of **Mohammed**. He taught that ◆ Allah (God) is all-powerful and determines each person's fate. The **Koran** is the sacred book of Islam, and contains Mohammed's teachings. The basic religious duties a good Muslim must follow are found in the **Five Pillars of Wisdom**.

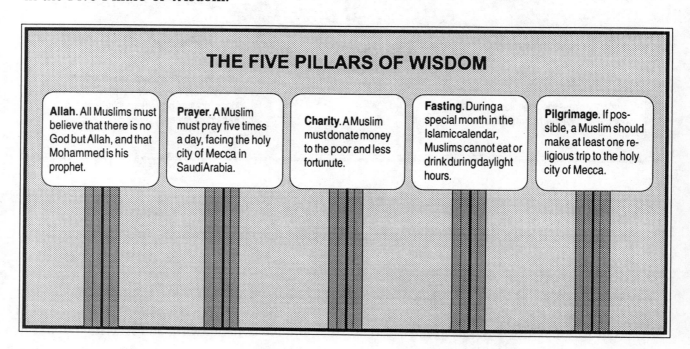

THE FIVE PILLARS OF WISDOM

Allah. All Muslims must believe that there is no God but Allah, and that Mohammed is his prophet.

Prayer. A Muslim must pray five times a day, facing the holy city of Mecca in Saudi Arabia.

Charity. A Muslim must donate money to the poor and less fortunate.

Fasting. During a special month in the Islamic calendar, Muslims cannot eat or drink during daylight hours.

Pilgrimage. If possible, a Muslim should make at least one religious trip to the holy city of Mecca.

THE ARTS

Most Middle Eastern culture has been heavily influenced by the Islamic religion. For example, Arabic literature is modeled after the style used in the Koran. Islam also influences other art forms — weaving, music and painting. The **Dome of the Rock**, an example of Islamic architecture, is one of holiest shrines in all Islam. Located in Jerusalem, it is built over the rock where Muslims believe Mohammed rose to heaven. The massive interior dome, tall pillars and wide arches of this mosque provide a dignified place for believers to pray.

SUMMING UP: SYSTEMS

GOVERNMENT. Since gaining independence, most Middle East nations have been ruled by kings or military dictators; a few countries are democracies.

ECONOMY. Many people in the Middle East today are still poor peasant farmers like their ancestors, following the traditional way of life.

SOCIETY. Many Middle Eastern people still follow their ancestors' way of life. However, a number of new ideas are being introduced to challenge the old traditions.

RELIGION. The Middle East is the birthplace of three of the world's major religions: Christianity, Judaism and Islam.

THE ARTS. Middle Eastern art is very heavily influenced by the Islamic religion.

THINKING IT OVER

Now that you have read the material in this section, were you correct in identifying the major

beliefs and key people of each religion? _____ What new information did you learn?

_____

_____

CHECKING YOUR UNDERSTANDING

Directions: Complete the following cards. Then answer the multiple choice questions that follow:

TORAH / BIBLE / KORAN

What are they? _____

Importance: _____

_____

JUDAISM

Describe it: _____

Major beliefs: _____

_____

CHRISTIANITY

Describe it: _____

Major beliefs: _____

_____

ISLAM

Describe it: _____

Major beliefs: _____

_____

1 The belief in a single God is called
   1 animism   3 capitalism
   2 monotheism   4 Communism

2 Judaism, Christianity, and Islam share a common belief in
   1 animism   3 reincarnation
   2 individualism   4 monotheism

3 A major belief of the Islamic religion is that
   1 there is but one God, Allah
   2 one should make a pilgrimage to Brazil
   3 the cow is a sacred animal
   4 the Church and State should be separated

4 Which city contains holy sites of the Jewish, Christian and Islamic religions?
   1 Mecca   3 Tel Aviv
   2 Rome   4 Jerusalem

5 As a result of greater income from oil prices, which statement about the Middle East is correct?
   1 Economic development has increased.
   2 There has been an elimination of all fighting.
   3 Learning and culture have decreased.
   4 New sources of water have been discovered.

6 There is a growing conflict in the Middle East between modernization and the
   1 traditional Islamic culture
   2 spread of Communism
   3 need to reduce the birth rate
   4 development of cities

7 The Ten Commandments and the Five Pillars of Wisdom are similar in that both
   1 question all authority
   2 establish rules for proper living
   3 establish rigid social classes
   4 promote military rule

8 The main characteristic of a traditional economy is
   1 a powerful labor union
   2 a centralized government
   3 following your ancestors' occupation
   4 private ownership

9 Which has had the greatest influence on Middle East culture and values?
   1 technological advances
   2 political leaders
   3 the Islamic religion
   4 democratic government

10 Which would most likely occur in a traditional society?
   1 a boy challenging his father's leadership
   2 a woman becoming a professional
   3 a boy learning his father's occupation
   4 a girl picking whom she wants to marry

4
IMPORTANT PEOPLE

In this section you will read about some important people who have had a great impact on the Middle East.

THINK ABOUT IT

Which person first comes to mind when you hear the term "Middle East?" _____

_____ Why? _____

_____

Important Names: As you read this section, look for the following names:

◆ **Anwar Sadat**   ◆ **Ayatollah Khomeini**
◆ **Golda Meir**   ◆ **Saddam Hussein**

 **THE MIDDLE EASTERN TIMES**

Volume 19   Number 4

ANWAR SADAT

As President of Egypt, Sadat was the first Arab leader to take steps toward peace with Israel. In 1977, Sadat visited Israel; he later signed a peace agreement with the Israeli Prime Minister. He was awarded the Nobel Peace Prize in 1978. Because of his peace efforts, extremists assassinated Sadat in 1981.

AYATOLLAH KHOMEINI

In 1979, Khomeini and his followers overthrew the leader of Iran. He turned Iran into a nation which followed orthodox Islamic rule—a strict interpretation of the Koran. As leader of Iran, Khomeini was strongly anti-Western, with a particular hatred for the U.S.

GOLDA MEIR

Golda Meir was a political leader who helped Israel become a powerful Mideast nation. She participated in the Jewish resistance to British rule in Palestine. Meir became Israel's Prime

Anwar Sadat at an international meeting, listening to a translator through headphones

Minister in 1973, the first woman to lead a modern Middle Eastern nation.

SADDAM HUSSEIN

Hussein has been dictator of Iraq since 1979. In 1990 he invaded Kuwait, a neighboring country, resulting in the Gulf War in which the U.S. and its allies drove Iraq out of Kuwait. Some of his supporters see him as trying to bring Arabs together. His opponents claim he is a ruthless dictator who threatens world peace.

SUMMING UP: PEOPLE IN THE NEWS

Middle East leaders such as Anwar Sadat, Golda Meir, Ayatollah Khomeini and Saddam Hussein have had an important influence on world events.

THINKING IT OVER

Would you now change your mind about the person you most identify with the Middle East?

(Yes ___ No ___)   If yes, why? _____

_____

If no, why not? _____

_____

CHECKING YOUR UNDERSTANDING

Directions: Complete the following cards. Then answer the multiple choice questions that follow.

ANWAR SADAT

Who was he? _____

Why is he important? _____

_____

GOLDA MEIR

Who was she? _____

Why is she important? _____

_____

AYATOLLAH KHOMEINI

Who was he? _____

Why was he important? _____

_____

SADDAM HUSSEIN

Who is he? _____

Why is he important? _____

_____

1 Which person is correctly paired with his country?
   1 Desmond Tutu - Egypt
   2 Fidel Castro - Mexico
   3 Anwar Sadat - France
   4 Saddam Hussein - Iraq

2 Which leader supported signing a peace treaty with Israel?
   1 Ayatollah Khomeini   3 Anwar Sadat
   2 Fidel Castro   4 Saddam Hussein

3 Which headline correctly pairs the person and the event they are associated with?
   1 "Construction Begins On The Suez Canal" — Fidel Castro
   2 "Israel and Egypt Go To War" — Nelson Mandela
   3 "Israel Signs A Treaty With Egypt" — Anwar Sadat
   4 "Jews Demand An Independent Israel" — Ayatollah Khomeini

4 Which event occurred while Saddam Hussein was in power?
   1 start of the Gulf War
   2 end of World War I
   3 issuance of the Monroe Doctrine
   4 creation of the state of Israel

5 Ayatollah Khomeini believed that the government of Iran should
   1 model its nation on religious principles
   2 allow women the right to vote
   3 follow Western ideas and technology
   4 expand democratic practices

6 Anwar Sadat, Fidel Castro and F.W. de Klerk are best known as
   1 nuclear scientists
   2 religious leaders
   3 Communist leaders
   4 political leaders

5 CONCERNS

In this section you will read about some of the major problems and issues currently facing the peoples of the Middle East.

THINK ABOUT IT

What do you think is the major problem facing the Middle East today? _____

_____

_____

Important Terms: As you read this section, look for the following terms:

   ◆ **Palestinian-Israeli Conflict**   ◆ **Islamic Fundamentalism**
   ◆ **Camp David Accords**   ◆ **Gulf War**

◆ THE CLASH BETWEEN ISRAEL AND THE PALESTINIANS

In 1917, the British promised the Jews a homeland in Palestine. After the deaths of over six million Jews in Europe during World War II at the hands of Nazi Germany, the surviving Jews wanted desperately to go to Palestine. However, it was not until three years after the war that a homeland for Jews finally became a reality. In 1948, the United Nations voted to divide the former British colony of Palestine into two parts. One part became the State of Israel—a homeland for the Jews—and the other part was for the Palestinian Arabs.

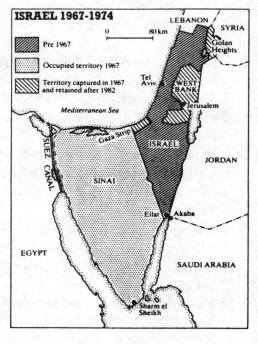

THE ARAB-ISRAELI WARS

Arab nations refused to recognize Israel as an independent country. They immediately declared war on the new nation. During the war, many Palestinians fled to neighboring Arab countries. These Palestinians refused to recognize the State of Israel, and demanded their own homeland. Some Palestinians formed the **Palestinian Liberation Organization (PLO)**, led by **Yassir Arafat**. The division of Palestine was the cause of three more wars between the Arabs and Israelis (in 1956, 1967 and 1973). As a result of winning, Israel gained land (now called the "occupied territories") from surrounding Arab countries. Israelis believed they had to maintain control of the "occupied territories" to defend themselves. Palestinians believed that they had a right to control their own lands, free of Israeli interference.

◆ PEACE BETWEEN ISRAEL AND EGYPT

In 1979, Egypt's President **Anwar Sadat** and Israel's Prime Minister **Menachem Begin,** with the help of U. S. President Jimmy Carter, signed the **Camp David Accords,** the first peace treaty to be signed between Israel and an Arab country. Israel gave back to Egypt some of the land it captured during wartime in return for peace. President Sadat's action angered some militant Arabs. In 1981, he was assassinated for his efforts to bring about a peace settlement with Israel.

THE MIDDLE EAST PEACE CONFERENCE

In 1991, the U.S. helped arrange a peace conference between Israel and many of the Arab states. Among the issues under discussion are control of the territories Israel had captured from the Arabs, and common problems such as the shortage of water. Recent progress has been made toward shaping agreements between Israel and Jordan, as well as Israel and Syria.

ISRAEL AND THE PALESTINIANS MAKE A DEAL

In September 1993, Israeli and Palestinian leaders signed an agreement. Israel officially recognized the PLO, and agreed to give the Palestinians control of the Gaza Strip and the town of Jericho (two of the "occupied territories"). Palestinians promised to give up their struggle against the existence of Israel. Many issues remain, such as the future of Jerusalem, Jewish settlements on the West Bank, and a separate Palestinian state. In addition, many Israelis and Palestinians oppose all attempts at compromise. Nevertheless, the agreement creates new hope for peace in the Middle East.

MIDDLE EAST OIL AND THE WEST

OPEC AND ITS EFFECT ON OIL PRICES

Many oil-producing countries are located around the Persian Gulf (Saudi Arabia, Iran and Iraq). In the early 1970s several Middle Eastern and other oil-producing countries formed the **Organization of Petroleum Exporting Countries (OPEC)** to try to control the production and price of oil. Acting together, OPEC sharply raised the price of oil, resulting in many Middle East nations becoming very wealthy. On the other hand, countries which relied heavily on imported oil suffered because they had to pay much higher prices. Eventually, Western countries reduced their dependence on oil from OPEC. As a result, the price of oil has remained steady throughout the 1980s and into the present.

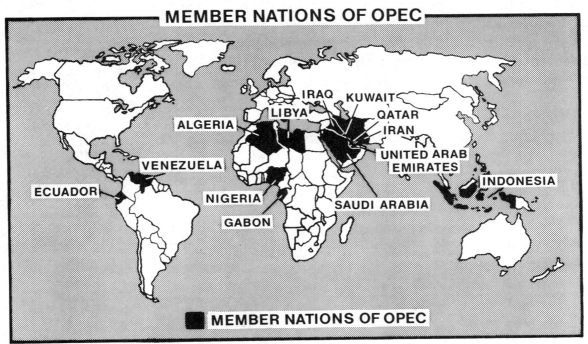

MEMBER NATIONS OF OPEC

IRAQ KUWAIT
LIBYA QATAR
ALGERIA IRAN
VENEZUELA UNITED ARAB EMIRATES
ECUADOR INDONESIA
NIGERIA SAUDI ARABIA
GABON

■ **MEMBER NATIONS OF OPEC**

THE IRANIAN REVOLUTION AND ISLAMIC FUNDAMENTALISM

Islamic Fundamentalism refers to the resolve of some Muslim groups to follow the laws of Islam very strictly, and reject more modern, Western kinds of lifestyles. It includes having women go back to traditional roles. This movement has occurred in:

➤ **Iran**. In 1979, Islamic Fundamentalists overthrew the Shah (king), who had made Iran into a modern, less religious society. **Ayatollah Khomeini**, who became Iran's new leader, set up a religious dictatorship. Under his control, religious leaders ran the government according to strict Islamic law. Opponents were dealt with harshly. Iraq invaded Iran in 1980, and the fighting lasted until the 1988 cease-fire. The war caused great loss of life and property.

➤ **Lebanon**. Islamic Fundamentalists, encouraged by events in Iran, became involved in a civil war between various groups which had been fighting in that country. Lebanese Fundamentalists, friendly to Iran, kidnapped several Westerners and held them hostage (since that time most of the hostages have been released). In 1980, Syria invaded Lebanon to end the civil war. Today, the Lebanese are trying to put their country back together again.

◆ THE GULF WAR (1990-1991)

In August 1990, Iraq invaded its much smaller neighbor, Kuwait. **Saddam Hussein**, Iraq's dictator, took over Kuwait's great oil wealth and territory. Hussein next threatened to invade Saudi Arabia, the world's largest supplier of oil. World leaders were greatly concerned, because many countries depend on Kuwait and Saudi Arabia for their oil.

OPERATION DESERT STORM

In an effort to get Iraq to withdraw from Kuwait, many nations sent troops, planes and ships to the area. The U.N. gave Hussein a deadline to leave Kuwait, but he refused. The war began soon after the deadline passed. The allies, led by the United States, launched an attack known as **Operation Desert Storm**. In just a few weeks, under massive bombing, Iraq was defeated.

RESULTS

The war resulted in much of Kuwait being destroyed. Despite the large loss of Iraqi lives and the damage which resulted from the war, Hussein remained in power. However, the war proved that the nations of the world, many of which do not get along together, could cooperate when faced with a crisis. The importance of the U. S. increased in the Middle East. The U.S. used its new influence to arrange a peace conference to try to help settle Arab-Israeli disputes.

SUMMING UP: CONCERNS

Differences between the Israelis and Palestinians over the land once called Palestine led to three wars. The recent agreement between Israel and the PLO, however, holds out hope for peace in the area. Other issues, such as the spread of Islamic Fundamentalism and reliable access to Middle Eastern oil, still concern much of the world today.

THINKING IT OVER

Now that you have finished reading this section, what do you think is the major problem or issue facing the Middle East? _____ Why? _____

_____

_____

CHECKING YOUR UNDERSTANDING

Directions: Complete the following cards. Then answer the multiple choice questions that follow.

PALESTINIAN / ISRAELI ISSUE

What is the issue? _____

Major effect on the area: _____

_____

CAMP DAVID ACCORDS

What were they? _____

Importance: _____

_____

ISLAMIC FUNDAMENTALISM

What is it? _____

Major effect on the area: _____

_____

GULF WAR

Cause: _____

Results: _____

_____

---

1 The main purpose of OPEC is to
1 limit nuclear weapons
2 save the rain forests
3 regulate oil production
4 guarantee freedom of minorities

2 A direct result of the Camp David Accords was that
1 the Suez Canal was given to Israel
2 Israel assassinated Yassir Arafat
3 Golda Meir was elected prime minister of Israel
4 Israel and Egypt signed a peace treaty

3 Which headline best reflects events in the Middle East during the 1990s?
1 "Gulf War Begins"
2 "European Powers Establish New Colonies"
3 "United Nations Creates An Israeli State"
4 "Israel and Egypt Sign A Peace Treaty"

4 The term "Islamic Fundamentalism" refers to
1 the worship of nature
2 adopting Western ideas of government
3 a movement to return to basic Islamic values
4 a strict code of non-violence

5 A major result of Iraq's invasion of Kuwait was
1 the immediate overthrow of Saddam Hussein
2 the introduction of Communism into Kuwait
3 lasting peace throughout the world
4 a show of international cooperation

6 Ayatollah Khomeini criticized the government in Iran because the Shah
1 was friendly with the Soviet Union
2 followed traditional Islamic values
3 allowed Western ideas to influence the nation
4 denied women the right to vote

7 The main source of conflict between Israel and the Palestinians has been
1 the presence of Israeli ships in the Suez Canal
2 the demand of Palestinians for their own homeland
3 Soviet support for the State of Israel
4 increased European interference in the Middle East

8 In which Middle East country is Islamic fundamentalism a major force?
1 Turkey   3 Israel
2 Iran   4 Egypt

9 During the 1990s, the United States and Iraq were engaged in a war because
1 Iraq used terrorism on Iran
2 Iraq invaded Kuwait
3 Israel threatened to invade Iraq
4 Kuwait signed a treaty with Israel

10 The main goals of the Palestinian Liberation Organization (PLO) have been to
1 establish a homeland for Palestinian Arabs
2 eliminate Communism in Palestine
3 make peace between Palestinians and Israelis
4 control the price of Palestinian oil

SUMMARIZING YOUR UNDERSTANDING

PARAGRAPH FRAME

To answer the following question, use the words in the Word Game box to fill in the paragraph.

Why does a conflict exist between Israel and the Palestinians?

word game

Camp David Accords	United Nations	Palestinian Arabs
Anwar Sadat	British	Israel
PLO	Egypt	Palestine

In 1917, the _____ government promised the Jewish people a homeland in _____. When the _____ voted to create an independent state of _____ in 1948, war broke out. The _____ refused to recognize this new nation. A new organization was begun, the _____, to win back from Israel the lands taken from the Palestinian people. Since that time, three wars have been fought. However, in 1977, the President of _____ signed a peace treaty with Menachem Begin of Israel. This new peace treaty, called the _____ _____, so angered some fundamentalists that in 1981 _____ was assassinated.

Directions: Fill in the information in the organizer below.

Deserts: _____

Rivers / River Valleys: _____

EFFECTS OF GEOGRAPHY ON THE PEOPLES AND HISTORY OF THE MIDDLE EAST

Climate: _____

Resources: _____

CROSSWORD PUZZLE

Building Your Vocabulary. Use your reading of this chapter and the clues below to complete the puzzle.

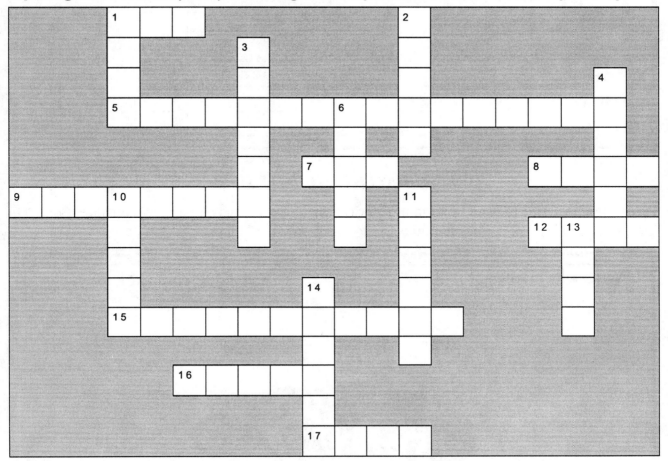

ACROSS
1. Much of the Middle East's wealth is based on this resource.
5. Peace treaty signed by Egypt and Israel in 1977.
7. Organization whose goal is the creation of a Palestinian state.
8. Nation that invaded Kuwait in 1990.
9. European attempts to recapture the Holy Land from the Muslims.
12. River where the ancient Egyptian civilization began.
15. Economic system in which sons follows their ancestors' occupation.
16. Natural resource that is most scarce in the Middle East
17. Canal used to connect Europe with Asia.

DOWN
1. Organization formed to regulate the price and supply of oil.
2. Holy book of the Islamic religion.
3. Religion of most people living in Israel.
4. Name of the Jewish nation in the Middle East.
6. Major religion of most people living in the Middle East.
10. Egyptian President assassinated for signing a treaty with Israel.
11. Leader of the PLO.
13. Nation once governed by Ayatollah Khomeini.
14. River near where the Mesopotamian civilization began.

Directions: Complete the information in the following chart on major religions:

	JUDAISM	CHRISTIANITY	ISLAM
Major Beliefs	1 _____ 2 _____	1 _____ 2 _____	1 _____ 2 _____
Key People	_____	_____	_____
Holy Books	_____	_____	_____
Holy Sites	_____	_____	_____

DESCRIBING HISTORICAL EVENTS

Directions: Describe fully an important historical event you learned about in this chapter. Complete the chart by filling in the information called for in each box.

WHO was involved?

_____

_____

WHEN did it happen?

_____

_____

THE GULF WAR

WHERE did it take place?

_____

_____

WHAT was its main cause?

_____

_____

RESULTS:

1. _____

2. _____

3. _____

4. _____

UNDERSTANDING THE WORLD'S RELIGIONS | TEST HELPER

This section will help prepare you to answer questions dealing with religions. Questions on global studies examinations often center around religions' **major beliefs**, how religions have influenced history, and the **conflicts** that often arise out of religious differences.

WHAT IS RELIGION?

All societies have some forms of religious beliefs. Because these beliefs touch on what people think life itself is about, religion has a tremendous impact on the way people behave. There is simply no way to understand world history and culture without the study of religion. Most religions have three common elements:

1. A set of *beliefs* about the nature of the universe, and the meaning of life.

2. A set of *practices* relating to worship and to proper conduct in life.

3. An *organization*, such as a church, which oversees the conduct of religious practices.

For example, Jews and Christians believe in one God and believe this God created the earth, but they differ from each other because they have their own unique forms of prayer to God. When studying a religion, you should ask yourself:

➤ What are its *beliefs*? Do its followers believe in a God or gods? Do they believe in life after death? Does the religion have prophets or holy persons?

➤ What are its *customs and practices*? Does it have rules for leading a moral life? Does it have holy places? Are there foods or actions that are forbidden to its followers?

➤ Does it have a religious *organization*? Is there a group of religious leaders? What are their powers and duties? Does it have houses of worship?

THE WORLD'S RELIGIONS

As you learn about each area of the world, you will come across a large number of religions. This chart shows where some of them started:

AFRICA	CHINA and JAPAN	AMERICAS
Ancient Egyptian religions Traditional African religions	Confucianism Taoism Shinto	Native American
EUROPE	INDIA	MIDDLE EAST
Ancient Greek and Roman religions	Hinduism Buddhism Sikhism	Judaism Christianity Islam

HISTORICAL DEVELOPMENT

One way to look at the world's religions is to organize them according to their history. For example, Christianity and Islam both developed out of Judaism. All three religions share a belief in the existence of one God. Christianity then later divided into Eastern Orthodoxy and Roman Catholicism. Finally, in the 1500s, Western Europe divided into Roman Catholicism and Protestantism. If we chart these relationships, they appear like this:

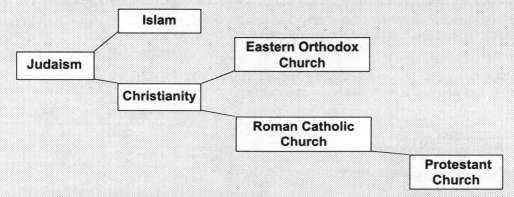

Other religions developed in India. Buddhism grew out of Hinduism. Sikhism was an attempt to bring together Hindu and Islamic beliefs. Zen Buddhism was a form of Buddhism that developed in Japan:

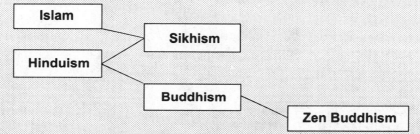

This way of thinking about religions is useful, because usually each new religion borrows some ideas and practices from the older religion it grew out of.

ONE OR MANY GODS?

Another way to describe religions is to look at their basic beliefs:

Animism	Belief that spirits are found in people and all natural objects	Traditional African religions; Shintoism
Polytheism	Belief in many gods and goddesses	Ancient Egyptian; Ancient Greek and Roman; Native American; Hinduism
Monotheism	Belief in one God	Judaism, Christianity, Islam, Sikhism

You might notice that some important religions are missing from this chart. These other religions are not especially concerned with the existence of gods. Both Buddhism and Confucianism, for example, are more interested in how people should best conduct their lives. For this reason Buddhists and Confucians often feel free to follow the teachings of more than one religion.

TESTING YOUR UNDERSTANDING

Directions: Base your answers to questions 1 and 2 on the political cartoon below and on your knowledge of global studies.

1 Which person is being depicted in the cartoon?
   1 Fidel Castro   3 Nelson Mandela
   2 Saddam Hussein   4 Anwar Sadat

2 Which event does the cartoon make reference to?
   1 Camp David Peace Accords
   2 The formation of OPEC
   3 Iraq's invasion of Kuwait
   4 Overthrow of the Shah of Iran

3 The Nile, the Tigris and Euphrates, and the Amazon are
   1 mountain ranges   3 lakes and streams
   2 river systems   4 deserts and plateaus

4 Which is a major geographic problem for the Middle East?
   1 extremely heavy rainfalls
   2 long cold summers
   3 frequent water shortages
   4 a lack of any natural resources

5 Which is usually a characteristic of a traditional economy?
   1 many consumer products
   2 production is restricted by law
   3 central government planning
   4 most people work at farming

6 Judaism, Christianity and Islam are similar in that each
   1 first developed in Asia
   2 has holy sites in Rome
   3 believes in one God
   4 prohibits the eating of pork

7 Which leader favored a government based on the Islamic religion?
   1 Jomo Kenyatta
   2 Ayatollah Khomeini
   3 Nelson Mandela
   4 Fidel Castro

8 A believer in Islamic customs and principles would agree that
   1 women should go to college
   2 charity is a religious obligation
   3 Muslims should eat pork products
   4 Islam must combine with Judaism

9 The cultural development of the Middle East has been most influenced by
   1 the words of the Koran
   2 international terrorism
   3 Arabic women leaders
   4 advances in science and mathematics

ESSAYS

1 Religion helps to shape the values and beliefs of a society.

Religions

Animism	Judaism
Christianity	Islam

Part A

Choose *two* of the religions listed, and for each one chosen, state *two* of its major beliefs.

RELIGION	MAJOR BELIEFS
A. _____	1. _____
	2. _____
B. _____	1. _____
	2. _____

Part B

In your part B answer, you should use information you gave in Part A. You may also include different or additional information in your Part B answer. (**NOTE:** Use the "cheeseburger method" on p. 75.)

Write an essay explaining how religion helps shape the values and beliefs of a society.

2 The clash between Israel and the Palestinians is a global problem.

Part A

State the cause of the clash between Israel and the Palestinians: _____

_____

Identify *one* effect this clash has had on another part of the world: _____

_____

Part B

In your part B answer, you should use information you gave in Part A. However, you may also include different or additional information in your Part B answer.

Write an essay showing how the clash between Israel and the Palestinians has had an effect on other parts of the world.

3 Individuals have often brought about important changes in their countries.

Individuals

Nelson Mandela	F.W. de Klerk
Fidel Castro	Anwar Sadat
Saddam Hussein	Ayatollah Khomeini

Part A

Select *two* individuals from the list: 1. _____ 2. _____

State how *each* individual has brought about important changes in his country:

1. _____

2. _____

Part B
In your part B answer, you should use information you gave in Part A. However, you may also include different or additional information in your Part B answer.

Write an essay showing how some individuals have brought about important changes in their countries.

GLOBAL CHECKLIST

THE MIDDLE EAST

Directions: Before going on to the next chapter, you should check your understanding of the important people, terms and concepts covered in this chapter. Place a check mark (✔) next to those that you are able to explain. If you have trouble remembering a term, refer to the page listed next to the item.

- ❑ Middle East (80)
- ❑ Suez Canal (80)
- ❑ Tigris River (80)
- ❑ Euphrates River (80)
- ❑ Oil Reserves (81)
- ❑ Mesopotamia (85)
- ❑ Cuneiform (85)
- ❑ Code of Hammurabi (85)
- ❑ Nile River (85)
- ❑ Hieroglyphics (85)
- ❑ Monotheism (85)
- ❑ Crusades (86)
- ❑ Judaism (91)
- ❑ Mohammed (92)
- ❑ Torah (92)
- ❑ Bible (92)
- ❑ Koran (92)
- ❑ Christianity (92)
- ❑ Islam (92)
- ❑ Anwar Sadat (95)
- ❑ Ayatollah Khomeini (95)
- ❑ Golda Meir (95)
- ❑ Saddam Hussein (95)
- ❑ Palestinian-Israeli Conflict (98)
- ❑ Camp David Accords (98)
- ❑ Islamic Fundamentalism (99)
- ❑ Gulf War (100)

GEOGRAPHY

- Size and Location
- Geographic Features and Their Effects

CONCERNS

- Rapid Population Growth
- Economic Development
- Group Conflicts
- Problems in Southeast Asia

CHAPTER 5

SOUTH AND SOUTHEAST ASIA

HISTORY

- Early Cultures
- India Under British Rule
- Indian Independence, and Partition
- South Asia Since Independence
- Southeast Asia: A Region with Many Influences
- Independence and War

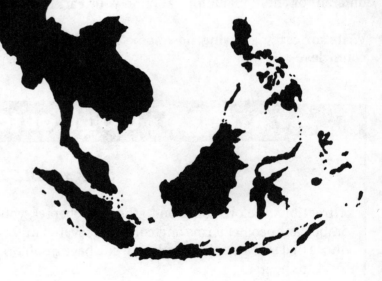

IMPORTANT PEOPLE

- Mohandas Gandhi
- Corazon Aquino
- Ho Chi Minh
- Mother Teresa

SYSTEMS

- Government
- Economy
- Society
- Religion
- The Arts

What do these pictures show you about South and Southeast Asia? _____
_____
_____
_____

1 GEOGRAPHY

In this section you will read about the major geographic features of South and Southeast Asia, and how these features have affected its people and history.

THINK ABOUT IT

Look at the maps of South and Southeast Asia on this and the next page. Can you name two countries in each of these areas?

SOUTH ASIA

1. _____

2. _____

SOUTHEAST ASIA

1. _____

2. _____

Important Terms: As you read this section, look for the following terms:

◆ **Subcontinent**
◆ **Himalayas**

◆ **Ganges River**
◆ **Monsoons**

SIZE AND LOCATION

— SOUTH ASIA —

◆ Most of South Asia is a **subcontinent** (*a large piece of land smaller than a continent*). The Indian subcontinent looks like a large triangle jutting out of Asia, pointing into the Indian Ocean. India, Pakistan and Bangladesh, and several smaller countries, make up this region.

— SOUTHEAST ASIA —

Southeast Asia is made up of a large **peninsula** (*land surrounded by water on three sides*) on the southeast corner of the Asian mainland, and several island nations. The peninsula includes Thailand, Cambodia, Laos and Vietnam. The island nations include Indonesia, Malaysia and the Philippines.

MAJOR GEOGRAPHIC FEATURES AND THEIR EFFECTS

MOUNTAINS

◆ The **Himalayas**, the highest mountains in the world, separate the Indian subcontinent from the rest of Asia. As a result, people on both sides of the Himalayas developed their own separate languages, customs and cultures. Despite these high mountains, India was invaded several times through the northwest mountain passes.

RIVERS AND RIVER VALLEYS

As in Africa and the Middle East, the earliest civilizations of South Asia and Southeast Asia developed
◆ in river valleys, like the Indus and Ganges river valleys in India. The **Ganges River** is considered holy by Hindus, the largest religious group in India. They believe that washing in this river can remove their sins and gain them rewards in the next life. In Southeast Asia, the Mekong and the Irrawaddy rivers serve as water routes.

CLIMATE

Both South and Southeast Asia have warm winters and hot summers. The most important feature
◆ of the climate are the **monsoons**. Monsoons are winds that bring heavy rains in the summer. They

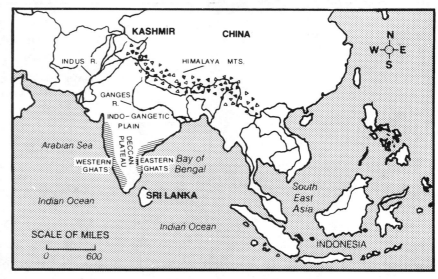

have both good and bad effects. The rain waters the crops and helps support life in the region. However, if they bring too much rain, the monsoons cause flooding, property damage and death.

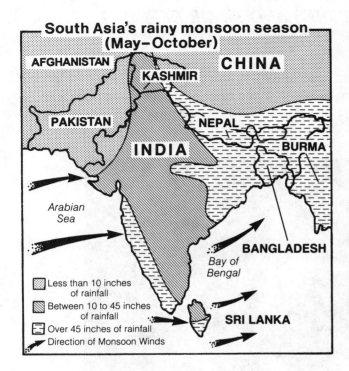

South Asia's rainy monsoon season (May–October)

AFGHANISTAN

CHINA

KASHMIR

PAKISTAN

NEPAL

INDIA

BURMA

Arabian Sea

BANGLADESH

Bay of Bengal

▦ Less than 10 inches of rainfall

▨ Between 10 to 45 inches of rainfall

▤ Over 45 inches of rainfall

➤ Direction of Monsoon Winds

SRI LANKA

RESOURCES

Western nations have long looked upon the lands of South and Southeast Asia as rich sources of spices, teas, rice, and tropical wood. These resources attracted imperialist nations, which conquered or colonized the area.

IMPORTANT LOCATION

Southeast Asia provides the shortest trade route between the Pacific and Indian Oceans. From the earliest times, people have passed through the area — as travelers, merchants or invaders. Therefore, Southeast Asia has been affected by the mix of peoples coming to the region, resulting in a culture that has been heavily influenced by the Indians and the Chinese.

SUMMING UP: GEOGRAPHY

Most of South Asia is a subcontinent; India forms its largest part. Southeast Asia consists of a large peninsula. The Himalayas, the highest mountains in the world, and the monsoons, the winds which bring heavy rains to the area in summer, are two geographic features which have had the greatest effect on South and Southeast Asia.

THINKING IT OVER

What do you think is the most important geographic feature of the region? _____

_____ Explain why: _____

_____

_____

CHECKING YOUR UNDERSTANDING

Directions: Complete the following cards. Then answer the multiple choice questions that follow.

MONSOONS

Definition: _____

Importance: _____

_____

GANGES

What is it? _____

Importance: _____

_____

HIMALAYAS

What are they? _____

Importance: _____

_____

SUBCONTINENT

Definition: _____

Two nations that are part of a subcontinent:

1 _____ 2 _____

1 India is a part of the continent of
   1 Asia   3 South America
   2 Australia   4 Europe

2 Monsoons can best be described as
   1 seasonal winds   3 mountain ranges
   2 river valleys   4 rain forests

3 Which geographic feature is correctly paired with its location?
   1 Sahara Desert — Vietnam
   2 Amazon River — Israel
   3 Nile River — Saudi Arabia
   4 Ganges River — India

4 A plane from Pakistan to Bangladesh would be flying in which general direction?
   1 east   3 north
   2 west   4 south

5 Which statement about India's geography is most accurate?
   1 India has high mountains.
   2 India has many oil wells.
   3 India lacks natural barriers.
   4 India lacks major rivers.

6 Which affects the climate of India most?
   1 melting of glaciers   3 large desert regions
   2 tropical rain forests   4 monsoon rains

2 HISTORY

In this section you will read about the historical developments in South and Southeast Asia, from their earliest civilizations to their achievement of independence from European imperialism.

TIMELINE OF HISTORICAL EVENTS							
700	**1857**	**1947**	**1948**	**1954**	**1971**	**1975**	**1986**
Muslims invade India	Sepoy Mutiny	India gains independence	Gandhi assassinated	Vietnam split in two	Bangladesh breaks from Pakistan	Communists take power in Cambodia	Aquino defeats Marcos

---

THINK ABOUT IT

India has been called "a land of foreign invaders?" Why do you think it was so named?

_____

_____

Important Terms: As you read this section, look for the following terms:

- "Divide and Conquer"
- Sepoy Mutiny
- Passive resistance
- Civil disobedience
- Genocide
- Vietnam War

— SOUTH ASIA —

AN EARLY CENTER OF CIVILIZATION

More than 5000 years ago, the Indus River Valley in northeast India was one of the earliest centers of human civilization. Throughout its history, India's wealth was the reason for frequent invasions. About 1,000 B.C., the Aryan peoples invaded and established the Hindu religion and the caste system.

CLASSICAL AGE OF HINDU CULTURE (321 B.C. - 500 A.D.)

During this 800-year period, India was united under the Maurya and Gupta Empires. This period is known as the classical period of Hindu civilization. It was famed for its important developments in the arts, literature, sciences, and mathematics (*development of the decimal point and the concept of zero*).

MUSLIM RULE (700-1760)

About 1,300 years ago, Muslims invaded and took control over most of India. These Muslims, called **Mughals**, united India by the 1550s. They made important contributions to Indian culture. For example, Muslims built the **Taj Mahal**, one of the world's most famous architectural achievements. The domes of the Taj Mahal show the influence of Islam on Indian art—an important example of **cultural diffusion**.

Pictured at right: The Taj Mahal. Its construction, begun in 1632, took almost 20 years and 20,0000 workers to complete.

INDIA UNDER BRITISH RULE

THE BRITISH GAIN CONTROL

By the early 1700s, the British, who were interested in Indian foodstuffs and cloth, established trading posts. Over time, the British gained control over India by following a policy of "**divide and conquer.**"

Under this policy, the British maintained friendship with some states, while using force against other states. This prevented the Indian states from uniting against British rule. However, a few uprisings were carried out against British control. In 1857, during the **Sepoy Mutiny**, a group of **sepoys** (Indian soldiers in the British Army in India) rose up against their British officers. The British government put down this revolt, using it as an excuse to take official control of India.

CHANGES UNDER BRITISH RULE

During the two centuries of British rule, life in India changed a great deal.

Indian weavers working with a hand loom

> **Government.** The British united India under one government and system of law, similar to Great Britain's.

> **Economic Development.** The British built roads, bridges and railroads, and set up telegraph wires.

> **Employment.** Many Indians found jobs working for the British government. However, those who had earned a living making products in their homes lost their jobs, as people began to buy cloth and other goods made in English factories. Other Indians worked long hours for low wages under terrible conditions, to serve their British rulers.

> **Social Changes.** Schools and hospitals were built. However, the subjects taught in the schools were those which the British thought were important, such as the English language. In general, Indians and Indian culture were treated as inferior to the British.

INDIAN INDEPENDENCE

British rule gradually stirred strong feelings of nationalism among the Indian people, who began to look for ways to gain their independence.

THE INDIAN NATIONALIST MOVEMENT

Mohandas Gandhi was a leader in the struggle for Indian independence. He believed that violence should not be used to achieve independence from the powerful British. Instead, Gandhi urged Indians to use the non-violent, peaceful methods of passive resistance and civil disobedience.

> **Passive Resistance.** Gandhi developed a policy known as passive resistance. He told his followers that rather than fight back when the British tried to enforce their laws, they should peacefully suffer beatings and violence. Gandhi believed that this would gain world attention and lead to increased support for the cause of Indian independence. Eventually the British would see their mistakes and, Gandhi hoped, they would withdraw peacefully.

> **Civil Disobedience.** Gandhi advised Indians to use civil disobedience to protest unjust British laws. He instructed his followers to disobey laws with fasts, marches, sit-ins and strikes. He pro-

tested the British salt tax by making a famous "march to the sea." He encouraged people to **boycott** (refuse to buy) British goods, and to buy only items made locally.

THE ESTABLISHMENT OF INDIA AND PAKISTAN (1947)

World War II (1939-1945) weakened the British a great deal. As a result of Gandhi's efforts and its own weakness, Great Britain decided to grant India its independence after the war. However, it soon became obvious that India's Hindu and Muslim populations could not get along peacefully. Gandhi wanted a unified India, but Muslim leaders wanted to set up their own state. Therefore, in 1947 when the British granted India its independence, they made two separate nations—India and Pakistan—out of the former British colony. Since religious differences were the main cause of violence, the division was made along religious lines: India became a Hindu nation and Pakistan a Muslim nation. Millions of Indians had to move from their homes to India or Pakistan, depending on their religion. Thousands of Muslims and Hindus were killed in the riots that followed. Religious differences between the two groups have created much bitterness.

SOUTH ASIA SINCE INDEPENDENCE

INDIA

After independence, India became the leader of a group of **non-aligned** nations—countries that refused to become allies of either the Western democracies or the Communist nations. India still stands as a leader of the countries of the developing world.

PAKISTAN

When Pakistan was established in 1947, it consisted of two parts: one on the east and the other on the west side of India, separated by 1000 miles. Ethnic differences between the people in the eastern and western parts of Pakistan led to fighting. In 1971, the people in the eastern part of Pakistan broke away from the western part of Pakistan to form a new nation called Bangladesh.

BANGLADESH

Bangladesh is one of the world's poorest nations. Since its independence in 1971, it has been suffering from overpopulation and flooding. Bangladesh is the most densely populated nation in the world, with over 120 million people in an area the size of New York State.

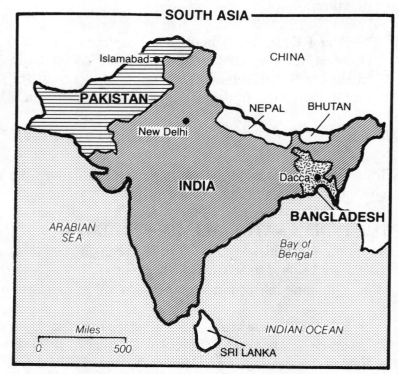

Melting snows from the Himalayan Mountains often cause severe flooding, which results in the destruction of crops, property loss and death.

— SOUTHEAST ASIA —

A REGION WITH MANY INFLUENCES

Separate river valley kingdoms (for example, Vietnam, Burma and Laos) existed in Southeast Asia thousands of years ago. This region was strongly influenced by both Indian and Chinese culture. Other parts of the area, such as Indonesia, were affected by Islamic culture. Beginning in the 1500s, attracted by spices found in the area, European imperial powers began to take colonies in Southeast Asia.

INDEPENDENCE AND WAR

During World War II, Japan occupied most of Southeast Asia, driving out the European powers. Once the war was over, the Europeans returned. However, a spirit of nationalism took hold in the region. In the years following the war the people of Southeast Asia struggled to obtain their independence.

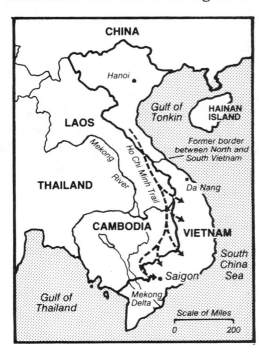

VIETNAM

After Japan's defeat, France tried to take back control of its colonies in Southeast Asia. In Vietnam, nationalists led by **Ho Chi Minh** defeated the French by 1954. Vietnam was then divided in two — a Communist North Vietnam and a non-Communist South. Attempts to reunite the country failed. The North Vietnamese Communists (**Vietcong**) attempted to take over South Vietnam, which led to the **Vietnam War**. Troops from the United States, South Vietnam, and their allies attempted to stop the spread of Communism, but the South Vietnamese government was unpopular and foreign attempts to save it did not work. In 1973, a peace agreement led to the withdrawal of U.S. troops, and in 1975, Vietnam was reunited under Communist rule.

CAMBODIA (Kampuchea)

The withdrawal of U.S. forces from Vietnam led to the collapse of the neighboring government in Cambodia. In 1975, local Communists called the **Khmer Rouge** took control of Cambodia, turning it into a Communist nation. A policy of **genocide** (*mass murder*) was carried out by the new government. People suspected of not supporting the Communist cause were murdered. It is estimated that over 4 million Cambodians were killed for this reason. In 1978, Vietnam invaded Cambodia, and forced the Khmer Rouge government out of power.

THE PHILIPPINES

The Philippines, a U.S. colony since 1898, achieved independence in 1946. **Ferdinand Marcos** was elected President in 1965. He established stability but

Opened grave pits of victims of the Khmer Rouge

proved to be a dishonest leader who used government money to make himself rich. In 1986, he was defeated in a democratic election by **Corazon Aquino**. Aquino attempted to restore democracy and to solve such problems as widespread poverty and unemployment. She left office in 1992.

ANALYSIS

What do you think are some of the major problems facing newly independent countries?

_____

_____

_____

SUMMING UP: HISTORY

The Indus River Valley of India was one of the early centers of civilization. During its long history, India has been invaded and controlled by foreign groups several times. Led by Mohandas Gandhi, India achieved independence after World War II, which led to the creation of two separate nations, Hindu India and Muslim Pakistan. Southeast Asia also has been the object of foreign control. After gaining independence, some Southeast Asian nations set up Communist governments.

THINKING IT OVER

Now add to or correct your statement about why India has been called "a land of foreign invaders": _____

_____

CHECKING YOUR UNDERSTANDING

Directions: Complete the following cards. Then answer the multiple choice questions that follow.

"DIVIDE AND CONQUER"

Define: _____

Results: _____

_____

SEPOY MUTINY

Describe it: _____

Importance: _____

_____

```
┌─────────────────────────────────┐   ┌─────────────────────────────────┐
│        PASSIVE RESISTANCE        │   │        CIVIL DISOBEDIENCE        │
│                                  │   │                                  │
│   Define: _____ │   │   What is it? _____  │
│                                  │   │                                  │
│   Example: _____ │   │   Example: _____   │
│                                  │   │                                  │
│   _____│   │   _____ │
└─────────────────────────────────┘   └─────────────────────────────────┘
```

```
┌─────────────────────────────────┐   ┌─────────────────────────────────┐
│          VIETNAM WAR             │   │            GENOCIDE              │
│                                  │   │                                  │
│   Causes: _____ │   │   Define: _____    │
│                                  │   │                                  │
│   Results: _____ │   │   Example: _____    │
│                                  │   │                                  │
│   _____│   │   _____ │
└─────────────────────────────────┘   └─────────────────────────────────┘
```

1 A study of India's history shows that the Muslim and the British were similar in that both
   1 were foreign invaders
   2 supported India's independence
   3 opposed imperialism
   4 were defeated by India

2 Two countries, India and Pakistan, were formed from the single British colony of India mainly because of
   1 religious and cultural differences
   2 demands made by the Soviet Union
   3 geographic factors making it easier to have two nations
   4 demands made by the United Nations

3 Which development came last?
   1 India and Pakistan were partitioned
   2 the Sepoy Mutiny broke out
   3 Bangladesh was established
   4 the British colonized India

4 The term "passive resistance" means
   1 violent uprisings against the government
   2 a movement to overthrow democracy
   3 a change in the way goods pass from business to consumers
   4 a policy of non-violent behavior in the face of government abuse

5 Which statement about India's history is most accurate?
   1 military conflicts are the only way to achieve independence
   2 religious conflicts can sometimes influence political events
   3 military conflicts lead to improved living standards
   4 religious conflicts help to promote unity among nations

6 The Taj Mahal is a classic example of
   1 Muslim literature   3 Indian architecture
   2 Vietnamese music   4 Pakistani technology

7 Which statement best characterizes India's official foreign policy?
   1 military alliances with Communist nations
   2 friendship with all Muslim nations
   3 non-alignment with the major powers
   4 selling raw materials only to the Europeans

8 The partition of India into two nations was a result of
   1 Communist revolutions
   2 conflicts between Hindus and Muslims
   3 fighting over natural resources
   4 environmental concerns

3 SYSTEMS

In this section you will read about the major political institutions, economic development, religions and cultural achievements in South and Southeast Asia.

THINK ABOUT IT

To understand everyday life in this region, you should know certain important terms. Can you identify the following?

Hinduism: _____

Caste System: _____

Find their meanings in this section, or in the glossary (located in the back of the book).

Important Terms: As you read this section, look for the following terms:

- ◆ **Green Revolution**   ◆ **Untouchables**
- ◆ **Social mobility**   ◆ **Reincarnation**

GOVERNMENT

INDIA
India has been a democracy since its independence in 1947. It has a Parliament which makes its laws, a Prime Minister who carries out those laws and a Supreme Court which interprets the laws.

OTHER COUNTRIES
Like India, several other countries in the area — the Philippines, for example — are democracies. In addition, some civilian and military dictatorships exist in the region. Vietnam is a Communist dictatorship.

ECONOMY

INDIA
Today India has a **mixed economy**, in which both private business and government play important roles. While the country has some industry, three-quarters of its people are farmers, who continue to work by hand or with a few farm animals. In the 1960s and 1970s, the Indian government introduced what is called the **Green Revolution**. This was a policy designed to improve food production by applying modern science and technology. It succeeded in increasing some production in India, but it has been less successful in other countries in the region because farmers are often too poor to make use of the new seeds, fertilizers and equipment.

SOUTH AND SOUTHEAST ASIA

Like India, most of the nations have a traditional economic system. People work on farms and there is little industry. Some countries have private businesses, but in many nations the government plays an important economic role. In Communist countries such as Vietnam, the government directs all major economic activities. Following China's example, however, Vietnam now permits some private enterprise and foreign investment.

SOCIETY

INDIA

In traditional India, people were organized into **castes** or social classes. Membership in a caste was based ◆ on a person's birth and lasted one's entire life. There was no **social mobility** (*moving from one social* ◆ *group to another*) because a person could not marry someone from another caste or move from one caste to another. Hindu priests called **Brahmins** belonged to the highest caste. At the bottom of the caste system were the Shudra (laborers and servants). Below them were the **Untouchables**, considered ◆ so lowly as to be outside the caste system. Untouchables were given work that no one else wanted to do, such as sweeping streets and handling dead animals. Although the caste tradition still exists, the government today is attempting to eliminate it. This is a difficult task, because it is an important part of Hindu religious beliefs.

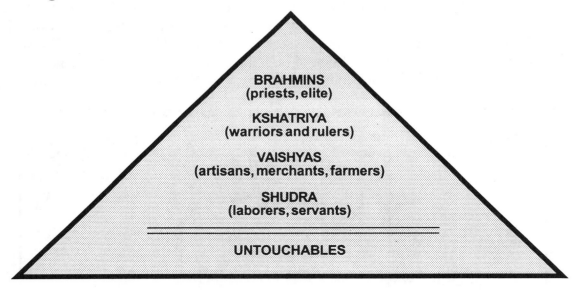

BRAHMINS
(priests, elite)

KSHATRIYA
(warriors and rulers)

VAISHYAS
(artisans, merchants, farmers)

SHUDRA
(laborers, servants)

UNTOUCHABLES

SOUTH AND SOUTHEAST ASIA

Most people live in small villages as part of **extended families**, with children, parents, and grandparents living under one roof. Usually, the oldest man is the decision-maker, with women and children having few rights. However, traditional values and customs are being weakened as a result of **urbanization** (*people moving to cities*), improvements in living conditions, and the introduction of radio and television in the countryside.

RELIGION

HINDUISM

Over 80% of India's people are Hindu. Hinduism is more than just a religion; its principles have an influence on how most Indians live.

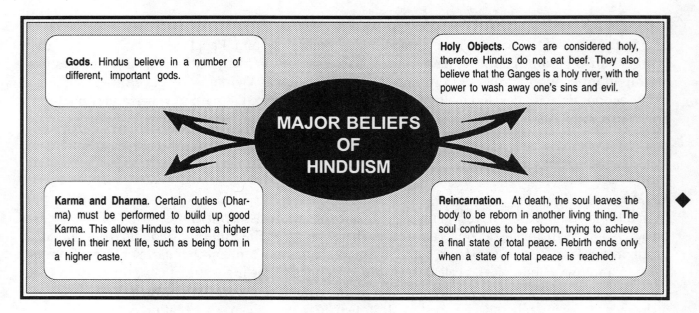

Gods. Hindus believe in a number of different, important gods.

Holy Objects. Cows are considered holy, therefore Hindus do not eat beef. They also believe that the Ganges is a holy river, with the power to wash away one's sins and evil.

MAJOR BELIEFS OF HINDUISM

Karma and Dharma. Certain duties (Dharma) must be performed to build up good Karma. This allows Hindus to reach a higher level in their next life, such as being born in a higher caste.

Reincarnation. At death, the soul leaves the body to be reborn in another living thing. The soul continues to be reborn, trying to achieve a final state of total peace. Rebirth ends only when a state of total peace is reached.

OTHER RELIGIONS

Many people in this area are Muslims or Christians, religions about which you have read earlier. The Sikhs in northwest India are another important religious group. They combine Hindu and Muslim religious ideas. For example, they believe in reincarnation, but also believe in only one God. Muslims are found in Bangladesh, Pakistan and Indonesia. Also, Buddhism had its origins in India, and spread to other countries in the region. (A discussion of Buddhism can be found in the chapter on China.) Christians are found in the Philippines and Vietnam.

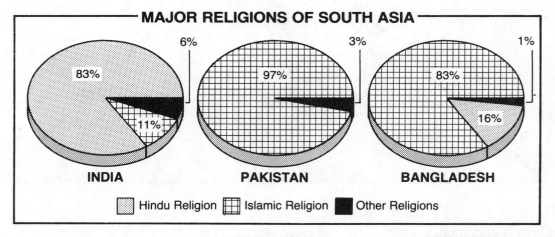

MAJOR RELIGIONS OF SOUTH ASIA

INDIA — 83%, 11%, 6%
PAKISTAN — 97%, 3%
BANGLADESH — 83%, 16%, 1%

▨ Hindu Religion   ▦ Islamic Religion   ■ Other Religions

THE ARTS

INDIA

As in other areas of the world, much of India's culture is based on its religious beliefs. This is especially true in the fields of architecture, art, music and dance — all heavily influenced by Hinduism. For example, classical dances in India tell stories about Hindu gods and heroes. The dancers are expected to learn more than 140 different poses when performing. They are often accompanied by flutes, drums and sitars (stringed instruments), all instruments used by earlier generations.

Indian dancer

Indian architecture was also greatly affected by its Muslim heritage. The Taj Mahal, built by the Mughals, is considered to be one of the world's most beautiful buildings.

SOUTHEAST ASIA

The arts of Southeast Asia show both Chinese and Indian cultural influences. Myanmar (Burma) and Thailand are famous for their many Buddhist temples. Indonesia is known for its masked dancing and shadow-puppet theater.

SUMMING UP: SYSTEMS

GOVERNMENT. India is the world's largest democracy. Other nations like Singapore have democracy, while nations like Myanmar (Burma) have dictatorships.

ECONOMY. India has a mixed economy, where private business and government play important roles. In other parts of South and Southeast Asia, the government has a more active role. This is especially true in communist economies like Vietnam.

SOCIETY. In India people are organized into separate groups called castes. The higher castes have more privileges than the lower ones. In many parts of South and Southeast Asia, people follow traditional lifestyles.

RELIGION. Hinduism is the major religion in India. Most people in Pakistan are Muslim. Buddhism, begun in India, is the religion of many people living in Southeast Asia.

THE ARTS. The Indian arts have been influenced by Hinduism, and by a Muslim heritage. Arts in Southeast Asia show a mixed Chinese-Indian influence.

THINKING IT OVER

Now that you have read this section, what key words do you think best reflect the kind of life found

in the region? _____

CHECKING YOUR UNDERSTANDING

Directions: Complete the following cards. Then answer the multiple choice questions that follow.

SOCIAL MOBILITY	CASTE SYSTEM
What is it? _____	Define it: _____
Importance: _____	Name two castes: 1 _____
_____	2 _____

UNTOUCHABLES

Who are they? _____

What do they do? _____

_____

HINDUISM

Definition: _____

Major beliefs: _____

_____

REINCARNATION

Define it: _____

Importance in Asian life: _____

_____

GREEN REVOLUTION

What is it? _____

How successful was it? _____

_____

1 Hinduism and Buddhism are both examples of Indian
   1 religious beliefs   3 social classes
   2 educational groups 4 official agencies

2 A major belief of Hindus is that
   1 the goal of all people should be to achieve wealth
   2 the soul continues to be reborn
   3 humans are born perfect
   4 Allah is the one true God

3 Which is the religion of most people in India and Pakistan?
   1 Islam and Judaism
   2 Animism and Hinduism
   3 Judaism and Christianity
   4 Islam and Hinduism

4 Belief in reincarnation is primarily associated with the beliefs of
   1 Islam   3 Judaism
   2 Animism   4 Hinduism

5 In India, the term "caste" refers to
   1 government members
   2 a hereditary social class
   3 an increase in urbanization
   4 traditional farming methods

6 The caste system has been most weakened by
   1 enforcing military laws against the system
   2 people moving from villages to cities
   3 the discovery of large oil deposits in India
   4 the refusal of Western nations to trade with India

7 The major goal of the Green Revolution was to
   1 decrease population growth
   2 increase agricultural production
   3 limit military alliances
   4 eliminate castes in India

8 Traditional values in India are being weakened by the
   1 movement of people to the cities
   2 shift in population to rural areas
   3 strengthening of the caste system
   4 new limitations being put on women

4 IMPORTANT PEOPLE

In this section you will read about some important individuals who have had a great impact on life in South and Southeast Asia.

THINK ABOUT IT

Which person first comes to mind when you think about South and Southeast Asia?_____

_____ Why? _____

Important Names: As you read this section, look for the following names:

◆ **Mohandas Gandhi** ◆ **Corazon Aquino**
◆ **Mother Teresa** ◆ **Ho Chi Minh**

 **THE NEW ASIAN TIMES**

Volume XXIV   Number 9

MOHANDAS GANDHI

Gandhi is often called the "the Father of Modern

India." By using acts of civil disobedience, he was able to end British rule of India. Gandhi used a non-violent approach called "passive resistance." He was assassinated soon after India became independent. Many of his ideas of non-violent resistance were later used in the U.S. by Martin Luther King Jr. during the 1960s Civil Rights Movement.

CORAZON AQUINO

Although elected President of the Philippines, Ferdinand Marcos became a dictator, enriching himself by stealing government money. Corazon Aquino's husband opposed Marcos's rule. After her husband was assassinated, Corazon Aquino defeated Marcos in a free election. Marcos tried to claim

victory anyway, but the people rose up against him and Aquino became President—a success for democracy in the Philippines.

MOTHER TERESA

Mother Teresa is a nun who has devoted her life to

providing health care, food and education to India's poorest people. She established a new religious order, The Missionaries of Charity. Known as the "Saint of the Gutters," Mother Teresa was awarded the Nobel Peace Prize in 1979.

HO CHI MINH

A Communist and nationalist, Ho Chi Minh was known as the "George Washington of Vietnam." He fought for independence from the French following World War II. After Vietnam was divided into a Communist North and a non-Communist South, he fought against the South Vietnamese, the U.S. and their allies. Vietnam was reunited as a Communist nation shortly after his death.

SUMMING UP: IMPORTANT PEOPLE

Leaders like Mohandas Gandhi of India and Ho Chi Minh of Vietnam have been able to rally their nations in the struggle for independence. Corazon Aquino has helped promote democracy in the region, while Mother Theresa has drawn world attention to the problems of the poor.

THINKING IT OVER

Have you **now** changed your mind as to the person you would identify with the area? (Yes ___

No ___) If yes, why? _____

_____ If no, why not? _____

_____

CHECKING YOUR UNDERSTANDING

Directions: Complete the following cards. Then answer the multiple choice questions that follow.

MOHANDAS GANDHI

Who was he? _____

Why was he important? _____

_____

MOTHER TERESA

Who is she? _____

What has she done? _____

_____

CORAZON AQUINO

Who is she? _____

Why is she important? _____

_____

HO CHI MINH

Who was he? _____

What did he accomplish? _____

_____

1 With which idea is Mohandas Gandhi most closely associated?
   1 providing free medical care for everyone
   2 using force to remove the British from India
   3 isolating India from the rest of Southeast Asia
   4 achieving Indian independence through civil disobedience

2 Ho Chi Minh was important to Vietnam because
   1 he was the first elected prime minister
   2 he introduced capitalism into Vietnam
   3 he helped reunify the Vietnamese
   4 he established freedom of religion in Vietnam

3 Mohandas Gandhi was important to India because he
   1 created the Muslim League
   2 developed a modern economy in India
   3 brought a peaceful end to British rule
   4 led India in a war against Pakistan

4 Which method did Gandhi use in his struggle against British imperialism in India?
   1 supporting armed uprisings
   2 enlisting foreign help
   3 using passive resistance
   4 demanding Soviet help

In this section you will read about some of the major problems and issues currently facing the peoples of South and Southeast Asia.

THINK ABOUT IT

Look at the graph on page 130. It shows how the population in India has grown. What effect do you think this population growth has had on the country? (**Note:** If you are not familiar with interpreting line graphs, read the Skill Builder that follows, before answering this question.)

_____

_____

Important Terms: As you read this section, look for the following terms:

◆ **Population Growth**   ◆ **"Boat People"**
◆ **Cultural Diversity**   ◆ **Sikhs**

Sometimes global studies examinations have line graphs and questions about how to interpret them. In this section you will read about India's increasing population. A line graph helps to illustrate the problem that India is facing. The following **Skill Builder** will help you understand and interpret line graphs.

What Is a Line Graph?

A line graph is a chart made up of a series of points connected by a line. It is used to show how something has increased, decreased, or remained the same.

Keys to Understanding a Line Graph

First, look at its different parts:

Title. The title tells you the major focus of the line graph. For example, the title of this graph is "**India's Growing Population.**" Thus you expect the graph to show something about how India's population is increasing.

Vertical and Horizontal Axis. Line graphs include a vertical (*up and down*) and a horizontal (*side to side*) axis (*line*). These tell you what items are being compared. In our line graph, the vertical axis, which runs from bottom to top, lists "Population" measured in *millions* of people — 300 million, 400 million, etc. Notice that as you move up from the bottom, the numbers get larger. The horizontal axis, which runs from left to right, shows the years in ascending (*lower to higher*) order.

Legend. If the graph has two or more lines, a legend is necessary to indicate what each line represents. If the graph has only one connecting line, as in our graph, there is no need for a legend.

Interpreting a Line Graph

First read the title, to find out the overall meaning of the graph. To find specific information, usually you must examine several items in the graph. For example, what was the population of India in 1968? To find out, run your finger across the "years" until you reach 1968. Now, move your finger up until you reach where the line representing population crosses the year 1968. To find the actual number, slide your finger over to the left, to the population figures given on the vertical axis (left side). These lines cross at about 525 million people. Thus, the answer to the question — "What was the population of India in 1968?" — is about 525 million people.

Note: Sometime in line graph questions you are asked to identify a **trend** (*a general direction or tendency*). You can figure out a trend by looking at the points on the line. For example, the trend indicated by our graph is that India's population is continuing to rise.

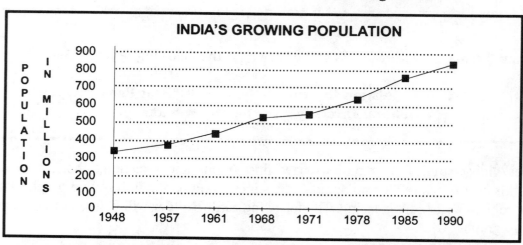

RAPID POPULATION GROWTH

THE PROBLEM. Population growth is a serious problem for India and other nations in the area. Growth rates in this region are among the highest in the world. Large increases in population have led to food shortages, overcrowded cities and slums. If these populations continue to grow at present rates, there will not be enough food or resources to go around. Living standards will decline instead of improving.

SOLUTIONS. Indian leaders have suggested that people use modern methods of birth control. Many have been unwilling to do so, because they see it as a threat to their traditional way of life. To encourage population limits, the Indian government now gives extra benefits to families with two children or less.

ECONOMIC DEVELOPMENT

PROBLEMS. India faces a number of serious economic problems. It must depend on money and other kinds of help from foreign countries to build factories and to make other needed improvements. Taxes on businesses are very high. More than half of India's workers cannot read or write. Ethnic, religious and caste differences also slow down economic growth.

SOLUTIONS. India must continue to seek money from other countries. Building schools has become very important for the training of more skilled workers. There is a large middle class which is playing an important role in helping India in its push for economic development. Limiting population growth and reducing clashes between ethnic groups would also help.

CONFLICTS BETWEEN DIFFERENT GROUPS

Cultural diversity (*differences in religion, language, and traditions*) is found everywhere in South and Southeast Asia. For example, Hindi is the national language of India, but there are over 15 major languages and some 850 dialects.

— MAJOR LANGUAGES SPOKEN IN INDIA —

URDU
PUNJABI
ENGLISH
ASSAMESE
ENGLISH
MANIPURI
HINDI
HINDI
ENGLISH
GUJARATI
BENGALI
MARATHI
ORIYA
MARATHI
TELEGU
KONKANI
KANNADA
FRENCH
TAMIL
MALAYALAM
SINHALESE

If cultural differences are too great, they can lead to conflict and violence. In recent years, clashes between members of different religious and ethnic groups has been on the rise. Fighting between Hindus and Muslims still occurs in India. Early in 1993, for example. Hindu rioters in Bombay attacked Muslims' homes, resulting in over a thousand deaths. In addition, the **Sikhs**, another religious group in India wishing to form their own nation, have often clashed with the Hindu majority.

PROBLEMS IN SOUTHEAST ASIA

Starting in the 1500s, Southeast Asia gradually came under European control. It wasn't until after World War II that the area achieved independence. Since independence, many nations in Southeast Asia have faced similar problems.

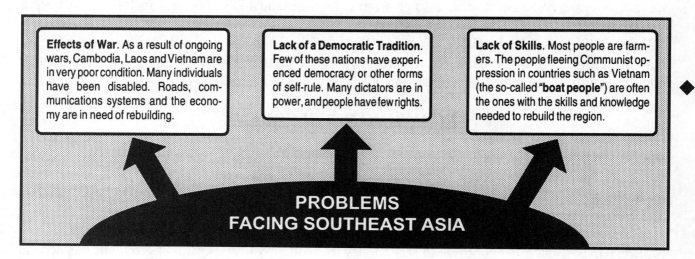

Effects of War. As a result of ongoing wars, Cambodia, Laos and Vietnam are in very poor condition. Many individuals have been disabled. Roads, communications systems and the economy are in need of rebuilding.

Lack of a Democratic Tradition. Few of these nations have experienced democracy or other forms of self-rule. Many dictators are in power, and people have few rights.

Lack of Skills. Most people are farmers. The people fleeing Communist oppression in countries such as Vietnam (the so-called "**boat people**") are often the ones with the skills and knowledge needed to rebuild the region.

PROBLEMS FACING SOUTHEAST ASIA

To improve standards of living and rebuild the educational system, the nations of Southeast Asia are looking to others outside of the area for help. Vietnam has recently passed new laws inviting foreign investment. However, improvements are coming about very slowly.

ANALYSIS

Should the U.S. help nations in Southeast Asia? If so, why? _____

_____ If not, why not? _____

_____

SUMMING UP: CONCERNS

Among the problems facing people in this area are overpopulation, the need to develop their economies, and a lack of a democratic tradition (especially in Southeast Asia). Attempted solutions to these problems have still not met with success.

THINKING IT OVER

What can you **now** add about the effects of population growth in India? _____

_____

_____

CHECKING YOUR UNDERSTANDING

Directions: Complete the following cards. Then answer the multiple choice questions that follow.

POPULATION GROWTH

Define it: _____

Why is it a problem? _____

_____

CULTURAL DIVERSITY

Definition: _____

Example: _____

_____

"BOAT PEOPLE"

Who are they? _____

Problem caused by their leaving: _____

_____

SIKHS

Who are they? _____

Their goal: _____

Why is this a problem? _____

---

1 In an outline, one of these is a main topic, the others are sub-topics. Which is the main topic?
1 Lack of Democratic Traditions
2 Heavy War Damages
3 Problems Facing Southeast Asia
4 Lack of Skilled Workers

2 A major goal of the Sikhs in India is to
1 establish their own nation
2 limit nuclear weapons
3 merge with the Hindus
4 Westernize their religion

3 Which statement best illustrates the existence of cultural diversity of India?
1 A majority of Indians are Hindus.
2 India has a two-house legislature.
3 Many languages are spoken in India.
4 India depends on hand labor.

4 A major problem facing India today is that
1 there is an over-production of farm crops
2 there have been continuous wars with China
3 the population is growing faster than food production
4 modernization has led to an excessive amount of housing

SUMMARIZING YOUR UNDERSTANDING

MAP PUZZLE

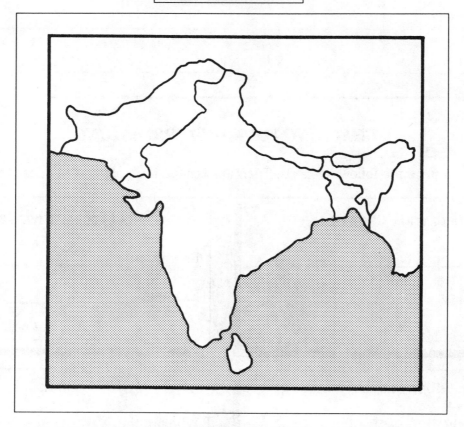

Directions: Put each number in its correct location on the map.

1	India	6	China	11	Indian Ocean
2	Bangladesh	7	Sri Lanka	12	Deccan Plateau
3	Pakistan	8	Bay of Bengal	13	Himalayan Mountains
4	Bhutan	9	Kashmir	14	Ganges River
5	Nepal	10	Arabian Sea	15	Indus River

Directions: Fill in the information in the organizer below, and in the organizer on the next page.

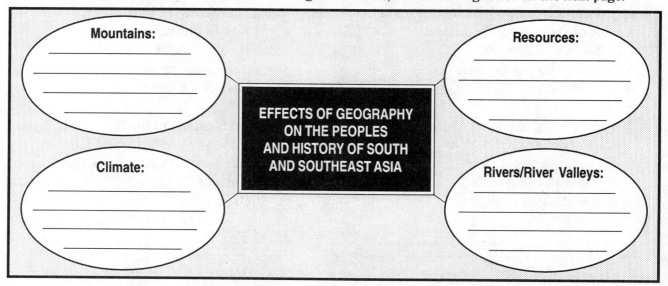

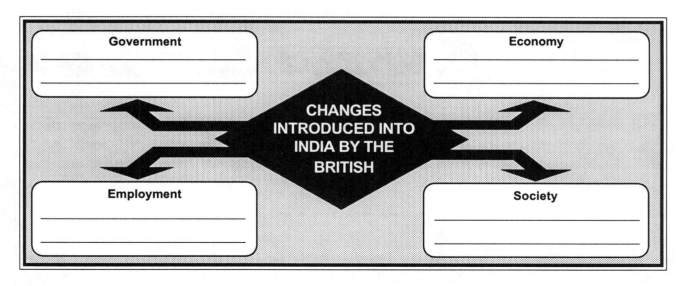

DESCRIBING HISTORICAL EVENTS

Directions: Describe fully the following important historical event that you learned about in this chapter. Fill in the information called for in each box.

WHO was involved?

WHEN did it happen?

THE PARTITION OF INDIA

WHY was it necessary?

RESULTS:

1. _____

2. _____

3. _____

People like to be with other people, and as a result they organize themselves into societies. **Sociologists** (*scholars who study society*) refer to the way in which society is organized as its **social structure**. Social structure consists of the institutions of a particular society and the division of its members into different groups, called **classes**.

MEETING SOCIAL NEEDS

Every human society has essentially the same basic needs. For example, each society tries to provide food and shelter to its members; protects itself from other groups; brings about cooperation among its members; and raises and educates its young.

CUSTOMS AND ROLES

Each society develops its own patterns of behavior to meet these needs. These patterns are known as **customs**, and are passed from one generation to the next. **Roles** are social rules for the proper behavior of individuals in particular positions and situations. A mother, for instance, is expected to behave in a certain way toward her children. Once a role in society is learned, people know how they are "supposed" to act.

INSTITUTIONS

Entire organizations, known as **institutions**, are developed by each society to help make roles clear, and to take care of social needs. For example:

- **Families** arrange for reproduction, the care of family members and raising children.

- **Governments** protect societies from hostile outsiders, promote social cooperation and regulate behavior.

- **Schools** teach the young the values of the society and prepare them for the responsibilities of adulthood.

SOCIAL CLASSES

In most societies, some members enjoy privileges and wide opportunities, while others suffer hardships. People who share similar characteristics are said to belong to the same **social class**. The following social classes exist in most societies:

■ **Upper Class**. This group is usually wealthy and owns a large share of a society's property. Its members often fill leadership positions within society. This is usually the smallest class.

■ **Middle Class**. This is an intermediate group of educated and relatively successful people, who act as managers, professionals, shopkeepers, owners or service providers.

■ **Working Class**. This group is composed of people who work in factories, mining, transportation, or as independent craftsmen.

■ **Peasants**. These are small farmers or farm workers mainly engaged in subsistence agriculture. They have little education and limited experience of the world outside their own villages. In most non-industrialized societies, this is the largest group.

■ **Lower Class**. They are often uneducated, unskilled and either unemployed or work at the least desirable and worst-paying jobs. Often, members of lower classes face prejudice, suffer from physical or mental problems or face other social handicaps.

SOCIAL MOBILITY

Social mobility (*the ability to move from one social class to another*) varies greatly, depending on the kind of social system people live under.

SOCIETIES WHERE RACE OR CASTE PREVENT MOBILITY
In some societies, social mobility is not possible. Each person is assigned a social position inherited from his or her parents. Usually this is based on racial or cultural characteristics. In South Africa, blacks were treated as an inferior social class: until recently, they had no political rights and very little economic opportunity. Traditional Indian society was divided into castes. There was no movement from one caste to another. Your caste determined what work you did and who your friends were. Your children also remained in the same caste and were limited to the same range of jobs.

SOCIETIES WITH SOCIAL MOBILITY
In other societies, class is defined in terms of wealth, education and type of occupation. Each person is born into a particular social class, but it is possible to move from one class to another. In some societies, the movement is limited, while in others—like the United States—people may move more easily from one class to another.

ANSWERING QUESTIONS ON SOCIAL CONFLICT

Because people often feel deeply about their race, ethnic group, or religion, members of different groups often do not trust one another. History is full of examples of conflict between ethnic, racial and religious groups.

At times on a global studies examination you will be asked to discuss conflicts that exist between different groups and to examine the effects of these conflicts on those involved. As you read through this book, you will learn about different social conflicts that exist in various parts of the world. To help you answer any type of question dealing with this topic, each area chapter in this book contains a **History** section which discusses the major social conflicts and their causes. In addition, the **Systems** section contains important information about the principal conflicts in the area.

TESTING YOUR UNDERSTANDING

Directions: Circle the number in front of the word or expression that correctly answers the statement or question. Following the multiple choice questions, answer the essay questions.

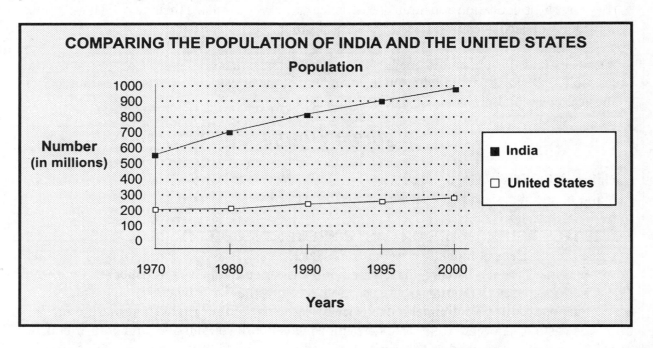

1 Based on the line graph, what was the population of the United States in 1990?
   1 about 200 million   3 about 550 million
   2 about 250 million   4 about 820 million

2 Which statement is best supported by the information in the graph?
   1 By the year 2000, India will probably have the largest population in the world.
   2 From 1970 to 2000, India's population will triple.
   3 By the year 2000, the United States and India will have the same size population.
   4 By the year 2000, India's gain in population will be larger than the gain in the U.S.

3 Which geographical feature is correctly paired with its location?
   1 Sahara Desert - Brazil
   2 Himalayan Mountains - Egypt
   3 Amazon River - Philippines
   4 Ganges River - India

4 The Indus, Amazon, and Nile are the names of
   1 mountain ranges   3 islands
   2 river systems   4 plateaus

5 Mohandas Gandhi and Martin Luther King, Jr. both believed
   1 that total power should be in the hands of government
   2 that violence is the best way to achieve political power
   3 in using non-violent methods to achieve a goal
   4 in one-man rule of the government

6 Which newspaper headline correctly pairs the person with the event?
   1 "Monroe Doctrine Introduced"— Fidel Castro
   2 "Atlantic Slave Trade Begins" — Ayatollah Khomeini
   3 "Israel Signs Treaty With Egypt" — Saddam Hussein
   4 "India Achieves Independence" — Mohandas Gandhi

7 The Buddhist religion spread from India to other parts of Asia. This illustrates
1 urbanization
2 nationalism
3 democratic reforms
4 cultural diffusion

8 • The U.S. buys raw materials from India.
• India buys manufactured goods from the U.S.

These statements are examples of
1 India's social independence
2 global interdependence
3 that India has industrialized
4 that economic warfare is inevitable

9 Traditional Indian society was organized into social classes known as
1 castes
2 families
3 clans
4 tribes

10 If India's population continues to grow faster than its food production, it is likely that India's
1 standard of living will decline
2 government will remain unchanged
3 exports will decline
4 people will move from cities to mountain areas

ESSAYS

1 Religious conflicts can play an important role in the history of an area.

Religious Conflicts

Muslims / Jews in the Middle East
Hindus / Muslims in South Asia
Sikhs / Hindus in South Asia

Part A

Choose *one* of the religious conflicts listed: _____

State the reason for the conflict between the two groups: _____

_____

_____

Part B

In your Part B answer, you should use information you gave in Part A. However, you may also include different or additional information in your Part B answer.

Write an essay discussing how religious differences can play an important role in the history of an area.

2 Developing nations often have similar problems that slow or prevent their economic growth.

Part A

Define the term *economic growth*: _____

_____

List *two* problems that have slowed or prevented the economic growth of nations in South or Southeast Asia.

1 _____

2 _____

Part B
In your Part B answer, you should use information you gave in Part A. However, you may also include different or additional information in your Part B answer.

Write an essay showing how developing nations often have similar problems that slow or prevent their economic growth.

3 Some individuals have brought about important changes in their countries.

Individuals

Mohandas Gandhi   F.W. De Klerk
Ho Chi Minh   Nelson Mandela
Anwar Sadat   Saddam Hussein

Part A

Select *two* individuals from the list, and for *each one* state how that individual has brought about an important change in his country:

INDIVIDUAL	CHANGE
1. _____	_____
2. _____	_____

Part B
In your Part B answer, you should use information you gave in Part A. However, you may also include different or additional information in your Part B answer.

Write an essay showing how some individuals have brought about important changes in their countries.

GLOBAL CHECKLIST

SOUTH AND SOUTHEAST ASIA

Directions: Before going on to the next chapter, you should check your understanding of the important people, terms and concepts covered in this chapter. Place a check mark (✔) next to those that you are able to explain. If you have trouble remembering a term, refer to the page listed next to the item.

An Indian fisherman

❑ Ganges River (113)
❑ Monsoons (113)
❑ "Divide and Conquer" (116)
❑ Sepoy Mutiny (117)
❑ Passive Resistance (117)
❑ Civil Disobedience (117)
❑ Genocide (119)

❑ Vietnam War (119)
❑ Green Revolution (122)
❑ Caste System (123)
❑ Hinduism (123-124)
❑ Social Mobility (123)
❑ Untouchables (123)
❑ Reincarnation (124)

❑ Mohandas Gandhi (127)
❑ Mother Teresa (127)
❑ Corazon Aquino (127)
❑ Ho Chi Minh (127)
❑ Population Growth (131)
❑ Cultural Diversity (131)
❑ "Boat People" (132)

GEOGRAPHY

- Size and Location
- Geographic Features and Their Effects

CONCERNS

- Chinese-American Relations
- Population Growth
- World Trade and Political Reform

HISTORY

- Early Civilization
- European Imperialism
- From Republic to Communist Nation
- China under Mao Zedong
- China under Deng Xiaoping

CHAPTER 6

CHINA

IMPORTANT PEOPLE

- Confucius
- Sun Yat-Sen
- Mao Zedong
- Chiang Kai-Shek

SYSTEMS

- Government
- Economy
- Religion
- Society
- The Arts

What do these pictures show you about China? _____

_____

_____

_____

1 GEOGRAPHY

In this section you will read about the major geographic features of China, and how these features have affected its people and history.

THINK ABOUT IT

Look at the map of China on page 145. Where do you think the majority of China's population lives? _____

Why? _____

Important Terms: As you read this section, look for the following terms:

♦ **Hwang Ho / Yangtze**   ♦ **Ethnocentrism**

SIZE AND LOCATION

China is one of the largest countries in the world. It occupies most of the mainland of East Asia, covering 3.7 million square miles. The map below shows that China is slightly larger than the United States. China's neighbors to the north and west are Russia and Mongolia. To the east lies the Pacific Ocean.

MAJOR GEOGRAPHIC FEATURES AND THEIR EFFECTS

MOUNTAINS

On the southern and western borders of China are some of the world's high mountains, including the **Himalayas**, the highest in the world. These mountains have protected and isolated China from other nations. Cut off from the outside world, China's people developed a unified culture. This help-
♦ ed promote **ethnocentrism** (*the belief that one's culture is superior to all other cultures*) among the Chinese.

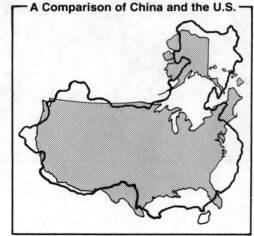

┌─ **A Comparison of China and the U.S.** ─┐

DESERTS

Much of western China is made up of deserts; the Gobi Desert is the largest. Because of this geographic feature, a high **population density** exists in the eastern part of the country (*the greater the number of people, the higher the population density*).

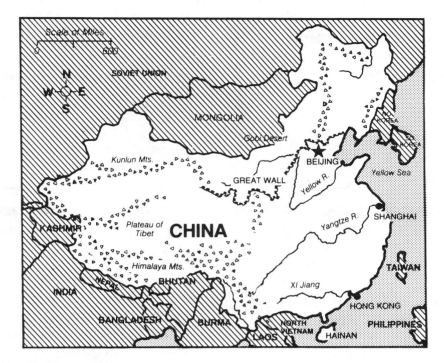

RIVERS AND RIVER VALLEYS

Like other ancient civilizations (*the Egyptians along the Nile and the Indians along the Indus River*) the Chinese developed their earliest civilization in river valleys. River valleys such as the **Hwang Ho** ◆ (*Yellow River*) and the **Yangtze** have been very important to China, providing water for transportation ◆ and agriculture.

CLIMATE

Because of its large size, China's climate varies greatly from one part of the country to another. Most Chinese live in the eastern part of the nation where the most fertile soil is found. The southeast part of China receives plenty of rainfall from monsoons, making it easier to grow rice and other crops.

SUMMING UP: GEOGRAPHY

China, located in eastern Asia, is one of the largest countries in the world. Mountains have played an important role in China's history, allowing it to develop apart from the rest of the world.

THINKING IT OVER

Were you correct in locating the most populated area of China? _____

What might you now answer? _____

Why? _____

CHECKING YOUR UNDERSTANDING

Directions: Complete the following cards. Then answer the multiple choice questions that follow.

HWANG HO / YANGTZE

What are they? _____

Effects on China: _____

_____

ETHNOCENTRISM

Definition: _____

Why did it develop in China? _____

_____

---

1 The Indus, Yangtze, and Amazon are
   1 mountain ranges   3 lakes
   2 river systems   4 deserts

2 If you were to take a trip from California to China, in which general direction would you travel?
   1 north   3 south
   2 east   4 west

3 Which statement about China is most accurate?
   1 China's mountains and deserts allowed it to develop a separate culture.
   2 Chinese civilization first developed along the Nile River.
   3 The best farm land is found in western China.
   4 China has the world's largest oil resources.

4 China is a part of which continent?
   1 Asia   3 South America
   2 Australia   4 Europe

5 A main characteristic of ethnocentrism is
   1 believing your culture is superior to others
   2 promoting energy conservation
   3 providing foreigners with trading rights
   4 thinking your culture is backward

6 China's highest population density is found in
   1 its western desert sections
   2 the Himalayan Mountains
   3 the east
   4 its tropical rain forests

2 HISTORY

In this section you will read about China's earliest civilization and how it developed. Then you will read about western imperialism in China, and how in 1949 it became a Communist nation under Mao Zedong.

THINK ABOUT IT

The History section on China is divided into **five** major topics or themes. List them below:

1. _____   2. _____

3. _____   4. _____

   5. _____

Important Terms: As you read this section, look for the following terms:

◆ **Dynasties**   ◆ **Boxer Rebellion**
◆ **Spheres of Influence**   ◆ **Cultural Revolution**
◆ **Open Door Policy**   ◆ **Tiananmen Square**

TIMELINE OF HISTORICAL EVENTS

214	1894	1900	1911	1949	1971	1979	1982
Great Wall completed	Sino-Japanese War begins	Boxer Rebellion starts	Manchu Dynasty ends	Communists seize power	Communist China admitted to U.N.	U.S. resumes diplomatic relations with China	China's population reaches 1 billion

CHINESE CIVILIZATION (4000 BC-1912)

EARLY CHINESE CIVILIZATION

The world's first civilizations developed in valleys by the banks of rivers. Ancient peoples were attracted to river valleys because they offered a mild climate, fertile soil, protection from invasions and a water highway to other areas. About six thousand years ago—in the same period that early river valley civilizations began in other parts of the world—China's first civilization developed along the Hwang Ho (*Yellow River*).

CHINA'S DYNASTIES (2000 B.C.-1912 A.D.)

From about 2000 B.C., China was ruled by emperors belonging to a series of **dynasties**, (*a succession of rulers from the same family*). During the long period from 618-1279 A.D. China experienced its **Golden Age**, filled with cultural achievements and inventions. Peace and stability were achieved partly because the government was run by those with the greatest abilities, which they proved by passing a test based on the teachings of **Confucius**. For a fuller discussion of Confucius, see page 158.

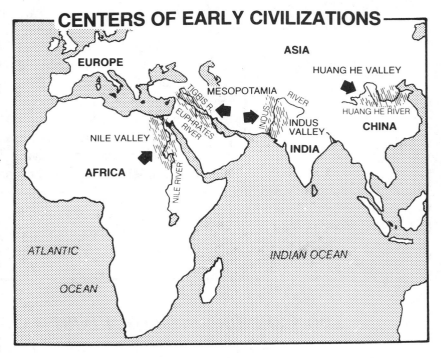

CENTERS OF EARLY CIVILIZATIONS

ANCIENT CHINA'S CONTRIBUTION TO WORLD CIVILIZATION

For much of its history, China was the world's most advanced civilization. The Chinese invented paper, the compass, printing, silk, porcelain and gunpowder. To protect themselves from invasions, they built a 25-foot-high wall stretching thousands of miles in western China. This **Great Wall** helped to isolate China from the rest of the world.

CHINA AND EUROPEAN IMPERIALISM

By the middle of the 1800s, European nations began to show an interest in China. Its large population could serve as a market for manufactured goods, and it had valuable resources and raw materials. China, cut off from the world for so long, lacked the military technology to prevent Western **imperialism** (*the takeover of a weak nation by a stronger one*). As a result, China fell under Western influence and control.

◆ Each powerful European country rushed to control part of China by creating its own "**sphere of influence.**" The United States also became interested in Chinese trade, although it opposed the idea of "spheres of influence."

HISTORY OF IMPERIALISM IN CHINA

EVENT	YEAR	RESULTS
Opium Wars	1839	China lost the war to Great Britain, and was forced to open its ports to allow Europeans trading rights inside China. A major rebellion broke out against the Chinese government, but the rebellion was brutally crushed.
Sino-Japanese War	1894	Japan easily defeated China. As a result, Japan took some Chinese land and created its own area of economic control.
◆ **Open Door Policy**	1899	The U.S. proposed equal trading rights for all nations in China, saving China from being divided up by foreign powers. This policy helped open China to trade with all nations.
◆ **Boxer Rebellion**	1900	Chinese "Boxers" (*a group opposed to foreign influences*) rebelled against Western ideas and imperialism, and attacked foreigners living in China. Foreign powers sent armies to China and crushed the rebellion.
Russo-Japanese War	1904	Japan defeated Russia and seized the province of Manchuria. This takeover showed that China was too weak to prevent others from fighting over its territory.

FROM REPUBLIC TO COMMUNIST NATION (1912-1949)

The Chinese people became angry about their country's weakness and backwardness; in 1912 they overthrew the imperial government. The new leader, **Sun Yat-Sen**, tried to establish a democratic government. This was difficult, however, because many local rulers (called warlords) refused to give up their powers.

Finally, in 1928, **Chiang Kai-Shek** defeated the local warlords and united most of China. Next, Chiang tried to destroy the growing Communist movement in China. He was interrupted in this when China was invaded by Japan in 1937. The Chinese spent most of World War II fighting to free themselves from the Japanese, who had conquered much of the country.

Following World War II (in 1949), the Chinese Communists, led by **Mao Zedong**, defeated the nationalist forces of Chiang Kai-Shek and took control of China. Chiang had failed to win the support of the Chinese people, who were tired of war, high prices and government corruption. Chiang and his followers fled from mainland China to **Taiwan**, an island off the coast.

CHINA UNDER MAO ZEDONG (1949-1976)

After taking control, Mao Zedong moved to bring all aspects of Chinese life under the control of the Communist Party. The changes he introduced are known as the **Chinese Revolution of 1949**.

MAO ZEDONG INTRODUCES CHANGES

Mao brought great changes to Chinese life. The most important group in traditional China had always been the family, but now Mao made the Communist Party the most important group. The father's traditional role as head of the family was greatly weakened. The practice of ancestor worship was forbidden. Communist beliefs were required learning in all universities and schools, factories and villages. All newspapers, books, music and art were expected to promote Communism. Opponents of Communism were forced to publicly declare their support for the new government, and those who did not were either jailed or killed. Mao made himself a god-like figure, and everyone had to study and memorize many of his writings and sayings. He also introduced economic changes, discussed later in the chapter.

THE CULTURAL REVOLUTION (1966-1975)

By 1966, Mao felt the Communist revolution was losing support in China. He decided to make one last attempt to achieve his goal of total Communism. Mao closed the schools and universities and invited China's youths, whom he called the **Red Guards**, to travel throughout the country attacking anyone who opposed Communism. Eventually the Red Guards got out of control, and Mao had to use the army to restore order, bringing an end to the Cultural Revolution.

CHINA UNDER DENG XIAOPING (1976-PRESENT)

When Mao died in 1976, he was replaced by **Deng Xiaoping** as China's new leader. Although a Communist, Deng seemed willing to change the way of life imposed by Mao in order to make China into a more modern nation.

CHANGES INTRODUCED BY DENG

Deng aimed to show the Chinese people that not all of Mao's actions had been perfect. He allowed the people more freedom of thought, greater contact with other nations, and a new legal code. He also introduced greater economic freedom by permitting some limited private enterprise. Despite these changes, critics of the Communist system were still arrested.

◆ PROTESTS IN TIANANMEN SQUARE

In Beijing (*China's capital city*) in 1989, large numbers of Chinese peacefully protested in Tiananmen Square for more democracy. Angered by these demonstrations, the government sent in tanks and soldiers, resulting in the deaths of many protesters. Others were executed afterwards. This showed the world what Deng could do when he believed the Communist system was threatened. Since 1989, China has continued to introduce economic reforms, but without advancing towards greater democracy.

Protesters about to be executed, shortly after the Tiananmen Square demonstrations

SUMMING UP: HISTORY

One of the world's first civilizations developed along the Huang Ho (Yellow) River valley. From about 2000 B.C. to 1912 A.D., China was ruled by powerful emperors. In the mid-1800s, European nations, and later Japan, gained control over parts of China. The rule of the emperors ended in 1912, when a republic was established. China became a Communist state in 1949, when Mao Zedong succeeded in taking over the government. Recently, the Communist leadership under Deng Xiaoping has supported economic reforms, but crushed an attempt to make China more democratic.

THINKING IT OVER

Which time period in China's history do you think is the most important? _____

_____ Why? _____

_____

CHECKING YOUR UNDERSTANDING

Directions: Complete the following cards. Then answer the multiple choice questions that follow.

DYNASTIES

What were they? _____

Contributions: _____

_____

SPHERES OF INFLUENCE

What were they? _____

Effect on China: _____

_____

BOXER REBELLION

What was it? _____

When did it happen?_____

Result:_____

OPEN DOOR POLICY

What was it? _____

When did it start? _____

Result:_____

CULTURAL REVOLUTION

What was it? _____

When did it happen? _____

Result: _____

TIANANMEN SQUARE DEMONSTRATIONS

Describe:_____

Results:_____

Importance: _____

1 The aim of the Open Door Policy in China was to
   1 introduce democratic reforms
   2 encourage Chinese immigration
   3 prevent China's division by foreign powers
   4 develop Chinese industries

2 Which leader would most agree with the ideas of Communism?
   1 Confucius   3 Mao Zedong
   2 Nelson Mandela   4 Chiang Kai-Shek

3 Before the 20th century, China's history was best characterized by
   1 many violent revolutions
   2 rule by dynasties
   3 being Communist
   4 rule by democratic leaders

4 The Golden Age in China was a period in which
   1 gold was discovered
   2 the government ended hunger
   3 great cultural achievements took place
   4 China defeated the U.S.

5 Which group would have supported the Boxer Rebellion?
   1 European imperialists
   2 Westerners living in China
   3 Chinese opposed to foreigners
   4 Christian missionaries

6 Which best describes China's relations with the outside world before 1850?
   1 isolationist   3 militarist
   2 imperialist   4 expansionist

7 The leader of the Communist forces of China in 1949 was
  1 Sun Yat-sen
  2 Chiang Kai-shek
  3 Mao Zedong
  4 Confucius

8 Which headline is associated with China's Cultural Revolution?
  1 "Red Guards Attack Doubters of Communist Ideals"
  2 "China's Emperor is Overthrown"
  3 "Japan Invades China"
  4 "United States Announces Open Door Policy"

9 A major goal of Deng Xiaoping has been to
  1 modernize China's economy
  2 limit farm production
  3 make China into a farming nation
  4 eliminate all foreign trade

10 The failure of the demonstrations in Tiananmen Square illustrated the fact that
  1 creating a democracy is important to Chinese leaders
  2 young people want to fight hunger in China
  3 certain democratic demands are unacceptable in China
  4 there is increased participation of women in government

3

SYSTEMS

In this section you will read about China's major political institutions, economic development, social structure, religions and cultural achievements.

THINK ABOUT IT

It has been said that China can only be understood if one knows China's "isms:" Confucianism, Buddhism and Communism. How many of these can you describe? What do you know about each of these "isms"?

Confucianism _____

Buddhism _____

Communism _____

Important Terms: As you read this section, look for the following terms:

◆ **Communism**   ◆ **Confucianism**
◆ **Communes**   ◆ **Buddhism**

GOVERNMENT

Since the Communist takeover in 1949, China has been ruled by a single leader, the head of the Communist Party. Today, China is the world's largest and most powerful Communist country.

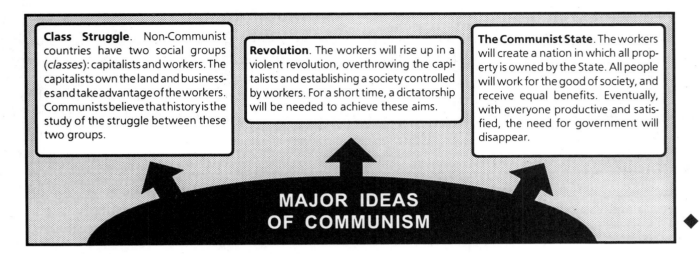

Class Struggle. Non-Communist countries have two social groups (*classes*): capitalists and workers. The capitalists own the land and businesses and take advantage of the workers. Communists believe that history is the study of the struggle between these two groups.

Revolution. The workers will rise up in a violent revolution, overthrowing the capitalists and establishing a society controlled by workers. For a short time, a dictatorship will be needed to achieve these aims.

The Communist State. The workers will create a nation in which all property is owned by the State. All people will work for the good of society, and receive equal benefits. Eventually, with everyone productive and satisfied, the need for government will disappear.

MAJOR IDEAS OF COMMUNISM

ECONOMY

THE ECONOMY UNDER MAO ZEDONG

Farms were taken away from their owners and given to peasants. Eventually, the farms became **communes** — smaller farms merged into one common farm of at least 20,000 people. Mao forced peasants and their families to live and work on these communes. All property was turned over to the commune. Peasants had to work in the fields together, eat in a central dining hall together, and place their children in government-run nurseries and schools.

THE GREAT LEAP FORWARD

Mao created a plan, known as the "**Great Leap Forward**," to increase agricultural production and turn China into an industrial power. He directed all of China's resources into achieving industrialization. People worked long hours and had little to eat. They built dams, bridges and factories. After a while, an economic and political crisis came about in China. Mao was forced to admit that his Great Leap Forward was a failure because of poor planning, a lack of cooperation from the peasants, and a lack of aid from the Soviet Union.

THE ECONOMY UNDER DENG XIAOPING

Deng faced many economic problems when he replaced Mao as leader. The most serious problem was China's growing population. Deng changed Communism in China by adding some capitalist features to its economy. For example, farmers were now able to own land, people could run their own small businesses, and productive workers were able to earn bonuses. New rules allowed foreign companies to start businesses in China. These reforms were very successful. China started producing more radios, television sets and other consumer goods for its people. It also began to export goods to Western countries like the United States. In 1992, China's economy was one of the fastest growing in the world.

RELIGIOUS SYSTEM

Chinese religious beliefs are more concerned with how to conduct one's life than with the nature of God. Confucianism and Buddhism are two of the key religions in China.

◆ CONFUCIANISM

Named after the ancient philosopher **Confucius** (551-479 B.C.), Confucianism stressed the natural order existing in the universe and in all human relationships. A person can achieve harmony and peace if he or she follows tradition — putting the needs of the family over individual needs, having good manners, respecting others, and worshipping one's ancestors. Eventually, Confucianism became the official belief of the Chinese empire, and to get a government job a person had to pass a test based on the ideas of Confucius.

◆ BUDDHISM

Buddhism came into China from India. It is a religion based on the belief that desires are the main cause of pain and suffering in life. Instead of being concerned with obtaining wealth and trying to reach a high social position, a person should try to discover the true meaning of life. Buddhists believe that this is the only way to achieve inner peace.

COMMUNISM AND RELIGION

Communism looks down on all religious beliefs and practices. Communists believe that religion keeps people from seeing that the capitalists are their enemy. Despite this, religion still plays an important role in Chinese life.

SOCIETY

In traditional China people lived in villages, in extended families. The center of all authority was the male head of the family, and women had few rights. Peasants raised crops on small plots of land, growing only enough to feed their families. Many of the ideas introduced by the Communists went against those of traditional China. Individuals are forced to work for the benefit of the state rather than for the benefit of their families. Loyalty to the Communist Party was considered more important than family loyalty. The power of the oldest male in the family was reduced, and women were given equal rights with males.

Although China has a large population, most Chinese still live in rural villages, spending their entire lives there. Most feel very attached to the land, and few move to the cities.

SELECTED STATISTICS ABOUT CHINA AND ITS NEIGHBORS

Nation	Current Population (in millions)	Population Density (people per sq. mile)	Urban Population (percent)	Rural Population (percent)
China	1069.6	288	37	63
Mongolia	2.0	3	52	48
Taiwan	20.2	1460	72	28
Nepal	18.7	334	8	92

The above table provides information about China's population. However, if you have difficulty understanding it, you should read the following Skill Builder on interpreting tables.

SKILL BUILDER: INTERPRETING A TABLE

What Is a Table?

A table is an arrangement of words or numbers in columns. It helps us to organize large amounts of information so that specific items can be more easily located and compared.

Keys to Understanding a Table

First, look at its major parts:

Title. The title tells you the overall topic. For example, our table on page 154 is entitled: **"Selected Statistics About China and its Neighbors."** It tells us what information is in the table. The table lists statistics (*collected numbers*) that compare China's population with those of its neighbors.

Categories. Tables are made up of categories of information. These categories are found in the **headings** across the top of the table. In our table, the categories listed along the top row are: "Nation," "Current Population," "Population Density," "Urban Population" and "Rural Population."

Interpreting a Table

To locate specific information, you must find the nation you wish to learn about. For example, if you want to find information about Nepal's population density, move your finger down the "Nation" column until you reach "Nepal." Next, using your other hand, slide a finger down the column labeled "Population Density." Now slide from "Nepal" across to the "Population Density" column. Where the two columns meet tells you Nepal's population density: 334 persons per square mile.

THE ARTS

Chinese civilization is rich in cultural achievements, many of them influenced by Confucianism. Chinese writing is based on *characters*, in which a separate symbol is used for each word, instead of an alphabetic system. For example, the following character means "tree:"

Art forms such as painting, lacquerware, woodcuts and ceramics are inspired by nature and are decorated with flowers, birds and animals. Chinese literature, dance and music emphasize morality and virtue.

Today, the arts are greatly influenced by Communist propaganda. Culture is used to promote Communism. As in most countries where governments control all aspects of life, Chinese artists must follow official government policy.

A performer in the Beijing Opera

SUMMING UP: SYSTEMS

GOVERNMENT. Since 1949, China has been ruled by a single leader, the head of the Communist Party. The people have very few democratic rights.

ECONOMY. At first, Communist leaders tried to control the entire economy. Today, some private ownership and profit-making are allowed.

RELIGION. Confucianism and Buddhism have had a great influence on Chinese history. Today the Communists discourage religion.

SOCIETY. Many traditional Chinese practices were opposed by Communists. Under Communism, people work for the benefit of the state, and not for their individual families.

THE ARTS. Traditional Chinese art was most influenced by Confucianism. Under the Communists, artists must reflect official government policy.

THINKING IT OVER

What new things can you **now** add about each of China's "isms"?

Confucianism: _____

Buddhism: _____

Communism: _____

CHECKING YOUR UNDERSTANDING

Directions: Complete the following cards. Then answer the multiple choice questions that follow.

COMMUNISM

Major beliefs: _____

Effects on China: _____

_____

COMMUNES

Definition: _____

Effect on China: _____

_____

```
┌─────────────────────────────────┐
│           CONFUCIANISM          │
│                                 │
│  What is it? _____  │
│                                 │
│  Major beliefs: _____  │
│                                 │
│  _____  │
└─────────────────────────────────┘
```

```
┌─────────────────────────────────┐
│            BUDDHISM             │
│                                 │
│  What is it? _____  │
│                                 │
│  Major beliefs: _____  │
│                                 │
│  _____  │
└─────────────────────────────────┘
```

1 Which is an important belief of Communism?
   1 freedom of religion
   2 state ownership of property
   3 peaceful social change
   4 the profit motive

2 What do Communists predict will take place in most societies?
   1 violent revolution and a classless society
   2 private property ownership and freedom of religion
   3 peaceful change and freedom of the press
   4 social classes and a traditional economy

3 Confucianism is mainly concerned with
   1 respecting God
   2 learning about suffering
   3 achieving money and glory
   4 seeking harmony in relationships

4 Communist ideals emphasize
   1 individual gains
   2 the welfare of the group
   3 wealth and status
   4 the importance of religion

5 Which did Mao Zedong introduce into China under Communism?
   1 the importance of family matters
   2 the need for profits
   3 the importance of the individual
   4 the establishment of communes

6 An important belief of Buddhism is that
   1 one should not eat meat products
   2 suffering is caused by desire
   3 persons should travel to Mecca
   4 one should pray to Allah

7 Which value was considered important in traditional Chinese society?
   1 family loyalty
   2 nationalism
   3 individualism
   4 Christianity

8 Which philosophy had the greatest influence on traditional Chinese culture?
   1 Animism
   2 Communism
   3 Confucianism
   4 Christianity

9 Which best describes the goal of the Great Leap Forward?
   1 establish China as a great military power
   2 chase all Westerners out of China
   3 increase China's industrial production
   4 reduce the influence of the Communists

10 Buddhism came to China from India. This is an example of
   1 cultural diffusion
   2 racism
   3 cultural isolation
   4 imperialism

4

IMPORTANT PEOPLE

In this section you will read about some of the most important individuals who have helped to shape China in the past, as well as today.

THINK ABOUT IT

Which person first comes to mind when you think of China? _____

Why? _____

Important Names: As you read this section, look for the following names:

◆ **Confucius**   ◆ **Mao Zedong**
◆ **Sun Yat-sen**   ◆ **Deng Xiaoping**

   ꬠꞪꞮ ꞨꞪꟺ ꞬꞪꞮꞨꞪ ꞮꞮꞪꞬꞪꞨ

THE NEW CHINA TIMES

Volume XXVVL   Number 11

CONFUCIUS

Confucius, a scholar who lived about 2500 years ago, was China's most famous teacher and philosopher. His ideas about the individual, family and government helped to influence China and most of eastern Asia for over 2000 years. He stressed the importance of family, individual behavior, virtue and respect for one's ancestors. Confucius believed that each person had a role to play in life, and should fill that role properly. These ideals helped to promote harmonious social relations.

SUN YAT-SEN

Sun Yat-Sen devoted himself to overthrowing the rule of the emperor and establishing democracy in China. Sun hoped to make China a republic in which the people elected their leaders. He believed that to survive, the Chinese had to develop a sense of nationalism. Regarded as the "Father of Modern China," he died in 1925 and was succeeded by Chiang Kai-Shek.

MAO ZEDONG

In 1949, Mao became China's first Communist ruler. He led China for the next 25 years, introducing economic and political changes that affected Chinese life in almost every way. He was determined to increase farm production, reduce the rate of population growth, and to turn China into an industrial power. Mao and the Communist Party had total control. Going against tradition, he reduced the importance of the family and raised women's position in society.

DENG XIAOPING

After Mao died, Deng became China's ruler. He realized that some changes had to be made if Communism was to succeed. To modernize China, he moved away from some of Mao's ideas. He allowed some limited forms of capitalism, like the private sale of crops. Although not as harsh a ruler as Mao, Deng showed during the Tiananmen Square protests that he was willing to use force.

SUMMING UP: IMPORTANT PEOPLE

Leaders like Confucius, Sun Yat-Sen, Mao Zedong and Deng Xiaoping have had a very important influence on China.

THINKING IT OVER

Now, who is the first person that comes to mind when you think about China? _____

Why? _____

CHECKING YOUR UNDERSTANDING

Directions: Complete the following cards. Then answer the multiple choice questions that follow.

CONFUCIUS
Who was he? _____
Major ideas: _____
Importance: _____

SUN YAT-SEN
Who was he? _____
Major ideas: _____
Importance: _____

MAO ZEDONG
Who was he? _____
Major ideas: _____
Importance: _____

DENG XIAOPING
Who is he? _____
Major ideas: _____
Importance: _____

1 Respect for tradition and honoring one's parents were practices encouraged by
   1 Confucius   3 Chiang Kai-Shek
   2 Mao Zedong   4 Deng Xiaoping

2 Which would Mao Zedong have favored most?
   1 showing respect for one's ancestors
   2 increasing industrial production
   3 establishing imperialism in Africa
   4 establishing Confucian traditions

3 Which person is correctly paired with his country?
   1 Desmond Tutu — Israel
   2 Sun Yat Sen — Korea
   3 Anwar Sadat — Mexico
   4 Nelson Mandela — South Africa

4 Which leader supported limited capitalism in Communist China?
   1 Confucius   3 Mohandas Gandhi
   2 Mao Zedong   4 Deng Xiaoping

5 Which person tried to make China into a democratic republic?
   1 Sun Yat-Sen
   2 Mao Zedong
   3 Ho Chi Minh
   4 Saddam Hussein

6 Which headline correctly pairs the person with
   the event?
   1 "Panama Canal Completed" — Anwar Sadat
   2 "Communists Come To Power in China" —
     Mao Zedong
   3 "Tiananmen Square Protests Crushed" —
     Sun Yat-Sen
   4 "The Gulf War Begins" — Fidel Castro

5

CONCERNS

In this section you will read about
some of the major problems and
concerns currently facing the
government and people of China.

THINK ABOUT IT

Why did the 1989 demonstrations in Tiananmen Square capture the world's attention?

_____

_____

Important Terms: As you read this section, look for the following terms:

◆ **Population Growth**   ◆ **One-Child Policy**

AMERICAN RELATIONS WITH COMMUNIST CHINA

UNFRIENDLY RELATIONS (1949-1972)

The period following the 1949 Communist takeover in China was marked by distrust and bad feelings
between China and the United States. The United States refused to
recognize the Communists as China's legal government. Instead, the
U. S. recognized **Chiang Kai-Shek**, who had fled to Taiwan with his
followers, as the leader of the government of China.

In 1950, the Communist government of North Korea invaded non-
Communist South Korea. During the **Korean War** which followed
(1950-1953), the United States supported South Korea and sent in
troops. The Chinese sent in a large military force in support of
Communist North Korea. In 1953, a compromise ended the war,
leaving Korea divided exactly as it was before the war began. This
war increased the distrust between China and the United States,
because each thought the other was interfering where it did not
belong.

Chiang Kai-Shek

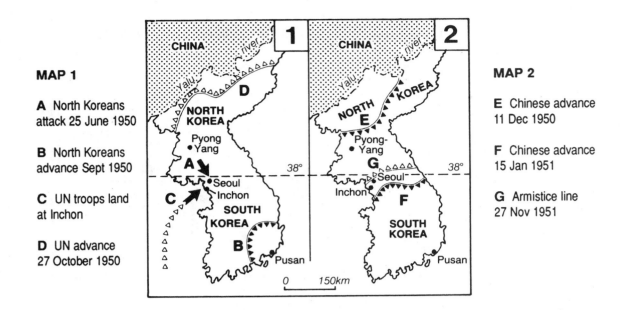

MAP 1

A North Koreans attack 25 June 1950

B North Koreans advance Sept 1950

C UN troops land at Inchon

D UN advance 27 October 1950

MAP 2

E Chinese advance 11 Dec 1950

F Chinese advance 15 Jan 1951

G Armistice line 27 Nov 1951

IMPROVED RELATIONS (1973-PRESENT)

In the 1960s the leaders of the two largest Communist nations, the Soviet Union and China, became increasingly unfriendly. This led the U.S. to seek better relations with China. Since the U.S. was involved in the Vietnam War at the time, it hoped that opening relations with China might give it some advantage in negotiating a peace settlement with North Vietnam. In 1972, **Richard Nixon** became the first American President to visit Communist China. In 1979, the U.S. reversed its long-standing policy and gave official recognition to the Chinese Communist government. This began a period of improved relations between the two countries. However, after the mass arrests and killings by the Chinese government of the demonstrators for democracy in Tiananmen Square, relations cooled between the U.S. and China. Since 1989, tensions have eased somewhat. China is now a major trading partner of the U.S., and many American companies are investing there.

POPULATION GROWTH

THE PROBLEM. With over 1 billion people, China has the world's largest population. Such a growing population makes it very difficult for China to feed its people or to raise their standard of living. Whatever gains China makes in food production are often used up by having more mouths to feed.

ATTEMPTED SOLUTIONS. In an effort to control the rapid population growth, the government began a program known as the "**one-child policy.**" Each family was told how many children it was allowed to have (usually one child), and the policy was carried out by force. Recently the Chinese government has modified this policy, and the number of children allowed in each family depends upon where the family lives (city or country), their jobs and their ethnic group. Parents who follow the government's rules about the size of their family receive free medical care, cash awards, and favored treatment in government housing and jobs. However, solutions to the overpopulation problem have not completely succeeded, because peasants want larger families to help with farm work. Also, if their first child is a girl, most Chinese couples want a second child, hoping to have a boy.

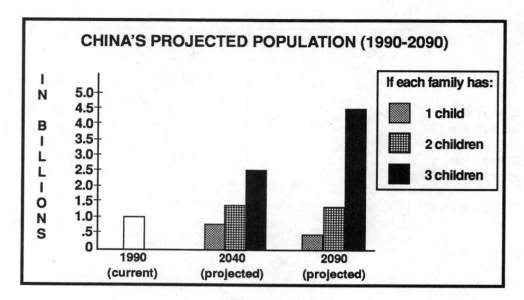

WORLD TRADE AND POLITICAL REFORM

THE PROBLEM. China needs to trade with other nations in order to improve the standard of living of its people. Increased trade would allow China to buy more equipment and machinery, making it more prosperous. Most of the trade would be with democratic nations like the U.S. — yet China is still a very undemocratic country; there is only one political party, and no freedom to express different ideas. Democratic nations are angered over China's crushing of the movement for democracy in Tiananmen Square, and also because China is selling weapons of war to certain countries in violation of international law. China has also oppressed the people of Tibet — a small mountainous country that China invaded in 1950 and has controlled ever since. Critics say that U.S. trade with China should be reduced.

ATTEMPTED SOLUTIONS. Chinese leaders are trying to convince the U.S. and other democracies that they are introducing changes that will make China a freer country. Many Chinese say that increasing trade remains the best way to encourage more democracy.

SUMMING UP: CONCERNS

Overpopulation continues to be China's most serious problem, and attempted solutions have not completely succeeded. From 1949 to 1979, the United States did not recognize the Chinese Communist government. Today relations between the two countries are far better.

CHECKING YOUR UNDERSTANDING

THINKING IT OVER

Did you give the correct reasons as to why the demonstrations in Tiananmen Square captured the world's attention? _____ What effects have these protests had on China? _____

_____

ANALYSIS

Many people believe that although China's leaders have crushed the movement for democracy, increasing trade with China is the best way to encourage democracy. Do you agree?

_____ Explain:_____

_____

Directions: Complete the following cards. Then answer the multiple choice questions.

POPULATION GROWTH

Why is it a problem? _____

Importance:_____

Attempted solutions:_____

ONE-CHILD POLICY

What is it? _____

How has it changed? _____

_____

1 The primary reason for China's policy of one child per family was to
1 introduce labor-saving devices
2 add unskilled workers
3 limit the need for doctors
4 prevent population increases

2 Communist China is undemocratic in part because
1 it has only one political party
2 the press may print anything it wishes
3 candidates must be Buddhists
4 elections take place too often

3 If China's population continues to increase faster than its production of goods, then
1 its standards of living will decline
2 industrialization will remain unchanged
3 people will move from cities to rural areas
4 capitalism will be adopted as China's economic system

4 One immediate result of the Korean War was to
1 lead to U.S. support of North Korea
2 bring about friendly relations between China and the U.S.
3 increase distrust between the U.S. and China
4 end Communism in China

5 The terms "one-child policy," "cash awards" and "favored treatment" are most closly associated with the problem of
1 overpopulation
2 Communist leadership
3 foreign trade
4 dynastic government

6 In an outlines, one of these is the main topic; the other three are sub-topics. Which is the main topic?
1 Reaction to Tiananmen Square
2 Nixon Visits China
3 The Korean War
4 Chinese-American relations

7 A major problem facing the government of China in the 1980s and 1990s is
1 environmental pollution
2 religious unity
3 population control
4 racial differences

8 Which event occurred last?
1 India gains its independence
2 Demonstrations break out in Tiananmen Square
3 The Korean War begins
4 Castro comes to power in Cuba

SUMMARIZING YOUR UNDERSTANDING

WORDCIRCLING

Directions. Use the information you have learned in this chapter and other chapters to circle the word being described.

```
T  E  T  H  N  O  C  E  N  T  R  I  S  M  C
M  I  B  C  E  F  T  N  I  X  O  N  N  O  O
O  P  A  C  D  R  S  T  E  F  G  O  B  N  M
N  D  Y  N  A  S  T  Y  R  A  I  O  C  M  M
O  C  R  B  A  N  G  L  A  D  E  S  H  O  U
T  D  S  P  U  N  T  A  I  W  A  N  C  N  N
H  E  O  T  I  S  M  D  E  F  A  I  O  S  I
E  F  S  T  U  L  D  E  N  G  F  A  D  O  S
I  M  J  O  N  L  M  S  N  E  A  S  T  O  M
S  B  U  D  D  H  I  S  M  N  C  A  B  N  C
M  C  O  M  M  U  N  E  B  O  X  E  R  S  D
M  A  O  E  D  H  O  N  G  C  L  F  L  M  O
C  O  N  F  U  C  I  A  N  I  S  M  R  S  T
B  C  R  E  D  G  U  A  R  D  S  B  E  A  U
O  R  A  I  C  G  A  N  G  E  S  O  D  E  F
```

Succession of rulers from the same family. D _ _ _ _ _ Y

Ancient Chinese ideas concerning how to act in society. C _ _ _ _ _ _ _ _ _ M

Belief in one God. M _ _ _ _ _ _ M

Belief that one's race is superior to other races. E _ _ _ _ _ _ _ _ _ M

Considered a holy river by the Hindus of India. G _ _ _ S

Group of Chinese that rebelled against foreigners. B _ _ _ S

First U.S. President to visit China. N _ _ N

Name of man who introduced Communism into China. M _ _

Square where Chinese students protested for democracy. T _ _ _ _ _ N

Mass murder of a group. `G` `|` `|` `|` `|` `|` `E` `|`

Area of China in which most of its population is located. `E` `|` `|` `T`

Name of man who replaced Mao as leader of China. `D` `|` `|` `G`

Nation split from Pakistan in 1971. `B` `|` `|` `|` `|` `|` `|` `H`

Island off mainland China where Chiang Kai-Shek fled. `T` `|` `|` `|` `N`

Religion that recommends avoiding wealth and high social position. `B` `|` `|` `|` `|` `M`

Students used by Mao to carry out the Cultural Revolution. `R` `|` `|` `|` `|` `|` `S`

Economic system introduced into China by Mao Zedong. `C` `|` `|` `|` `|` `|` `M`

Merging of many smaller farms into one larger collective farm. `C` `|` `|` `|` `E`

Summer winds that bring heavy rains to China. `M` `|` `|` `|` `S`

Directions: Fill in the necessary information on the following two visual organizers.

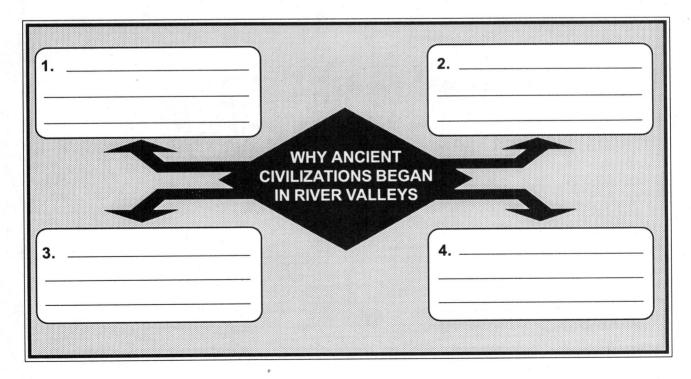

1. _____

2. _____

WHY ANCIENT
CIVILIZATIONS BEGAN
IN RIVER VALLEYS

3. _____

4. _____

Role of the Father _____

_____

_____

Ancestor Worship _____

_____

_____

CHANGES INTRODUCED INTO CHINA BY THE COMMUNISTS

Property _____

_____

_____

Women _____

_____

_____

DESCRIBING HISTORICAL EVENTS

Directions: Fully describe a historical event you learned about in this chapter, by filling in each box.

WHEN did it happen?

_____

WHERE did it happen?

_____

THE COMMUNIST TAKEOVER OF CHINA

WHO was involved?

_____

_____

_____

WHAT were the causes?

_____

_____

_____

RESULTS:

1. _____

2. _____

3. _____

LOOKING AT IMPORTANT PEOPLE   TEST HELPER

One way to study history is to look at the impact of great men and women. Each of these people has had an important effect on the lives of millions of others. In studying any of these individuals, the key question to focus on is: How has the world been changed by the existence of this person?

Two types of people who often have a major impact on others are *leaders* and *thinkers*.

Leaders are people who usually head a government or an organization. They affect history because they persuade or force millions of people to follow their commands. When studying leaders, you should ask yourself the following questions:

- What country or group did he or she lead?
- When was he/she active?
- What problems did the country or organization face?
- What actions were taken by the leader?
- What were the effects of the leader's policies?

For this last question, you should consider the effects both on the leader's country and on the rest of the world. For example, did the policies lead to independence, peace, war, prosperity or depression? How was the world changed by the activities of this leader?

Thinkers are people who, by their ideas, stimulate others to act or lead others to technological or artistic changes. When studying these thinkers, you should ask yourself:

- In what field did this thinker (writer, scientist) make a contribution?
- What was the contribution?
- What was the impact of this contribution?

For this last question, you should consider how the world has been changed by the contribution of this person.

Following is a list of important individuals that you should pay particular attention to when you read about them. You know some of these names already. Others will appear in later chapters.

LEADERS		THINKERS
Adolf Hitler	Fidel Castro	Karl Marx
Peter the Great	Corazon Aquino	Mother Teresa
Elizabeth I	Mao Zedong	Martin Luther
Mikhail Gorbachev	Mohandas Gandhi	Albert Einstein
Napoleon Bonaparte	Nelson Mandela	Confucius
Anwar Sadat	Vladimir Lenin	Galileo Galilei

TESTING YOUR UNDERSTANDING

Directions: Circle the number preceding the word or expression that correctly answers the statement or question. Following the multiple choice questions, answer the essay questions.

Base your answers to questions 1 through 3 on the table below and on your knowledge of global studies.

HOW THE WORLD'S MOST POPULATED NATIONS COMPARE
(in millions of people)

NATION	1960	1970	1987	2000	2020
CHINA	650	820	1,067	1,200	1,361
INDIA	438	547	800	1,013	1,310
U.S.	180	205	243	268	296

1 What was the population of China in 1970?
1 820
2 82,000
3 820,000
4 820 million

2 Which nation is expected to show the greatest increase in population between 1987 and the year 2000?
1 China
2 India
3 Russia
4 U. S.

3 If the population trend in China continues, there is a possibility of a
1 decline in farm production
2 need for slower trains
3 reduced rate of illiteracy
4 serious shortage of food

4 Which geographical feature is correctly paired with its location?
1 Sahara Desert / Brazil
2 Gobi Desert / China
3 Amazon River / Egypt
4 Nile River / India

5 Ancient Chinese civilization was similar to other ancient civilizations in that it
1 developed near river valleys
2 shared a common language
3 originally began in Africa
4 had a democratic government

6 The flight of Chiang Kai-Shek from mainland China and Mao Zedong's taking control of China are events most closely related to the
1 Japanese invasion of China (1937)
2 Korean War (1950)
3 Communist Revolution of 1949
4 Gulf War of 1991

7 The fact that Chinese foods are eaten by many Americans is an example of
1 nationalism
2 cultural diffusion
3 ethnocentrism
4 cultural isolation

8 Confucianism is most concerned with a person's
1 physical appearance
2 inherited traits
3 social relationships
4 emotional makeup

9 In China, Mao Zedong introduced the Great Leap Forward in order to
1 break up the communes
2 stress religious values
3 increase production
4 introduce capitalism

10 The Boxer Rebellion was an attempt to rid China of
1 dynastic control
2 Communists
3 illegal drug traffic
4 foreigners

ESSAYS

1 Communist beliefs have influenced the political, economic, and social life of China.

Part A

List *two* beliefs of Communism. For *each* belief, state an effect it has had on Chinese life.

BELIEF	EFFECT ON CHINESE LIFE
1 _____	1 _____ _____
2 _____	2 _____ _____

Part B

In your part B answer, you should use information you gave in Part A. However, you may also include different or additional information in your Part B answer.

Write an essay explaining how Communist beliefs have influenced the political, economic, and social life of China.

2 China faces many problems that make economic growth difficult.

Part A

Define the term "economic growth:" _____

List *two* problems making economic growth difficult in China.

1. _____

2. _____

Part B

In your part B answer, you should use information you gave in Part A. However, you may also include different or additional information in your Part B answer.

Write an essay beginning with this topic sentence:

Many problems have made economic growth difficult in China.

3 Events in one part of the world often affect other areas of the world.

Events

Open Door Policy (1899-1900)   Iraq's invasion of Kuwait (1990)
Communist takeover in China (1949)   Korean War (1950)

Part A

Select an event: _____

State what happened: _____

State how this event affected another part of the world: _____

_____

Part B

In your part B answer, you should use information you gave in Part A. However, you may also include different or additional information in your Part B answer.

Write an essay describing how events in one part of the world often affect other areas of the world.

4 Some individuals have brought about important changes in their countries.

Individuals

Mao Zedong   Deng Xiaoping
Nelson Mandela   Anwar Sadat
Mohandas Gandhi   Ayatollah Khomeini

Part A

Choose *two* individuals from the list. For *each* individual, state *one* important change brought about by that individual.

INDIVIDUAL	CHANGE
1 _____	1 _____ _____
2 _____	2 _____ _____

Part B

In your part B answer, you should use information you gave in Part A. However, you may also include different or additional information in your Part B answer.

Write an essay showing how some individuals have brought about important changes in their country.

GLOBAL CHECKLIST

CHINA

Directions: Before going on to the next chapter, you should check your understanding of the important people, terms and concepts covered in this chapter. Place a check (✔) mark next to those that you are able to explain. If you have trouble remembering a term, refer to the page listed next to the item.

Terraced rice paddies

❑ Ethnocentrism (144)
❑ Hwang Ho River (145)
❑ Dynasty (147)
❑ Spheres of Influence (147)
❑ Open Door Policy (148)
❑ Boxer Rebellion (148)
❑ Chiang Kai-Shek (148)

❑ Cultural Revolution (149)
❑ Red Guards (149)
❑ Communism (150)
❑ Tiananmen Square (150)
❑ Communes (153)
❑ Confucianism (154)
❑ Buddhism (154)

❑ Confucius (158)
❑ Sun Yat Sen (158)
❑ Mao Zedong (158)
❑ Deng Xiaoping (158)
❑ Korean War (1600
❑ Population Growth (161)
❑ One-Child Policy (161)

GEOGRAPHY

- Size and Location
- Geographic Features and Their Effects

CONCERNS

- Trade Imbalance with Other Nations

IMPORTANT PEOPLE

- Matthew Perry
- Emperor Hirohito
- Douglas MacArthur
- Soichiro Honda

CHAPTER 7

JAPAN

HISTORY

- Early History
- The Feudal Period
- The Opening of Japan to the West
- The Meiji Restoration
- Japan Becomes a World Power
- The U.S. Occupation of Japan

SYSTEMS

- Government
- Economy
- Society
- Religion
- The Arts

What do these pictures show you about Japan? _____
_____
_____
_____

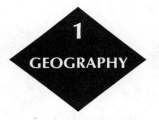

In this section you will read about the major geographic features of Japan and how these features have affected its people and history.

THINK ABOUT IT

Japan is a group of four islands off the coast of Asia. What effect do you think this has had on the

lives of the Japanese? _____

Why? _____

Important Terms: As you read this section, look for the following terms:

◆ **archipelago**　　　　◆ **population density**

SIZE AND LOCATION

◆ Japan is an **archipelago** (*a group of islands*)1,500 miles long. It is east of the Asian mainland, separated from China, Korea and Russia by the Sea of Japan. Its four main islands are Honshu, Hokkaido, Kyushu, and Shikoku. During its early history, Japan was greatly influenced by Chinese culture—its religion, method of writing and way of life. Although Japan is small in land area, it has a population of
◆ over 120 million, about half the number of people in the U.S. This results in a very high **population density** (*the number of people living in a given area*) in Japan — 844 people per square mile.

Comparison Map: Japan and the U.S.

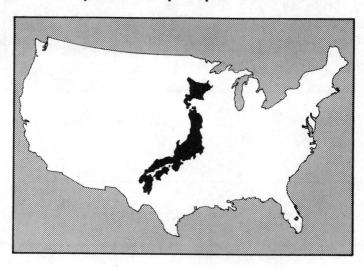

MAJOR GEOGRAPHIC FEATURES AND THEIR EFFECTS

MOUNTAINS
About 85% of Japan consists of mountains and hills. Since this makes much of the land difficult to farm, most people live on the lower plains near the coast.

SEAS AND OCEANS
Japan is surrounded by seas and oceans, separating it from the rest of Asia. This protected Japan from the outside world, making it possible for Japan to develop its own way of life, government and culture.

This general separation from others also allowed Japan to borrow ideas from various cultures, especially from China, without being controlled by them.

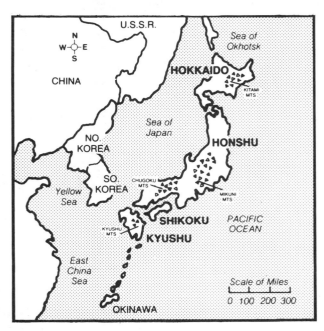

VOLCANOES AND EARTHQUAKES
Japan has many active volcanoes. Earthquakes are also common, and most homes and office buildings are constructed to withstand them. This has forced most of Japan's cities to spread outward, covering large areas, rather than having very tall buildings like the cities of some other parts of the world.

COASTLINE
The islands of Japan have long coastlines and excellent harbors, which allowed Japan to become an important trading center. This also helps explains why the Japanese depend so much on fishing, and why seafood is such an important part of their diet.

RESOURCES
Except for coal, Japan lacks most other natural resources—such as oil—that are needed for its industries. This created a major economic problem for Japan in the past, and it got its raw materials from other countries by using military force. Since its defeat in World War II, however, Japan gets the raw materials it needs by trading for them.

ANALYSIS

Which geographic feature do you think has had the most impact on Japan's history and culture? _____ Explain:

_____

_____

SUMMING UP: GEOGRAPHY

Japan is a country of islands. The seas and oceans surrounding kept it separated from other parts of the world for much of its history. However, Japan was greatly influenced by its neighbor, China. Japan lacks most of the resources needed for industry, making it necessary for Japan to trade with other nations in order to maintain a high standard of living.

THINKING IT OVER

Were you correct in guessing one of the effects that being surrounded by water has had on the history of the Japanese people? (Yes ___ No ___) What other effects have you learned about?

_____

CHECKING YOUR UNDERSTANDING

Directions: Complete the following cards. Then answer the multiple choice questions that follow.

ARCHIPELAGO

Definition: _____

Name one: _____

_____

POPULATION DENSITY

Define it: _____

Effect on Japan: _____

_____

1 If you took a plane trip from California to Japan, in which general direction would you fly?
   1 north   3 south
   2 east   4 west

2 Japan is an archipelago. This means that it
   1 is a group of islands
   2 lacks tall mountain ranges
   3 has many high plateau regions
   4 receives heavy rainfall

3 Japan is off the coast of which continent?
   1 Asia   3 South America
   2 Australia   4 Europe

4 In Japan a major economic problem has been its lack of
   1 natural resources
   2 skilled labor
   3 investment capital
   4 experienced managers

5 Which statement about Japan's geography is correct?
  1 Japan is a nation blessed with many natural resources.
  2 Volcanoes and earthquakes have influenced the way homes are built.
  3 Because of the extreme heat, most people live in the mountain areas.
  4 Japan's location led to frequent invasions by its neighbors

6 Because of its geography, Japan primarily relies on its exports of
  1 oil and petroleum
  2 raw materials
  3 farm products
  4 manufactured items

2 HISTORY

In this section you will read about the major historical events in Japan, from its earliest days as an isolated state under the rule of emperors and shoguns, to its present role as an economic superpower.

THINK ABOUT IT

Complete the first two columns of the chart, leaving the last column blank.

THE HISTORY OF JAPAN

What I Know	What I Want To Learn	What I Have Learned

Important Terms: As you read this section, look for the following terms:

◆ Feudalism
◆ Samurai
◆ Meiji Restoration
◆ Attack on Pearl Harbor
◆ Bombing of Hiroshima and Nagasaki
◆ Constitution of 1947

TIMELINE OF HISTORICAL EVENTS

1853	1868	1894	1904	1941	1942	1945	1989
Perry goes to Japan	Meiji Restoration	Sino-Japanese War	Russo-Japanese War	Japan attacks Pearl Harbor	Japan's empire reaches its height	U.S. drops atom bomb	Emperor Hirohito dies

JAPAN'S EARLY HISTORY (660 B. C.- 1185 A. D.)

The islands of Japan were first settled about 2,600 years ago by immigrants, probably from China, Korea and other parts of Asia. An emperor, supported by powerful families, ruled over the islands.

CHINA'S INFLUENCE ON JAPAN

Since its earliest history, Japan was deeply influenced by its neighbor, China. Buddhism, Confucianism, the use of word-symbols for writing, the calendar, tea and silk were all adopted from the Chinese culture. The exchange of different ideas and goods between cultures is called **cultural diffusion.**

FEUDAL PERIOD (1185-1600)

◆ Constant fighting among the powerful families led to a weakening of the emperor's power. As a result, **feudalism**, a political, economic and social system, developed.

KEY DEFINITIONS

Political: having to do with government
Economic: having to do with ways of earning a living
Social: ways in which people deal with each other

Two important characteristics of feudalism in Japan were the exchange of land for military service, and a strict class structure:

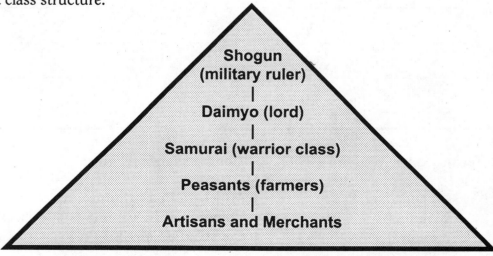

Shogun (military ruler)
|
Daimyo (lord)
|
Samurai (warrior class)
|
Peasants (farmers)
|
Artisans and Merchants

During the years when the Japanese lived under a feudal system, the leaders of local areas had more power than the Emperor. Eventually, one family became the most powerful and established its leader as the **Shogun** (*military ruler of the country*). The shogun allowed the Emperor to remain on his throne as a symbol of unity. Meanwhile, the local nobles hired warriors called **samurai** to protect them. The samurai lived by a strict code of honor in which suicide was preferred to disloyalty or defeat. Each samurai swore an oath of loyalty to the Emperor and to his **daimyo** (lord). Peasants worked the land of these local lords in return for protection by the samurai. This type of political arrangement lasted until the late 1800s.

THE OPENING OF JAPAN TO THE WEST (1854)

PERIOD OF ISOLATIONISM
European traders established contact with the Japanese in the 1500s. Fearing the negative effects of foreign influence, Japan cut itself off from trade with Europe in 1639. The Japanese were forbidden to travel to other countries, and foreigners were banned from entering Japan. This isolation from the outside world made it necessary for the Japanese to rely on themselves and their limited resources. It also shut them off from available scientific and technical knowledge, and made the Japanese uneasy and distrustful of outsiders.

THE UNITED STATES OPENS JAPAN
Americans were seeking better trade relations with Asian nations across the Pacific. In 1853, the United States sent **Commodore Matthew Perry** with a fleet of naval ships to Japan. Perry presented the American government's demands that the Japanese open their nation to trade with the United States and give better treatment to American sailors who might be shipwrecked in the area. Fearing Commodore Perry's military power, Japanese leaders opened their ports: first to the United States, and later to other nations. This brought an end to two hundred years of Japanese isolation from the Western world.

Pictured at right: Members of the first Japanese mission to the United States.

THE MEIJI RESTORATION (1868-1912)

Japan's military ruler, the Shogun, was forced out of power because of his decision to open Japan to the West. This event permitted the **Emperor Meiji** to regain the powers traditionally held by emperors. Emperor Meiji realized that if Japan were to avoid coming under foreign control, it would have to adopt Western ways. These developments are known as the **Meiji Restoration**.

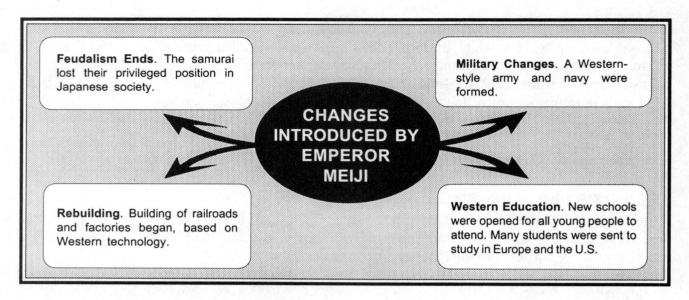

JAPAN BECOMES A WORLD POWER (1894-1941)

The **Meiji Restoration** helped Japan become a much more wealthy and powerful country. The Japanese borrowed the technology and inventions of others and adapted them to their own needs. Following the example of leading European nations, Japan became an imperialist nation, taking over weaker countries to gain natural resources, raw materials and markets in which to sell its goods. Japan set out on a series of wars that was to change it from an isolated, backward nation into a major world power.

SINO-JAPANESE WAR (1894-1895). Japan defeated China and took over control of Korea. This alerted the world to Japan's new-found military strength.

RUSSO-JAPANESE WAR (1904-05). Japan defeated Russia and gained additional territory. This further shocked the world, since it was the first time that Asians had defeated a major European power like Russia.

WORLD WAR I (1914-1918). Japan fought on the side of the Allies and, as a result, gained some territories from defeated Germany.

JAPAN ATTACKS CHINA (1937). In the 1930s, Japanese military leaders took over the government of Japan. Its foreign policy became more aggressive. Japan occupied northern China in 1931, and attacked the rest of China in 1937. The Japanese leaders hoped to build a vast empire over most of East Asia.

WORLD WAR II (1941-1945). During World War II, Japan fought on the side of Germany and Italy. On December 7, 1941, Japan launched a surprise attack on the U.S. naval base at **Pearl Harbor,** Hawaii. Japan won some early victories against the United States. In time, however, the United States defeated Japan after dropping two atomic bombs on the Japanese cities of **Hiroshima** and **Nagasaki** in August 1945. The atomic bombing of these two cities has been a hotly debated topic ever since. People have different opinions on whether the United States should have used the bombs on civilian targets.

Sometimes a test question requires you to distinguish a **fact** from an **opinion**. The following will help you to tell the difference between them.

- A *fact* is something that can be proven to be true. Facts often give a basic description of an event. An example of a factual statement would be:

  "The United States dropped an atomic bomb on Hiroshima on August 6, 1945."

- An *opinion* is someone's belief, and cannot be completely proven or disproven. Opinions are often about what **should** or **should not** be done. An example of an opinion would be:

  "Dropping the atomic bomb on Hiroshima was the best policy for the United States to follow at that time."

ALLIED ADVANCES IN THE PACIFIC

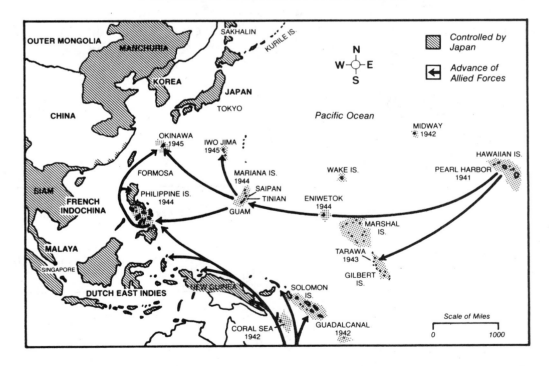

THE U.S. OCCUPIES JAPAN (1945-1952)

After the defeat of Japan in World War II, the United States sent soldiers to reorganize Japan. During the American occupation of Japan, many changes took place.

Empire Eliminated. All of Japan's overseas territories were taken away.

Power to Wage War Ends. Japan was forbidden to have an army or navy, ending its ability to make war. Japan also promised never to use nuclear weapons.

CHANGES IN JAPAN AFTER DEFEAT IN WORLD WAR II

Constitution. In 1947, the U.S. made Japan adopt a constitution establishing a democracy. Political power was given to the people.

Economy. The United States helped rebuild Japan's economy, making Japan one of the world's leading economic powers.

SUMMING UP: HISTORY

From Japan's earliest history, it has been greatly influenced by China. During the feudal period, local lords using their samurai warriors had control over Japanese society. In 1853, by sending in Commodore Perry, the U. S. forced Japan to trade with the West. Perry's visit led to the Meiji Restoration (1868-1912), and Japan became a modern industrial nation. After the Meiji Restoration, Japan became an imperialist power, eventually attacking the U.S. during World War II. After Japan was defeated in 1945, it became a peaceful and democratic country.

THINKING IT OVER

Return to page 177, where you completed the first two columns of the chart. Now complete the third column of the chart, indicating what you have just learned.

CHECKING YOUR UNDERSTANDING

Directions: Complete the following cards. Then answer the multiple choice questions that follow.

FEUDALISM

Definition: _____

Major characteristics: _____

_____

SAMURAI

Who were they? _____

Position in society: _____

_____

MEIJI RESTORATION

Define it: _____

Why was it important? _____

_____

ATTACK ON PEARL HARBOR

What happened? _____

Importance: _____

_____

BOMBING OF HIROSHIMA/NAGASAKI

Type of bombs: _____

Why was it important? _____

_____

CONSTITUTION OF 1947

What is it? _____

Importance: _____

_____

1 A Japanese samurai would be most similar to an American
  1 politician   3 cowboy
  2 soldier   4 government official

2 Which event occurred first?
  1 World War II began
  2 U.S. dropped an atom bomb on Japan
  3 Commodore Perry arrived in Japan
  4 United States occupied Japan

3 A major result of the U.S. occupation of Japan after World War II was that
  1 Japan relied more on the use of nuclear weapons
  2 the Japanese military lost its power
  3 Communism was introduced into Japan's economy
  4 feudalism returned to Japan

4 The policy of invading other nations from 1894 to 1945 was due to Japan's
  1 being invaded by other nations
  2 attempts to obtain natural resources
  3 desire to spread apartheid
  4 attempts to spread its religious beliefs.

5 Which is an opinion rather than a fact?
  1 Emperor Meiji restored the powers of the Japanese emperor.
  2 China has a larger population than Japan.
  3 It was necessary to drop the atomic bomb on Japan in 1945 to end the war.
  4 Commodore Perry visited Japan in 1853.

6 A major reason for Japan's economic success before World War II was its
  1 ability to borrow and adapt from others
  2 government ownership of industry
  3 use of traditional methods of production
  4 establishment of a democratic government

7 The Sino-Japanese War, the Russo-Japanese War and World War I were similar in that in each of them Japan sought to
  1 rid Japan of foreign influence
  2 spread Buddhism in Asia
  3 obtain land and natural resources
  4 take over the United States

8 Which was a characteristic of feudal society in Japan?
  1 rapid social change   3 high literacy rate
  2 industrialization   4 rigid class structure

9 Which Western nation was responsible for opening Japan to outside trade?
   1 Great Britain
   2 France
   3 the United States
   4 Germany

10 A major characteristic of feudalism was
   1 a belief in the importance of farmers
   2 its emphasis on building up Japan's industries
   3 protection in exchange for labor or military service
   4 an acceptance of Western ideas and technology

3
SYSTEMS

In this section you will read about Japan's government, economy, social structure, religions, and cultural achievements.

THINK ABOUT IT

Traditional art forms play an important part in Japanese life. What do you know about each of the following Japanese art forms?

Origami: _____

Haiku Poetry: _____

Kabuki Theater: _____

Important Terms: As you read this section, look for the following terms:

◆ **Emperor**   ◆ **Shintoism**

GOVERNMENT

◆ Before World War II, the **Emperor** and his advisors had control of the government of Japan. The Emperor was considered "God-like." However, since the war, Japan has become a democracy. The Emperor is now a patriotic symbol for Japan and its people, but has no real political power. The government is a democracy based on the idea that all power comes from the people. The leader of the Japanese government is the prime minister. Laws are made by its legislature, called the **Diet**. The Diet, similar to the American Congress, is made up of a group of representatives elected by the Japanese people.

ECONOMY

Japan lacks important natural resources and has little land on which to grow crops. However, since the end of World War II Japan has become a great economic power.

After World War II, the United States wanted to build a strong Japan to serve as an ally against the spread of Communism in Asia. Japan rebuilt its cities, factories and industries with American support. This rebuilding process was so successful that by the 1960s Japan became one of the world's leading industrial nations. This rapid recovery has been called an "economic miracle."

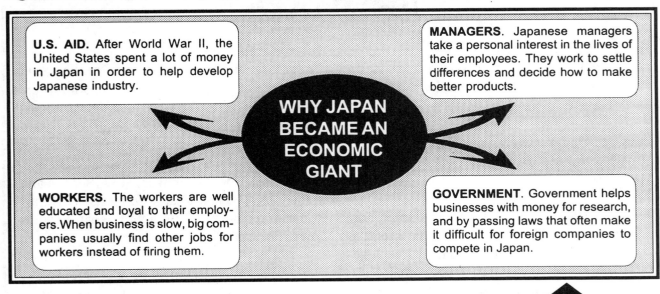

U.S. AID. After World War II, the United States spent a lot of money in Japan in order to help develop Japanese industry.

MANAGERS. Japanese managers take a personal interest in the lives of their employees. They work to settle differences and decide how to make better products.

WHY JAPAN BECAME AN ECONOMIC GIANT

WORKERS. The workers are well educated and loyal to their employers. When business is slow, big companies usually find other jobs for workers instead of firing them.

GOVERNMENT. Government helps businesses with money for research, and by passing laws that often make it difficult for foreign companies to compete in Japan.

ANALYSIS

Based on the example of Japan's economic success, what advice would you give to a developing nation today?

_____

_____

By the 1980s, Japanese companies dominated key industries such as electronics, steel and shipbuilding. They were also increasing their share of the U.S. market for cars and computer chips. Part of the credit goes to Japan's highly skilled and dedicated workforce. The following pie chart illustrates information about Japan's workforce. If you have any difficulty understanding the material in this chart, read the **Skill Builder** on page 186, which explains how to interpret a pie chart.

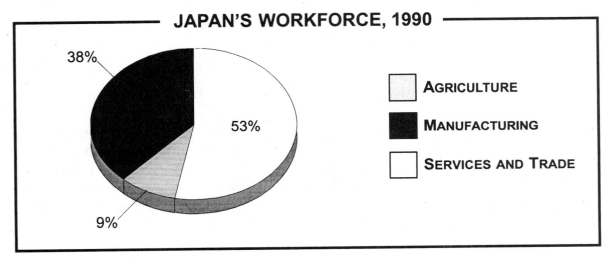

JAPAN'S WORKFORCE, 1990

38%

53%

9%

☐ AGRICULTURE

■ MANUFACTURING

☐ SERVICES AND TRADE

SKILL BUILDER: INTERPRETING PIE CHARTS

What Is a Pie Chart?
A pie chart is a circle divided into "pie slices" of different sizes. It shows the relationship between a whole and its parts.

Keys to Understanding a Pie Chart
To understand a pie chart, look at its major components:

Title. The title tells you the overall topic. For example, the title of our pie chart is "**Japan's Workforce, 1990.**" It shows the percentage of workers involved in each of the major job groups in Japan in 1990.

Legend. The legend shows what each slice of the "pie" represents. For example, in our chart, the gray slice represents workers in agriculture, while the black slice represents workers in manufacturing.

Slices Of The Pie. Each slice (piece) of the pie tells us what information is being examined and its size or relationship to the whole pie. Our pie chart shows that agricultural workers make up 9% of the workforce. This means out of every 100 people who work in Japan (the whole pie), nine of them (the gray slice) are employed in some form of agriculture.

Interpreting a Pie Chart
To find specific information, examine the size of each piece of the pie and its relationship to the other pieces, or to the whole pie. For example, you might want to find out the main occupation of most Japanese workers. We see that Services and Trade (53%) is the largest slice of the pie. Thus, most Japanese workers are in service and trade jobs. The chart can also be used to draw some other conclusions about Japan's workforce. For example:

- Only about 9% (1 in 10 people) of Japan's workforce is involved in farming. This might help us conclude that much of Japan's land is unsuited for growing crops.

- Since over half (53%) of the workforce is involved in services and trade, this might lead us to conclude that Japan does a great deal of trading with the outside world.

What other conclusions can you draw from the information in the pie chart?

_____

_____

SOCIETY

Since Japan has been isolated from the rest of the world for a large part of its history, local tradition has played an important part in Japanese life. In addition, Japan is a very **homogeneous** society (*almost all of the people have the same racial and ethnic identity*). Japan was also greatly influenced by the beliefs of the Chinese philosopher Confucius. His teachings stressed family loyalty and taught that the father was the head of the household. These beliefs encouraged the strong sense of discipline and loyalty in traditional Japanese life. Since World War II, Japanese society has undergone many changes.

➤ **Urbanization.** Today, three out of four Japanese live in cities. This leads to serious overcrowding. Japanese homes and apartments are small by American standards.

➤ **Education.** The Japanese place great importance on a good education. High school is especially important in Japan. What conclusions can you draw from the following chart?

A COMPARISON OF U.S. AND JAPANESE EDUCATION		
	U.S.	**JAPAN**
Literacy rate	99%	99%
Length of school week	5 days	5 + half-day Saturday
Days in school year	180	240
Students graduating from H.S.	under 80%	over 94%
Students going to college	58%	48%

➤ **Work.** In the workplace, managers and employees cooperate with each other. The managers frequently ask workers for their ideas. As a result, the Japanese are usually very loyal to their employers and work for the same company all their lives.

➤ **The Role of Women.** In traditional Japan, women were thought to be weak and inferior. Today, women are equal by law, but they still have fewer opportunities than men do in the workplace. In most Japanese families, the wife is expected to stay at home and raise the children.

RELIGION

Shintoism is a religion that began in Japan and is practiced only there. According to Shinto beliefs, gods ◆ or spirits are found in mountains, rivers, rocks and other parts of nature. Some believers also show great devotion to the Japanese Emperor. Shintoism has no sacred books or special codes of conduct. Besides Shintoism, many Japanese are followers of Buddhism, and some are Christians. The Japanese also developed their own form of Buddhism, known as **Zen Buddhism**, which emphasizes quiet contemplation and meditation.

THE ARTS

Japan's rich cultural heritage draws heavily from its association with China. Traditional Japanese arts also emphasize the values of simplicity, harmony and order, and the beauty of nature. Many of its art forms are uniquely Japanese — such as **haiku poetry** (short poems reflecting on the beauty of nature and life) and **Kabuki theater** (plays performed by an all-male cast in masks and elaborate traditional costumes). Other art forms

A Kabuki play

include **origami** (folding paper into animal and other interesting shapes); **ikebana** (artistic flower arranging emphasizing the beauty of nature); and the traditional Japanese tea ceremony.

SUMMING UP: SYSTEMS

GOVERNMENT. Today, Japan is a democracy. The Emperor serves as a symbol for the nation, but has no real power.

ECONOMY. Japan is an economic superpower with a capitalist system.

SOCIETY. Japan still follows many of its old ways, but changes take place as people move into the cities and become better educated.

RELIGION. Many Japanese follow Shintoism, a traditional religion concerned with the worship of nature.

THE ARTS. Japan has developed many unique art forms that reflect Chinese and Zen Buddhist influences and the traditional Japanese love of nature.

THINKING IT OVER

After reading about Japan's traditional arts, were you correct (on page 184) in identifying any of them? (Yes ___ No ___) Define the ones you did not know before: _____

_____

_____

CHECKING YOUR UNDERSTANDING

Directions: Complete the following cards. Then answer the multiple choice questions that follow.

EMPEROR

Traditional role: _____

Present role: _____

_____

SHINTOISM

What is it? _____

Major beliefs: _____

_____

1 Which statement best describes the current role of Japan's emperor?
   1 The position of Emperor has been abolished.
   2 The Emperor acts only as a symbol for Japan.
   3 Full power was restored to the Emperor after World War II.
   4 The Emperor is now elected by the Japanese people.

2 Which reform took place in Japan following World War II?
   1 Japan's nuclear arms were increased.
   2 Japan declared labor unions illegal.
   3 Japan became a democracy.
   4 The Emperor's position was abolished.

3 Which statement best describes modern-day Japan?
   1 Japan is primarily an agricultural society.
   2 Japan is a leading economic power in the world.
   3 Japan has returned to practicing feudalism.
   4 Japan follows a policy of strict isolation.

4 Since World War II, the Japanese government has been led by
   1 the Emperor   3 a prime minister
   2 an elected Cabinet   4 military advisors

5 Shintoism and Buddhism are Japanese
   1 government agencies   3 social classes
   2 educational reformers 4 religions

6 Which value was highly regarded by traditional Japanese society?
   1 family loyalty   3 female power
   2 material wealth   4 non-aggression

7 In a traditional Japanese family, a woman is expected to
   1 enter the business world
   2 stay at home and care for the children
   3 be the equal of males
   4 make major decisions for the family

8 A study of Japan's art, music, and theater best helps us to understand its
   1 foreign policy
   2 cultural values
   3 balance-of-trade policy
   4 technological advances

9 Haiku, origami and Kabuki are all examples of Japanese
   1 emperors   3 art forms
   2 religious groups 4 land areas

10 Which has had the greatest impact on Japanese art forms?
   1 European architecture
   2 Renaissance paintings
   3 the beauty of nature
   4 Japan's nearness to the equator

4

IMPORTANT PEOPLE

In this section you will read about some people who have had an important role in shaping Japan's history and culture.

THINK ABOUT IT

How many people can you name who had a role in shaping the history of Japan? _____ Who are they? _____

Important Names: As you read this section, look for the following names:

◆ Matthew Perry   ◆ Emperor Hirohito
◆ Douglas MacArthur   ◆ Soichiro Honda

THE JAPAN TIMES

Volume XI	No. 3

MATTHEW PERRY

Japan had closed itself off from contact with foreigners since the 1600s. In 1853, Commodore Perry was sent to Japan by the U.S. government with a fleet of warships, to demand better treatment for shipwrecked U.S. sailors who had been mistreated by the Japanese, and to demand that Japan open its ports to U.S. trade. The Emperor, fearing U.S. naval power, agreed. This ended more than 200 years of Japanese isolation and opened Japan's ports to foreign trade and Western influence.

EMPEROR MEIJI

In the late 1800s, Meiji restored the power of the Emperor and encouraged the modernization and industrialization of Japan.

DOUGLAS MacARTHUR

General Douglas MacArthur commanded Allied forces against Japan in World War II, and was put in charge of the occupying forces in Japan after the war. His task was to change Japan from a military to a peaceful state. MacArthur created a new democratic constitution for Japan, restored the Japanese economy, and redistributed land more fairly. He reformed Japan's educational system, improved working conditions, and expanded women's rights.

EMPEROR HIROHITO

Hirohito was the Emperor of Japan throughout World War II. After Japan's defeat in the war, he was forced to give up his claim of being "god-like." However, the emperor remained a popular and respected leader in Japan. Hirohito died in 1989 and was replaced by his son, **Emperor Akito.**

Hirohito as a young man.

SOICHIRO HONDA

Honda was an industrial pioneer who made his company one of the world's largest automakers. His hard work and leadership has made Honda the third best selling car in the United States. The Honda Company came to symbolize Japan's remarkable industrial rise after World War II. Soichiro Honda retired in 1973, claiming the company should be run by young, not aging, executives.

SUMMING UP: IMPORTANT PEOPLE

Matthew Perry opened Japan to western ideas and influences. Japan industrialized rapidly and adopted a policy of aggressive imperialism. After World War II, General Douglas MacArthur reshaped Japan into a democratic nation. Emperor Hirohito helped the Japanese adjust to these changes. Soichiro Honda was one of many outstanding businessmen who made Japan an industrial leader.

THINKING IT OVER

Look on page 189 at the list you made before reading this section. What other people can you now

add to it? _____

_____

CHECKING YOUR UNDERSTANDING

Directions: Complete the following cards. Then answer the multiple choice questions that follow.

MATTHEW PERRY

Who was he? _____

Why was he important? _____

_____

EMPEROR HIROHITO

When did he rule Japan? _____

Why was he important? _____

_____

DOUGLAS MACARTHUR

Who was he? _____

Achievements: _____

_____

SOICHIRO HONDA

Who is he? _____

Achievements: _____

_____

1 Which term best describes Japan before the arrival of Commodore Perry?
   1 imperialistic
   2 militaristic
   3 isolationist
   4 expansionist

2 Commodore Perry visited Japan to
   1 open Japanese ports to U.S. trade
   2 break Japan's control over China
   3 protect Japan
   4 invade Japan

3 Which person is correctly paired with his country?
   1 Desmond Tutu - Israel
   2 Anwar Sadat - Argentina
   3 Fidel Castro - Cuba
   4 Emperor Hirohito - China

4 Emperor Hirohito and General MacArthur are people most closely associated with
   1 Perry's visit to Japan
   2 the Meiji Restoration
   3 the Sino-Japanese War
   4 World War II

5
CONCERNS

In this section you will read about the major concerns facing Japan, and how Japan has looked for ways to make up for its shortage of natural resources.

THINK ABOUT IT

Japan has few natural resources, yet it became an economic giant in the world. How do you think

this was accomplished? _____

_____

Important Terms: As you read this section, look for the following terms:

◆ **Trade Deficit**   ◆ **Global Interdependence**

THE PROBLEM OF TRADE WITH OTHER COUNTRIES

In recent years, Japan has sold more goods to the United States than the United States has sold to Japan. For example, many Americans buy Japanese cars, but only a few Japanese buy American cars. This creates a **trade deficit** (*unequal exchange of goods*) favoring Japan. The U.S. is worried about this because American companies are losing business and workers are losing jobs. The Japanese say that the cause of the unequal trade is that Japanese goods are made better than American products. People in the U.S. argue that American-made goods would sell better in Japan if the Japanese government ended laws that make it difficult to sell foreign products there. If more American goods were sold in Japan, trade between the two countries would be more equal. In fact, in the early 1990s U.S. exports to Japan have increased at a faster rate than Japanese exports to the U.S. Many suggestions have been made for improving the U.S. trade imbalance with Japan:

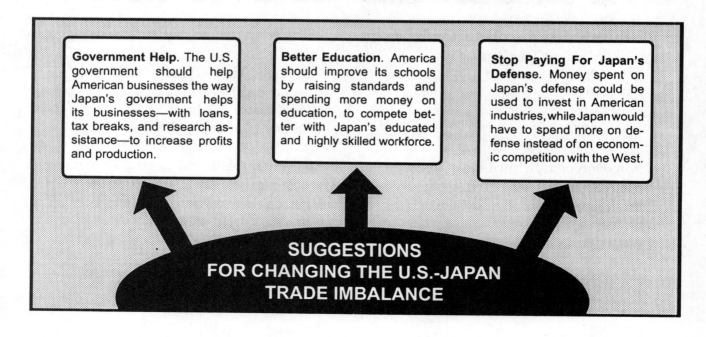

Government Help. The U.S. government should help American businesses the way Japan's government helps its businesses—with loans, tax breaks, and research assistance—to increase profits and production.

Better Education. America should improve its schools by raising standards and spending more money on education, to compete better with Japan's educated and highly skilled workforce.

Stop Paying For Japan's Defense. Money spent on Japan's defense could be used to invest in American industries, while Japan would have to spend more on defense instead of on economic competition with the West.

SUGGESTIONS FOR CHANGING THE U.S.-JAPAN TRADE IMBALANCE

Because of the trade deficit, American dollars leave the United States for Japan. Japan uses some of these dollars to buy raw materials it lacks, such as oil, and invests other dollars in businesses around the world. This illustrates the idea of **global interdependence**, showing that all nations depend on each ◆ other for trade and investment.

SUMMING UP: CONCERNS

Today Japan is an economic superpower. The fact that so many people in the United States buy Japanese rather than American products has caused some American workers to lose their jobs. People have suggested various ways for the United States to change this situation.

THINKING IT OVER

Were you correct in explaining why Japan, with limited resources, was able to become an economic superpower? ___ What additional information would you include now? _____

_____

CHECKING YOUR UNDERSTANDING

Directions: Complete the following cards. Then answer the multiple choice questions that follow.

TRADE DEFICIT
What is it? _____
What is its effect on the U.S.? _____
_____

GLOBAL INTERDEPENDENCE
Define it: _____
How does it work? _____
_____

1 Which is an example of global interdependence?
   1 Japan's government helps support a new industry.
   2 Japan halts all foreign imports into Japan.
   3 Japan buys U.S. clothing and sells Japanese cars in the United States.
   4 Japan passes a law attempting to stop environmental pollution.

2 Which statement best describes Japan since the end of World War II?
   1 Japan has become an economic superpower.
   2 Japan has rejected all contact with the foreign world.
   3 Japan has increased the Emperor's power.
   4 Japan has used imperialism to obtain new colonies.

3 U.S.-Japanese relations have sometimes been strained by Japan's
1 build-up of nuclear weapons
2 large volume of exports to the United States
3 close ties with China
4 close ties with South Africa

4 Following World War II, the Japanese government adopted policies designed to
1 increase its industrial production
2 gain colonies throughout Asia
3 establish Communism in Japan
4 return to a policy of isolationism

5 "Japanese imports cost American jobs." This statement reflects the belief that
1 too many Americans are moving to Japan to work
2 imports into the United States lead to American unemployment
3 Japan should not import so many U.S. products
4 the Japanese must make better goods if they expect Americans to buy them

6 Which group suffered the most from Japan's achievements as an economic superpower?
1 American importers of Japanese cars
2 Japanese farmers
3 American auto workers
4 Japanese auto manufacturers

7 Which is a major reason for the American trade deficit?
1 The government is printing too much money.
2 More foreign goods are sold in America than America is selling to foreigners.
3 The government spends more money than it can print.
4 Foreign-made goods are inferior to American-made goods.

8 One of Japan's most important economic advantages has been its
1 abundance of natural resources
2 highly skilled labor force
3 large amount of fertile land
4 government control of production

SUMMARIZING YOUR UNDERSTANDING

PARAGRAPH FRAME

Building Your Vocabulary. Use the words that appear in the box to fill in the blanks in the paragraph so that it answers the question below:

How has Japan been able to emerge as an economic superpower?

| nations' | exporter | United States |
| automobiles | World War II | natural resources |

Although Japan lacks many [＿＿＿＿＿], it has managed to overcome this problem. After [＿＿＿＿＿] Japan was faced with many burned cities, damaged transportation lines, and harbors in ruins. The [＿＿＿＿＿] provided a large amount of financial support to help rebuild Japan's economy. In rebuilding, the Japanese took advantage of many other [＿＿＿＿＿] scientific and technological advances. This allowed new industries to develop in postwar Japan that did not exist in prewar Japan. By the 1970s, Japan had become a major manufacturer of radios, televisions, and most of all [＿＿＿＿＿]. Today, Japan is a leading [＿＿＿＿＿] of products to all parts of the world.

WORD SCRAMBLE

Directions: Use the information you have learned from this and other chapters to unscramble the words below and spell them correctly in the boxes.

City bombed by United States with atomic weapons. (HIAMSOHRI)

H								

Emperor of Japan from 1926 to 1989. (TOROHIHI)

H							

Natural resource that is most scarce in the Middle East. (TWARE)

W				

U.S. General who introduced sweeping changes into Japan. (ACMRAHTRU)

M								

The art form of folding paper into animal and other unusual shapes. (GAIMORI)

O						

U.S. Commodore who opened Japan to foreign trade in 1853. (YERPR)

P				

Group of islands. (PLAIRHECAGO)

A										

Japanese religion based on the worship of nature. (THOSINIMS)

S								

Japanese warrior. (MAURISA)

S						

Leader who introduced Communism into Cuba. (TRASCO)

C					

Military ruler of feudal Japan. (HUNGSO)

S					

Nation once governed by Ayatollah Khomeini. (RIAN)

I			

Refers to a people's language, customs, attitudes and beliefs. (TURLCUE)

C						

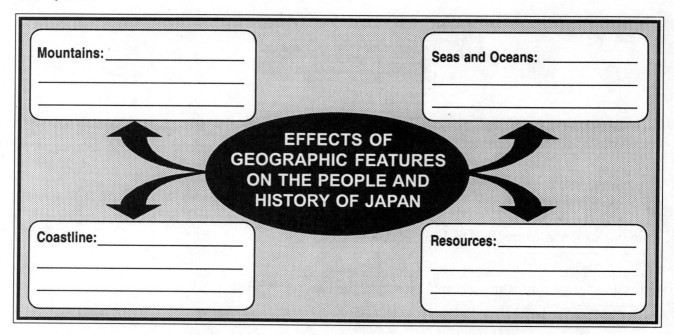

Mountains: _____
_____
_____

Seas and Oceans: _____
_____
_____

EFFECTS OF GEOGRAPHIC FEATURES ON THE PEOPLE AND HISTORY OF JAPAN

Coastline: _____
_____
_____

Resources: _____
_____
_____

DESCRIBING HISTORICAL EVENTS

Directions: Describe fully a historical event you learned about in this chapter, by filling in each box.

WHEN did it happen?
_____
_____

WHO was involved?
_____
_____

THE MEIJI RESTORATION

WHAT were the causes?
_____
_____
_____

RESULTS:
1. _____
2. _____
3. _____

LOOKING AT HISTORICAL EVENTS

TEST HELPER

This Test-Helper section will help you prepare to answer questions dealing with historical events.

In the movie *Back to the Future*, the main character travels back in time and meets his mother while she is a teenager. His appearance threatens to change events so that in the future he may never be born. Time travel is a fantasy, but part of the excitement of the film is that it suggests something true: if we could change a single past event, we might change the entire course of history. Why is this so?

CAUSE AND EFFECT

Every event has effects, and these effects have still further effects. Some events affect the entire development of a society—its social organization, government or economy. These changes then influence the later development of that society. At key times, choices by leaders can be especially important. If a leader decides to go to war, it can change a country's political, social and economic system. Historians are interested in examining how events are connected by causes and effects.

- The **causes** of something are the conditions that led to it or brought it about. An event would not have happened except for this cause. For example, turning a light switch that allows electric current to flow is the *cause* for the light to go on.

- The **effects** of something are any of the things that happen because of it — the results of a particular decision or event. For example, the light's going on was the *effect* of turning the switch.

Cause ——————————> Effect
I turned the switch.   The light went on.

ANSWERING AN ESSAY QUESTION ABOUT HISTORICAL EVENTS

Very often a test will have a question about historical events and their effects. The question will usually list events and ask you to discuss an event and its impact. For example, you may be asked about the opening of Japan to the West. Causes and effects are linked: the occupation of Japan by the U.S. eventually helped bring about Japan's development as an economic power. With this type of question, first think about the event (the **cause**), and write about the *who, what, when* and *where*. Then do the same for the **results** of the event. For example, your essay might read as follows:

After Japan was defeated in World War II, the United States sent soldiers to occupy its lands. The United States decided to spend money to help rebuild the destroyed Japanese economy. The United States was interested in doing this because it wanted a strong friend in East Asia to help it resist the growing threat of Communism. The United States therefore spent large amounts of money to help stimulate Japanese industries. From that boost, the Japanese went on to become an economic superpower in the world.

TESTING YOUR UNDERSTANDING

Directions: Circle the number preceding the word or expression that correctly answers the statement or question. Following the multiple choice questions, answer the essay questions.

Base your answers to questions 1 and 2 on the map and on your knowledge of social studies.

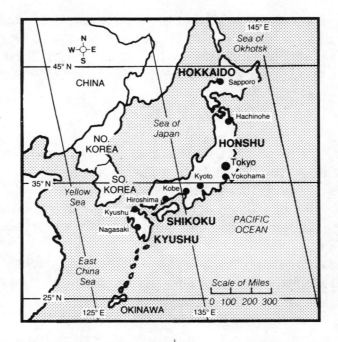

1 The most northern of Japan's four main islands is

1 Kyushu   3 Hokkaido
2 Nagasaki   4 Sapporo

2 According to the scale on the map, the distance between Tokyo and Hachinohe is

1 100 miles   3 400 miles
2 250 miles   4 500 miles

Base your answers to questions 3 and 4 on the pie charts and on your knowledge of social studies.

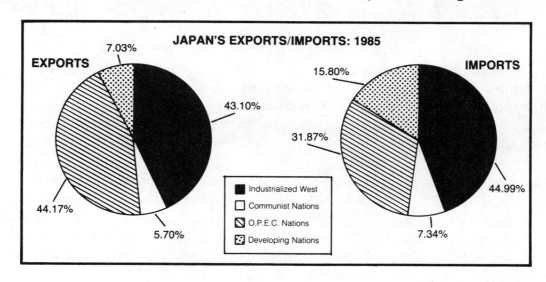

3 What is the percentage of goods Japan exported to the industrial West in 1985?
1 7.03%   3 43.10%
2 15.80%   4 44.90%

4 Which statement about 1985 is true according to the information in the pie charts?
1 Japan did not export any goods to the industrialized West.
2 Japan imported only from OPEC nations.
3 Japan exported mostly farm products.
4 Japan sold more goods to developing nations than to Communist nations.

5 Which is true about Japan's geography?
1 Japan has few natural resources.
2 Japan has few mountains.
3 Japan has two large deserts.
4 Japan has a large tropical rain forest.

6 Japan's invasion of China in the 1930s and its attack on Pearl Harbor in 1941 were results of Japanese
1 democracy   3 imperialism
2 feudalism   4 isolationism

7 Japan's emergence as a major power after World War II was a result of
1 colonial possessions   3 military forces
2 economic growth   4 nuclear arsenal

8 Which characteristic was found in traditional Japanese society?
1 All people were considered equal.
2 Individual rights were more important than family rights.
3 Women were expected to obey men.
4 Young people were free to marry whom they wished.

9 Much of Japan's history since 1853 has been influenced by its lack of
1 natural resources   3 skilled workers
2 educated managers   4 consumer goods

10 Which was a major factor in Japan's rapid recovery following World War II?
1 the threat of a Soviet invasion
2 the economic help of the United States
3 its oil production
4 its joining OPEC

ESSAYS

Directions: This part consists of several essay questions. You must answer two of them.

1 Since its defeat in World War II, Japan has emerged as an economic giant.

Part A

List *two* factors that have helped Japan's economic development.

1 _____

2 _____

Part B

In your part B answer, you should use information you gave in Part A. However, you may also include different or additional information in your Part B answer.

Write an essay showing how different factors have encouraged the economic development of Japan.

2 Religion shapes the values, beliefs and culture of a society.

Religions
Shintoism / Japan   Confucianism / China
Hinduism / India   Islam / Iran

Part A

Choose *two* of the religions listed. For *each* one chosen, state *one* belief and *one* way this religion has influenced the nation with which it is paired.

RELIGION	BELIEF	INFLUENCE ON THE NATION
A. _____	1. _____	1. _____
B. _____	2. _____	2. _____

Part B

In your part B answer, you should use information you gave in Part A. However, you may also include different or additional information in your Part B answer.

Write an essay explaining how religion helps shape the values, beliefs and culture of a society.

3 Events in one part of the world often affect other parts of the world.

Events
Commodore Perry's visit to Japan
Atomic bombs dropped on Hiroshima and Nagasaki
Great Britain grants India its independence
Iraq's invasion of Kuwait
Communist takeover of China

Part A

Select **one** event and identify what happened: _____

_____

State how it affected another part of the world: _____

_____

Select **another** event and identify what happened: _____

_____

State how it affected another part of the world: _____

_____

Part B

In your part B answer, you should use information you gave in Part A. However, you may also include different or additional information in your Part B answer.

Write an essay explaining how events in one part of the world often affect other parts of the world.

4 The way people live is usually influenced by the geographic features of the area.

Geographic Features

Deserts   Mountains
Rivers and River Valleys   Resources
Monsoons   Coastline

Part A

Select *two* features from the list. For *each* feature you selected, identify *one* geographic effect of this feature on the way people live in Africa, Latin America, the Middle East, India, China, or Japan.

FEATURE	EFFECT
1 _____	1 _____
2 _____	2 _____

Part B

In your part B answer, you should use information you gave in Part A. However, you may also include different or additional information in your Part B answer.

Write an essay explaining how people's lives are influenced by the geographic features of their area.

GLOBAL CHECKLIST

JAPAN

Directions: Before going on to the next chapter, check your understanding of the important people, terms and concepts covered in this chapter. Place a check (✔) mark next to those you can explain. If you have trouble recalling a term, refer to the page listed next to the item.

- ❑ Archipelago (174)
- ❑ Population Density (174)
- ❑ Cultural Diffusion (178)
- ❑ Feudalism (178)
- ❑ Samurai (179)
- ❑ Meiji Restoration (179)
- ❑ Pearl Harbor (180)
- ❑ Nagasaki (180)
- ❑ Constitution of 1947 (182)
- ❑ Homogeneous (186)
- ❑ Shintoism (187)
- ❑ Kabuki Theater (187)
- ❑ Matthew Perry (190)
- ❑ Douglas MacArthur (190)
- ❑ Emperor Hirohito (190)
- ❑ Trade imbalance (192)
- ❑ Global Interdependence (193)

GEOGRAPHY

- Size and Location
- Geographic Features and Their Effects

HISTORY

- Early History
- Imperial Russia Under the Czars
- Revolution of 1917
- Rise of the Communist State
- The Cold War
- Gorbachev Comes to Power
- The Countries of Eastern Europe

CONCERNS

- The Collapse of the Soviet Union
- The Changing Face of Eastern Europe

CHAPTER 8

THE COMMONWEALTH OF INDEPENDENT STATES AND EASTERN EUROPE

IMPORTANT PEOPLE

- Peter the Great
- Vladimir Lenin
- Josef Stalin
- Mikhail Gorbachev

SYSTEMS

- Government
- Economy
- Society
- Religion
- The Arts

What do these pictures show you about the Commonwealth of Independent States?

_____

_____

_____

_____

A SPECIAL NOTE ON THE SEVERAL NAMES GIVEN TO THIS AREA

Important changes have recently taken place in what was once the **Soviet Union**—now known as the **Commonwealth of Independent States (C.I.S.).** This area has been referred to by various names at different times in its history. In each time period the area had a different form of government and social organization, and different borders with its neighbors:

IMPERIAL RUSSIA (1480-1917)	Originally Russia was a small state centered in Moscow. Then the Russian Czars (emperors) began to conquer neighboring countries. By the 1800s Imperial Russia included the Baltic States, Finland and most of Poland. To the East, the Czars conquered lands stretching across Asia to the Pacific Ocean.
SOVIET UNION (U.S.S.R.) (1922-1991)	After the Russian Revolution of 1917, the Communists named their country the Soviet Union (U.S.S.R.) As in Czarist times, the country had many territories containing non-Russian peoples. Each major territory was called a "republic" and was given some local self-rule, but most decisions were made in Moscow.
COMMONWEALTH OF INDEPENDENT STATES (1991-Present)	After the breakup of the Soviet Union, many of the former republics agreed to become members of a loose association called the "Commonwealth of Independent States" (C.I.S.). Real power now lies with the governments of the independent republics. The largest and most powerful one is Russia.

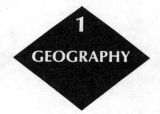

In this section you will read about the major geographic features of the Commonwealth of Independent States and of Eastern Europe, and how these features have affected the peoples and history of the area.

THINK ABOUT IT

What is meant by the following terms?

Russia:_____

Soviet Union (U.S.S.R.): _____

Commonwealth of Independent States: _____

Important Terms: As you read this section, look for the following terms:

◆ **Steppes**   ◆ **Tundra**

SIZE AND LOCATION

RUSSIA AND THE COMMONWEALTH OF INDEPENDENT STATES

The Commonwealth of Independent States occupies almost the same territory as the former Soviet Union. The largest country in the commonwealth is **Russia**—also the largest country in the world. Russia spans two continents—Europe and Asia. It extends from St. Petersburg on the Baltic Sea east to the Pacific Ocean. Almost all of Russia is north of the continental United States. The northernmost boundary is the Arctic Ocean. To the west and south of Russia are the other members of the Commonwealth of Independent States, also once part of the Soviet Union.

THE COUNTRIES OF EASTERN EUROPE

A group of independent countries separates the Commonwealth from Western Europe. These countries include Poland, Romania, Hungary, Bulgaria and Albania. They also include the **Baltic States** (bordering the Baltic Sea): Lithuania, Latvia and Estonia. Finally, the region includes some new smaller nations that were established when the former countries of Czechoslovakia and Yugoslavia split apart.

MAJOR GEOGRAPHIC FEATURES AND THEIR EFFECTS

RUSSIA AND THE COMMONWEALTH OF INDEPENDENT STATES

LACK OF WARM WATER PORTS

Because Russia is so far north, most of its ports are frozen throughout much of the year. The need for a port that would not freeze in winter was a major problem for much of Russian history. Because of its great distance from Western Europe and its lack of western ports, Russian culture was isolated from Western Europe until the time of Czar (Emperor) **Peter the Great** in the late 1600s. Peter fought several wars to extend Russia to the Baltic Sea, where he built the new city of Petersburg. Later Czars extended the Russian empire south to the Crimea on the Black Sea, gaining a warm water port.

During the existence of the Soviet Union, Russia had continuous access to the Black Sea, but now that the area is part of the independent republic of Ukraine, it is uncertain how much access Russia will have in the future. However, Russia does have an excellent network of rivers; the Don, the Volga, and the Ob.

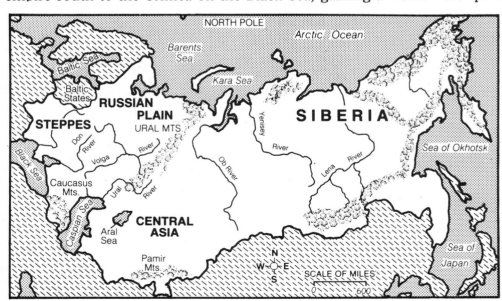

HARSH CLIMATE

◆ Most of Russia has long, cold winters and short, mild summers. Because of the harsh climate, farmers have very little time to grow and harvest crops. The Russian area farthest to the north is **tundra**—where little grows and the ground is frozen most of the year. South of it is a wide band of evergreen forests which also remains largely unsettled because of the harsh climatic conditions.

PLAINS AND STEPPES

◆ South of the forests is a large flat plain which begins in central Europe and sweeps across Russia and the Ukraine. The grasslands there are known as **steppes**, similar to the savannas of Africa, with fertile soil. Because this southernmost region has mild temperatures and rich soil, it was known as the "breadbasket" of the Soviet Union. Now much of the area belongs to the Ukraine, and it is uncertain how much food the Ukrainians will sell to Russia. Because the plains and steppes contained very few defensible borders such as mountains, the region was open to frequent invasions.

MOUNTAINS

There are several mountain ranges within the Commonwealth. The Caucasus mountains separates Russia from the countries of the Middle East, and the Pamir range separates it from China. The mountains made it possible for the native people of these regions to preserve something of their own cultures. Many of the new non-Russian countries of the Commonwealth are in the southern mountain areas.

NATURAL RESOURCES

The countries of the Commonwealth are rich in natural resources. Russia has gold, oil and natural gas. However, because of the harsh climate and great distance from centers of population, oil and gas were not developed until this past century. The republic of Kazakhstan also has important oil reserves. The northern forests of the area provide timber, furs and other valuable resources.

THE COUNTRIES OF EASTERN EUROPE

NORTHERN PLAINS AND SOUTHERN MOUNTAINS

The geography of Eastern Europe is similar to Russia's, but smaller in scale and generally further to the south. Poland is mainly flat, sharing the northern plain with Russia. South of Poland, the land becomes more mountainous. These mountains helped to divide the people living there into many nationalities. Each group spoke its own language and formed its own culture. Because of its closeness to Constantinople (Istanbul), this southern region came under strong Byzantine influence in earlier times.

RIVERS

The Danube River is the largest in Eastern Europe. It starts high in the Alps in Central Europe and flows through Austria and the plains of Hungary and Rumania, emptying into the Black Sea. The Danube River forms a vital link for trade, and once united these lands under the Austrian Empire.

Eastern Europe in 1991

SUMMING UP: GEOGRAPHY

The geography and climate of the Commonwealth of Independent States and of Eastern Europe help us to understand a great deal about the history and culture of the area.

THINKING IT OVER

How might you **now** describe what is meant by

Russia: _____

Soviet Union: _____

Commonwealth of Independent States: _____

CHECKING YOUR UNDERSTANDING

Directions: Complete the following cards. Then answer the multiple choice questions that follow.

STEPPES

What are they? _____

Other areas similar to steppes: _____

_____

TUNDRA

Where is it found? _____

Describe it: _____

_____

1 The Hwang Ho, the Nile and the Danube are
   1 mountains   3 lakes
   2 rivers   4 deserts

2 If you were to take a plane from Russia to India, in which general direction would you be traveling ?
   1 north   3 south
   2 east   4 west

3 On which two continents is Russia located?
   1 Asia and Africa
   2 Australia and Asia
   3 South America and Europe
   4 Europe and Asia

4 Which has been a problem through much of Russia's history?
   1 its very small size   3 no warm water port
   2 lack of resources   4 lack of fertile land

5 What do the Russian steppes and the African grasslands have in common?
   1 They are extremely cold areas.
   2 They are near large oil reserves.
   3 They are located in Asia.
   4 They contain rich fertile soil.

6 Which statement is correct about the geography of the former Soviet Union?
   1 It had a tropical climate.
   2 It was rich in natural resources.
   3 It was surrounded by water.
   4 It was mostly desert.

In this section you will read about the history of the Commonwealth of Independent States and of Eastern Europe, from early times through the Communist years, and into the uncertain times of today.

THINK ABOUT IT

Much of Russia's history has been filled with violence and revolution. Why do you think this occurred? _____

_____

Important Terms: As you read this section, look for the following terms:

- ◆ **Westernization**
- ◆ **Russification**
- ◆ **Revolution of 1917**
- ◆ **Communism**

- ◆ **Cold War**
- ◆ **Iron Curtain**
- ◆ **Glasnost**
- ◆ **Perestroika**

COMMONWEALTH OF INDEPENDENT STATES

TIMELINE OF HISTORICAL EVENTS

1682	1914	1917	1924	1945	1961	1985	1991
Peter the Great becomes Czar	Russia enters World War I	Start of the Russian Revolution	Stalin comes to power	Cold War begins	Berlin Wall is built	Gorbachev comes to power	Coup to overthrow Gorbachev fails; Soviet Union breaks up

EARLY HISTORY

Russia began as an organized state just over 1000 years ago, and came under the influence of the Byzantine Empire, adopting its alphabet and the Eastern Orthodox religion. During the 1200s, a warring people from Asia, known as the **Mongols**, invaded and gained control of most of Russia.

IMPERIAL RUSSIA UNDER THE CZARS

In 1480, **Ivan the Great** took the title of **Czar** (Emperor) and declared his independence from the Mongol overlords. He and the Czars that followed him were absolute rulers. Most of the people were

serfs — poor people who were treated like slaves and who worked the lands of the noble families. One of the most important Czars was **Peter the Great** (1682-1725), who believed that Russia needed **westernization**. By introducing western ideas, culture and technology, he tried to turn Imperial Russia from a backward nation into a modern world power. He also reinforced the dictatorial methods of earlier Czars.

PROFILES IN HISTORY

Catherine the Great

Catherine, a Czarina (empress) of Russia, ruled as an absolute dictator for 34 years. Known as Catherine the Great for her accomplishments in foreign affairs, she greatly expanded Imperial Russia's southern and western boundaries. She continued the policy of westernization by introducing European ideas and culture, and supported increased trade with Europe. Early in her reign, she toyed with the idea of freeing the serfs, but a serf rebellion in 1773 quickly changed her mind. By the time of her death in 1796, Imperial Russia had become a major European power.

THE RUSSIAN REVOLUTION OF 1917

During the 1800s, despite changes taking place in the rest of Europe, most of the Czars opposed doing anything that would make Imperial Russia more democratic or improve the conditions of life for the peasants. Serfdom did not end until 1861. By the start of the 20th century, many Russian people were desperate for a change. Finally, when Imperial Russia lost a war to Japan in 1905, workers, peasants and soldiers attempted to overthrow Czar **Nicholas II**. Fearing that he would lose his authority, the Czar agreed to give up some of his power. However, a short time later he withdrew his agreement to make reforms in Imperial Russia.

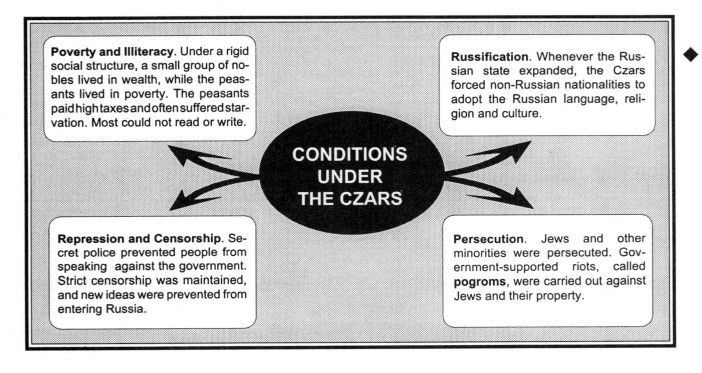

CONDITIONS UNDER THE CZARS

Poverty and Illiteracy. Under a rigid social structure, a small group of nobles lived in wealth, while the peasants lived in poverty. The peasants paid high taxes and often suffered starvation. Most could not read or write.

Russification. Whenever the Russian state expanded, the Czars forced non-Russian nationalities to adopt the Russian language, religion and culture.

Repression and Censorship. Secret police prevented people from speaking against the government. Strict censorship was maintained, and new ideas were prevented from entering Russia.

Persecution. Jews and other minorities were persecuted. Government-supported riots, called **pogroms**, were carried out against Jews and their property.

◆ THE RUSSIAN REVOLUTION BEGINS (1917)

In 1914, World War I began in Europe. Imperial Russia fought on the side of Britain and France against Germany. Russians suffered many defeats. At home, food supplies were low, leading to riots by city workers. Czar Nicholas II refused to withdraw from the war despite the great loss of life and widespread hunger. In February of 1917, soldiers refused to carry out the Czar's order to fire on striking workers. The Czar realized he was no longer in control, and he was forced to step down. A group of liberal democrats took charge and continued to fight the war, but conditions in Russia remained desperate. Finally a group calling themselves the **Bolsheviks** began a second revolution in October 1917. The Bolsheviks, or **Communists** as they are now called, were led by **Vladimir Lenin.** They won the support of the Russian people with their slogan, "**Peace, Bread and Land**" — promising peace to the soldiers, bread to the workers, and land to the peasants.

RISE OF THE MODERN COMMUNIST STATE

The main ideas of Communism were first developed in Germany by **Karl Marx** in the 1800s. These ideas were adopted, applied and modified by Lenin and Stalin.

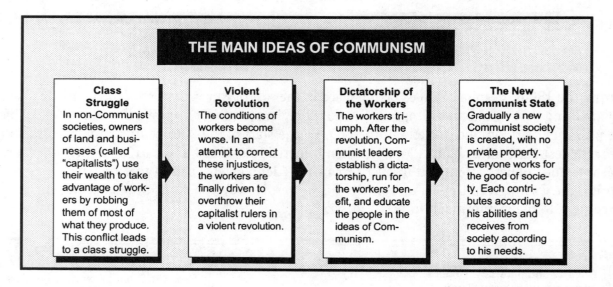

THE MAIN IDEAS OF COMMUNISM

Class Struggle
In non-Communist societies, owners of land and businesses (called "capitalists") use their wealth to take advantage of workers by robbing them of most of what they produce. This conflict leads to a class struggle.

Violent Revolution
The conditions of workers become worse. In an attempt to correct these injustices, the workers are finally driven to overthrow their capitalist rulers in a violent revolution.

Dictatorship of the Workers
The workers triumph. After the revolution, Communist leaders establish a dictatorship, run for the workers' benefit, and educate the people in the ideas of Communism.

The New Communist State
Gradually a new Communist society is created, with no private property. Everyone works for the good of society. Each contributes according to his abilities and receives from society according to his needs.

RULE UNDER LENIN (1917-1924)

Vladimir Lenin looked at Communism somewhat differently from Karl Marx. Lenin believed that a temporary dictatorship, led by a small group of Communists, was a necessary first step to making the nation into a Communist society. One of Lenin's first decisions was to withdraw from World War I and to sign a separate peace treaty with the Germans. Another was to order the execution of the Czar and his wife and children. Under Lenin, all industries were **nationalized** (*taken away from private owners*) and put under the control of the government. However, by 1920, Lenin realized his economic plan was not working. He introduced his **New Economic Policy** (N.E.P.) which permitted some private ownership of small-scale manufacturing and agriculture, while the government continued to control the major industries.

THE SOVIET UNION IS BORN

During Lenin's rule, some of the possessions of Imperial Russia, such as Finland and Poland, became independent. Other non-Russian territories, such as the Ukraine and White Russia, remained part of the Communist state. Lenin renamed this new communist country the **Union of Soviet Socialist**

Republics or **Soviet Union (USSR)**. Each republic had some limited powers of local government, but most decisions were made by Communist Party leaders in Moscow, the country's capital. The Russian Republic was the largest one, and Russian was the official language of government in the new Soviet state. In 1924, Lenin died.

SOVIET UNION UNDER STALIN (1924-1953)

After Lenin's death, there was a struggle over who should succeed him, and Josef Stalin won. Once in power, Stalin brought about many important changes.

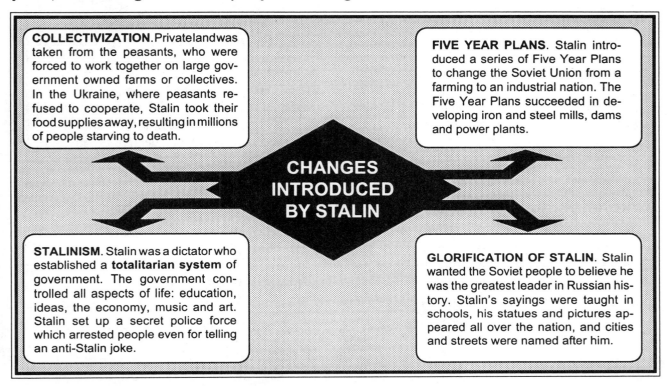

COLLECTIVIZATION. Private land was taken from the peasants, who were forced to work together on large government owned farms or collectives. In the Ukraine, where peasants refused to cooperate, Stalin took their food supplies away, resulting in millions of people starving to death.

FIVE YEAR PLANS. Stalin introduced a series of Five Year Plans to change the Soviet Union from a farming to an industrial nation. The Five Year Plans succeeded in developing iron and steel mills, dams and power plants.

CHANGES INTRODUCED BY STALIN

STALINISM. Stalin was a dictator who established a **totalitarian system** of government. The government controlled all aspects of life: education, ideas, the economy, music and art. Stalin set up a secret police force which arrested people even for telling an anti-Stalin joke.

GLORIFICATION OF STALIN. Stalin wanted the Soviet people to believe he was the greatest leader in Russian history. Stalin's sayings were taught in schools, his statues and pictures appeared all over the nation, and cities and streets were named after him.

WORLD WAR II (1939-1945)

While Stalin was imposing Communism in the Soviet Union, Adolf Hitler took power in Germany. In 1939, Hitler began World War II by attacking Poland. After making a deal with Stalin in which he promised not to attack, Hitler double-crossed Stalin by invading the Soviet Union in 1941. Fighting on the side of the United States and Great Britain, the Soviet Union helped defeat Germany by 1945. The Soviets lost 21 million people in World War II, much more than any other nation.

THE COLD WAR (1945-1985)

THE COLD WAR BEGINS (1945-1949)

Even though they were allies during World War II, the United States and Soviet Union had little in common. The United States represented capitalism and freedom, while the Soviet Union represented Communism and oppression. The Soviets used their victories in World War II to extend their system into Eastern European countries. Communist puppet governments were installed there, and Soviet troops remained there to make sure the governments stayed in power. This action alarmed the nations in the West, especially the United States. Although the United States and the Soviet Union remained enemies, they were afraid to go into direct conflict with each other because both had nuclear

weapons. Most of the armed conflicts were fought in smaller countries like Korea and Vietnam. This
◆ competition between the United States and the Soviet Union was known as the "**Cold War.**"

Who was to blame for starting the Cold War?	
THE AMERICAN VIEWPOINT U.S. leaders felt that Eastern European countries wanted to become democratic societies, but that the Soviet Union was preventing this. They also believed that it would be a mistake to turn their backs on European affairs as they had done after World War I. Americans felt that Stalin could not be trusted, since he had promised elections in Poland and other Eastern European countries but had backed away from this promise. Communism was seen as a dangerous revolutionary system that had to be stopped before it spread.	**THE SOVIET VIEWPOINT** Soviet leaders believed they had a right to control Eastern Europe. They felt that just as the United States controlled Latin America through the Monroe Doctrine, the Soviet Union should have the final say over its Eastern European neighbors. Stalin believed that the Western powers had no direct interests in Eastern Europe and should not interfere. Soviet leaders also believed they could not trust the United States and other Western countries because they had delayed the invasion of Germany during World War II, leading to very heavy military losses by the Soviet Union.

To stop the spread of Communism, the United States sent money and weapons to countries threatened
by Communism. The U.S. also organized its allies into a military organization called the **North Atlantic Treaty Organization (NATO)**. Its chief goal was to protect Western Europe from falling under
Communist control, by opposing Soviet aggression. In response to the creation of NATO, the Soviets
organized the Communist nations of Eastern Europe into a military alliance called the **Warsaw Pact**.

MEMBERS OF NATO AND THE WARSAW PACT

In the period from 1949 to 1963, Communism seemed to be spreading to Asia, Africa, the Middle East and Latin America. As a result, these areas became centers of competition between the Communists and the Western democracies.

PEACEFUL COEXISTENCE (1963-1985)

In the mid-1960s, the U.S. and U.S.S.R., decided to follow a policy of peaceful coexistence, in which they tried to avoid open conflicts which might lead to war. During the late 1970s they agreed to limit the number of missiles they would build. At the same time, both superpowers continued to compete with one another for influence in the newly emerging nations in Africa and Asia, which were following a policy of **non-alignment** (*not taking sides with either of the two superpowers*).

While the Soviet Union remained one of the world's leading military powers, it was unable to increase its industrial or agricultural production. Living standards remained low, and the Soviet economy kept falling further behind the West.

GORBACHEV COMES TO POWER (1985-1991)

When **Mikhail Gorbachev** came to power in 1985, relations between the two superpowers improved greatly. Gorbachev realized that Communism was in serious trouble, and introduced some immediate changes. In foreign affairs, Gorbachev and Presidents Reagan and Bush reached a number of agreements to make for a more peaceful world. Gorbachev allowed non-communist governments to take control in the countries of Eastern Europe. Inside the Soviet Union, he developed new policies to introduce reform, especially **glasnost** and **perestroika**.

GLASNOST	PERESTROIKA
Glasnost refers to Gorbachev's policy for making the Soviet Union more open and free. The people were allowed to criticize the government, freedom of the press was permitted, restrictions on travel were lifted, and Western ideas were allowed into the country.	Perestroika refers to the changes Gorbachev made in the Soviet economy. Believing Communism was in trouble economically, he sought to allow individuals more freedom to make economic decisions, instead of having them made by the central government.

Gorbachev hoped to preserve the Soviet Union while making some changes, but his policies released new forces that he was unable to control. This led to the breakup of the Soviet Union in December 1991.

THE COUNTRIES OF EASTERN EUROPE

Many different ethnic groups and religions are found in Eastern Europe. At various times in their history, Eastern Europeans have been ruled by Turkey, Austria, Germany and Russia. It wasn't until after World War I that most of these nations gained independence.

EASTERN EUROPE AS SOVIET SATELLITES

During World War II, Nazi Germany controlled most of Eastern Europe. At the end of the war, the Soviet army forced the Germans to retreat from Eastern Europe. The Soviets then set up **satellite** governments (*Communist-controlled governments whose leaders took their orders from the Soviet Union*). The countries that became satellites were Bulgaria, Poland, Hungary, Yugoslavia, Albania, Czechoslovakia and East Germany. The only political party allowed to exist was the Communist Party. People had little freedom, and trade could be conducted only with the Soviet Union and other Communist countries.

U.S.S.R. and Eastern Europe in 1991

◆ THE IRON CURTAIN FALLS ON EASTERN EUROPE (1945-1989)

The Soviets created an "**Iron Curtain**" — sealing off the borders of Western Europe from Eastern Europe and the Soviet Union. In Germany, they ordered the building of the Berlin Wall. The effect was to separate Eastern Europe from the Western democracies. During the 45 years of the Cold War, the Soviets forcefully put down every attempt by Eastern European nations to achieve their freedom.

RECENT CHANGES IN EASTERN EUROPE (1989-Present)

In 1989 Gorbachev stopped supporting the Communist puppet governments in Eastern Europe, and they collapsed. Now that these countries have democracy, they must rebuild their economies and make peace among ethnic groups. Czechoslovakia peacefully divided itself into two — the Czech Republic and Slovakia — but the former Yugoslavia has been torn apart by ethnic hatred and civil war.

SUMMING UP: HISTORY

The history of this area is divided into three major periods: Imperial Russia, the Soviet Union and the newly-created Commonwealth of Independent States. The countries of Eastern Europe became Soviet satellite states after World War II, but recently gained their independence.

THINKING IT OVER

Were you correct about why Russia's history has been filled with violence and revolutions?_____

Which event do you think has had the greatest impact on the Soviet Union? _____

Explain: _____

CHECKING YOUR UNDERSTANDING

Directions: Complete the following cards. Then answer the multiple choice questions that follow.

WESTERNIZATION

What was it? _____

Importance in Russian history: _____

_____

RUSSIFICATION

What was it? _____

Importance in Russian history: _____

_____

RUSSIAN REVOLUTION OF 1917

Describe it: _____

Why was it important? _____

_____

COMMUNISM

Whose idea was it? _____

Main beliefs: _____

_____

THE COLD WAR

Define it: _____

How did it begin? _____

_____

IRON CURTAIN

What was it? _____

Its effect: _____

_____

GLASNOST

Definition: _____

Examples: _____

_____

PERESTROIKA

Definition: _____

Examples: _____

_____

---

1 "Russification" refers to
   1 forcing Russian culture on others
   2 technology introduced into Russia
   3 the shift of wealth from Europe to Russia
   4 differences between Russian men and women

2 Which was a major result of the Russian Revolution of 1917?
   1 Russia became a Communist nation.
   2 Trade increased between the U.S. and Russia.
   3 Christianity became the state religion.
   4 Russia entered World War II on the U.S. side.

3   Who introduced Five Year Plans and collective farms into the Soviet Union?
   1 Josef Stalin   3 Peter the Great
   2 Nicholas II   4 Mikhail Gorbachev

4   In the period following World War II, differences between the United States and the Soviet Union led to
   1 the Green Revolution   3 the Cold War
   2 perestroika   4 pogroms

5   Who wrote about the idea of a classless society?
   1 Nicholas II   3 Peter the Great
   2 Karl Marx   4 Bishop Tutu

6   Which term best describes the position of Russian Jews under the Czars?
   1 a persecuted minority   3 military leaders
   2 supporters of the Czar 4 nobles

7   A major feature of perestroika was to
   1 increase oil production
   2 allow more individual economic decisions
   3 expand collectivization of farms
   4 rely on government decision-making

8   Which area was most influenced by the Soviet Union following World War II?
   1 North Africa   3 Eastern Europe
   2 South America   4 Africa

9   During the Russian Revolution of 1917, who promised the people "Peace, Bread and Land?"
   1 the Czars
   2 the Communists
   3 the Russian Orthodox Church
   4 the Russian nobles

10 Which statement best describes Russia before 1917?
   1 a democracy with elected officials
   2 a society with a strict class structure
   3 a rich nation
   4 a free and open society

11 Stalin's Five Year Plans attempted to
   1 introduce capitalism into the Soviet Union
   2 prevent Communism in Eastern Europe
   3 increase Russia's industrial production
   4 promote a military alliance with the U.S.

12 A result of World War II was that
   1 the United States and Soviet Union became superpowers
   2 Germany signed a separate treaty with Russia
   3 the Czar was overthrown
   4 the Soviet Union became a Communist country

3

SYSTEMS

In this section you will read about the political, economic, social, religious and cultural systems of the Commonwealth of Independent States and of Eastern Europe.

THINK ABOUT IT

After 75 years, Communism, the Soviet economic system, failed. Why do you think this occurred?

_____

_____

Important Terms: As you read this section, look for the following terms:

◆ **coup**   ◆ **Planned Economy**

COMMONWEALTH OF INDEPENDENT STATES

GOVERNMENT

THE SOVIET UNION UNDER COMMUNIST RULE (1917-1985)

In the USSR, the real power was held by the **Communist Party**. All important positions in the government, army and other institutions were held by Communist Party members. Important decisions were made by the **Politburo**, consisting of Party leaders and controlled by the General Secretary of the Communist Party, who ran the nation as a dictator. The government's secret police, or **KGB**, played an important role in denying people freedom and keeping the Communists in power.

THE PAST MAKE-UP OF THE SOVIET UNION
(YEAR OF ADMISSION TO THE SOVIET UNION)

THE SOVIET GOVERNMENT UNDER GORBACHEV (1985-1991)

Gorbachev came to power in 1985 and immediately began to introduce democratic changes in the Soviet Union. He allowed free speech and freedom of the press. People were permitted to criticize government officials. Gorbachev began to take power away from the Communist Party, in the hope of giving more power to the people. However, in August 1991 some Communist leaders, opposed to Gorbachev's changes, attempted a **coup** (*a takeover of the government by force*). The coup failed, and ◆ **Boris Yeltsin** emerged as the new leader. He banned the Communist Party and seized its assets. By December 1991, Gorbachev had to resign.

BIRTH OF THE COMMONWEALTH OF INDEPENDENT STATES (1991)

The republics that made up the Soviet Union began to declare their independence. By December 1991 the Soviet Union had come to an end. Most of the republics agreed to create a new organization called the **Commonwealth of Independent States**. However, this is only a loose association—each republic is an independent country with its own army and currency.

ECONOMY

THE ECONOMY UNDER COMMUNISM (1917-1985)

Under the Czars, most Russians were very poor. The Communists promised the people land and a better life. Once in power, they took control of all industries, businesses and banks. Large pieces of land formerly owned by nobles were broken up and sold to the peasants. At first, many people were better off under the Communists, but conditions soon changed for the worse. There was ◆ a **planned economy**: the government made all the decisions, such as what to produce, how much to produce and who got what was produced. Under Stalin, the peasants were forced to give up their lands and to work on large government-operated farms. By the 1980s it was obvious that the Communist system had failed to provide a better life for the average person. Farms did not produce enough food, factory goods were of poor quality, and corruption was widespread.

Peasants beg for bread during a Russian famine

GORBACHEV'S ECONOMIC CHANGES FAIL

Gorbachev, impressed by the prosperity of the West, tried to bring changes to the Soviet economy. He introduced a plan called **perestroika**, which rewarded those who did a better job, allowed some people to own their own land or a small business, and gave local factory managers an increased role in decision-making. However, Gorbachev's changes failed to improve the average standard of living, making him increasingly unpopular. Since the breakup of the Soviet Union, leaders of the former Soviet republics have been trying to improve conditions by introducing a free market economy like that of the United States. As these changes take place, the people in the Commonwealth States are experiencing very difficult times.

SOCIETY

Society in Russia and the other Commonwealth States is quite modern; most people live in cities and work in industry and service jobs. Similar conditions exist in the countries of Eastern Europe. Under Communism, the government provided low-cost housing, free health care, free education, guaranteed employment, and inexpensive public transport. Women achieved legal and social equality after the Russian Revolution of 1917. Although many work as doctors, factory managers or political leaders, the majority of women still hold the lowest-paying jobs.

A Russian Orthodox procession

RELIGION

Under the Czars, the official religion was the **Russian Orthodox Church**. Under Communism, religion was discouraged. Communists believed that religion was used by employers as a tool to control their workers. Recently, the Commonwealth States have restored the rights of the Orthodox Church. Throughout much of Russian history, Jews have been the victims of persecution and discrimination. Recent changes have made it much easier for Jews to leave, and many have gone to Israel and the United States.

THE ARTS

In the past, both Russians and non-Russians made major contributions to the arts. Russians developed the art of classical ballet. Tchaikovsky and Stravinsky composed beautiful ballet music. In literature, Russia had many great poets, playwrights and novelists, including Tolstoy, Dostoevsky, and Pushkin. Under Communism, the government provided funds to many artistic fields, but also limited the free expression of ideas. Many of Russia's greatest writers were imprisoned because of their work, and others fled (*left*) the country in order to continue writing freely.

EASTERN EUROPE

During the Communist period, the nations of Eastern Europe traded with the Soviet Union and helped in their defense against the West. However, strong feelings of nationalism often encouraged the nations of Eastern Europe to try to break away from Soviet control. Whenever an uprising occurred, Soviet leaders sent in tanks and troops to crush it. Religion has played an important role in many Eastern European nations. In Poland, the Roman Catholic church kept alive the movement to end Communism and Soviet control. When a Polish bishop was made Pope, it increased Polish patriotism and resistance to Communism. This resistance helped contribute to the collapse of Communism in Eastern Europe.

Some Eastern European countries contained many nationalities. The rivalries between them helped cause World War I in 1914. Under Communism, these rivalries were kept in check by military force. However, since the countries of Eastern Europe regained their independence in 1989, nationalism has been reshaping the area. For example, the fighting in the former nation of Yugoslavia is a direct result of nationalist and ethnic rivalries. The Serbs are Orthodox Christians, the Croats are Catholics, and the Bosnians are generally Muslims. Each group has its own traditions and history.

SUMMING UP: SYSTEMS

As a result of the events that have occurred since 1989, the systems of the Commonwealth of Independent States and Eastern Europe are undergoing important changes.

THINKING IT OVER

Were you correct in your opinion about why the Soviet economy failed? _____

What other factors might you now add to explain the failure of the Soviet economy?

_____

_____

CHECKING YOUR UNDERSTANDING

Directions: Complete the following cards. Then answer the multiple choice questions that follow.

COUP
Definition: _____
Example: _____
_____

PLANNED ECONOMY
What is it? _____
How does it work? _____
_____

1 An economic system characterized by a lack of private property ownership is
  1 feudalism
  2 capitalism
  3 Communism
  4 mercantilism

2 Under Communism, major economic decisions are made by
  1 farmers
  2 government officials
  3 consumers
  4 businessmen

3 Which policy, introduced by Gorbachev, was most different from the policies of Stalin?
  1 government control of production
  2 central planning of the economy
  3 the development of industries
  4 some private business ownership

4 Which characterized life in the Soviet Union under Communism?
  1 All government members were freely elected.
  2 People spent a great deal of money on health care.
  3 Women were considered to be inferior to men.
  4 The government provided housing and guaranteed jobs.

5 What did the economy of China and the former Soviet Union have in common?
  1 The main occupation was fishing.
  2 They were planned economies.
  3 They were led by the same person.
  4 They were opposed to heavy industry.

6 In the 1980s, Mikhail Gorbachev encouraged the Soviet Union to
  1 invade the nations of Eastern Europe
  2 introduce democracy and economic reforms
  3 limit the number of farms and factories
  4 build up its nuclear weapons

7 The Soviet Union established control over Eastern Europe following World War II
  1 because it feared an invasion by the West
  2 to spread the influence of Soviet literature
  3 to increase the power of the Catholic Church
  4 to prevent the spread of Communism

8 A major problem facing the new countries of the Commonwealth of Independent States is
  1 improving standards of living
  2 preventing invasions from Western Europe
  3 reducing the influence of religion
  4 eliminating military dictatorships

9 Which term best describes Soviet government under Communism?
  1 democracy
  2 monarchy
  3 dictatorship
  4 feudalism

10 Many Jews have fled Russia because
  1 there was overcrowding where Jews lived
  2 Jews experienced discrimination and persecution
  3 Jews were forced to work on collective farms
  4 Russia's climate was not suited to Jewish farming methods

4
IMPORTANT PEOPLE

In this section you will read about some of the people who have played a key role in shaping the history of the area.

THINK ABOUT IT

Russia's history has been greatly affected by certain key people. Which leader do you think has had the greatest impact on Russia? _____ Explain: _____

_____

Important Names: As you read this section, look for the following names:

◆ **Peter the Great**
◆ **Vladimir Lenin**
◆ **Josef Stalin**
◆ **Mikhail Gorbachev**

 **The Russian Times**

Volume XIX   Number 9

PETER THE GREAT

Czar Peter the Great traveled to Western Europe in the 1600s to learn about European ideas and technology. He applied many ideas that were to remodel Russia into a nation more like those of the West. His attempts to westernize Russia dramatically changed the country. For example, he ordered the Russian nobles to cut their long beards and wear European style clothes. He also made Russia into a great power by building a modern army and navy.

VLADIMIR LENIN

Lenin was dedicated to the ideas of Karl Marx. In 1917 Lenin led the Communist Revolution in Russia, and became the first leader of the Soviet Union. However, he died after only a few years in power.

JOSEF STALIN

Stalin replaced Lenin as leader of the Soviet Union in 1924. He ruled through fear; those who opposed him were either put in

prison camps or killed. He glorified himself as the "Father of the Soviet Union." His brutal methods achieved industrialization and helped the Soviet Union defeat Nazi Germany. After World War II, Stalin imposed Communism on the countries of Eastern Europe.

MIKHAIL GORBACHEV

Gorbachev, who led the Soviet Union from 1985 to 1991, is best known for his policies of **perestroika** (*changing the economic system to give people more control*) and **glasnost** (*allowing people greater political freedom*). He permitted Eastern Europe to free itself from Soviet control. However, his plans for improving the economy did not work, and the

Soviet Union broke apart. **Boris Yeltsin**, President of the Russian Republic, has now become the most powerful figure.

SUMMING UP: IMPORTANT PEOPLE

Certain leaders have greatly influenced events in the history of Imperial Russia, the Soviet Union, and the Commonwealth of Independent States, as well as Eastern Europe.

THINKING IT OVER

Do you still agree with your original choice of the leader who has had the most impact on Russian history? _____ If yes, explain why. _____

_____

If not, explain why not. _____

_____

CHECKING YOUR UNDERSTANDING

Directions: Complete the following cards. Then answer the multiple choice questions that follow.

PETER THE GREAT

Who was he? _____

What did he accomplish? _____

_____

VLADIMIR LENIN

Who was he? _____

What did he accomplish? _____

_____

JOSEF STALIN

Who was he? _____

What did he accomplish? _____

_____

MIKHAIL GORBACHEV

Who is he? _____

What did he accomplish? _____

_____

1 Which reforms were introduced by Mikhail Gorbachev?
1 perestroika and limited democracy
2 religious freedom and imperialism
3 free education and socialism
4 absolutism and glasnost

2 Which statement describes Lenin's role in the Russian Revolution of 1917?
1 He supported the Allies in World War I.
2 He opposed Communism.
3 He brought Communism to Russia.
4 He helped keep the Czar in power.

3 Which event occurred during Mikhail Gorbachev's time in power?
1 Russian Revolution of 1917
2 start of World War II
3 issuance of the Monroe Doctrine
4 reduction of Communist Party power

4 Peter the Great and Catherine the Great were similar in that both tried to
1 end Communism in Russia
2 introduce Western ideas into Russia
3 make Russia a democratic country
4 stop trade with the United States

5 Which was a principal belief of Peter the Great?
1 Communism is the best social system.
2 Serfs must be granted their freedom.
3 Russia must adopt Western technology.
4 Russification must be prevented.

6 Which description best fits Josef Stalin?
1 a deeply religious person
2 a brutal dictator
3 a supporter of democratic reforms
4 one who emphasized traditional values

7 Communism was established in Russia largely through the efforts of
1 Nicholas II   3 Vladimir Lenin
2 Boris Yeltsin   4 Fidel Castro

8 Mao Zedong was like Vladimir Lenin in that both
1 were leaders of Communist revolutions
2 used non-violent protests to obtain power
3 sought large colonial empires
4 introduced Western ideas and customs into Russia

5
CONCERNS

In this section you will read about some of the problems and concerns facing the Commonwealth of Independent States and Eastern European countries today.

THINK ABOUT IT

The events of 1989-1991 brought about tremendous changes to the former Soviet Union as well as to Eastern Europe. Can you name some of these key events? _____

_____

Important Terms: As you read this section, look for the following terms:

◆ **Boris Yeltsin**   ◆ **Berlin Wall**

THE COMMONWEALTH OF INDEPENDENT STATES

THE COLLAPSE OF THE SOVIET UNION

From 1940 to 1991, the Soviet Union was made up of 15 separate **republics**. Each was home to a separate nationality or group with its own language, traditions, religion and culture. In some ways these republics were similar to states in the United States, except that in the Soviet Union almost all powers were held by the central government.

THE AUGUST COUP AGAINST GORBACHEV

With the greater freedoms introduced by Gorbachev, non-Russian national groups living in the Soviet republics began to demand independence. Encouraged by the Soviet retreat from Eastern Europe, several republics declared their independence from Soviet control. The Soviet army failed to crush these uprisings. In August 1991 a group of Communists, unhappy with the new conditions in Eastern Europe and the Soviet Union, attempted a **coup** (*overthrow*) against Gorbachev. The coup attempt failed, since it did not have the support of the Soviet people. However, it was such an important event that it has been called the "Second Russian Revolution."

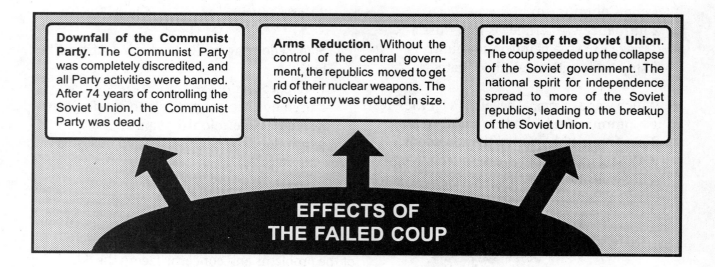

Downfall of the Communist Party. The Communist Party was completely discredited, and all Party activities were banned. After 74 years of controlling the Soviet Union, the Communist Party was dead.

Arms Reduction. Without the control of the central government, the republics moved to get rid of their nuclear weapons. The Soviet army was reduced in size.

Collapse of the Soviet Union. The coup speeded up the collapse of the Soviet government. The national spirit for independence spread to more of the Soviet republics, leading to the breakup of the Soviet Union.

EFFECTS OF THE FAILED COUP

BIRTH OF THE COMMONWEALTH OF INDEPENDENT STATES

No longer under Soviet central control, the peoples of the different republics now rule themselves in independent countries. Some of these newly independent republics have formed the **Commonwealth of Independent States** (C.I.S.) as a loose association to replace the former Soviet Union. **Boris Yeltsin**, the popularly-elected President of the Russian Republic, has promised his people democratic rule and a better life. However, Russians have little experience with democracy. In addition, in order to change the Russian economic system, Yeltsin took steps that resulted in the doubling of many prices. Food shortages exist in many areas, and there is a real threat of further unrest.

EASTERN EUROPE

In the years following World War II, whenever an uprising against Soviet control occurred in Eastern Europe, Soviets leaders sent in troops to crush the revolt. Gorbachev's policies changed that. When he permitted more freedom for the people of the Soviet Union, this idea also spread to Eastern Europe. Once it became clear that Soviet leaders would no longer support the Communist governments of Poland, Hungary, Bulgaria and Czechoslovakia, these governments were voted out of power. In East Germany the **Berlin Wall**, which had separated democratic West Berlin from Communist East Berlin since 1961, was torn down. After the Communists in East Germany were voted out of power, East and West Germany decided to reunite to form one Germany. In Romania, the Communist dictator refused to allow free elections and was toppled by force. Throughout Eastern Europe, former Communist countries have adopted democracy and are introducing free market economies. However, the end of Communism has not solved all the problems of Eastern Europe.

PROBLEMS FACING EASTERN EUROPE

NATIONALITY CONFLICTS
Several countries are made up of people from different national groups. These groups cooperated to get rid of Communism, but now fight each other — particularly in Yugoslavia.

ECONOMY
Living standards are lower than in the West. In changing from communism to capitalism, people have seen prices rise and now must pay for services that their former governments provided free.

POLLUTION
Under Communism, the aim was the production of more goods, without regard to the creation of waste and pollution. As a result, Eastern Europe has some of the worst environmental problems in the world.

The greatest turmoil is occurring in what was formerly Yugoslavia. Serb forces have been accused of "ethnic cleansing" — murdering or driving out Bosnians and Croats from lands claimed by Serbia. Fighting has led to the massacre of thousands of innocent civilians.

SUMMING UP: CONCERNS

The collapse of the Soviet Union and the birth of the Commonwealth of Independent States are bringing about enormous changes. Eastern Europe is also undergoing upheavals.

THINKING IT OVER

Which event do you think had the greatest impact in changing the Soviet Union into the Commonwealth of Independent States? _____ Why? _____

_____

CHECKING YOUR UNDERSTANDING

Directions: Complete the following cards Then answer the multiple choice questions that follow.

BORIS YELTSIN

Who is he? _____

Why is he important? _____

_____

BERLIN WALL

What was it? _____

When did it fall? _____

_____

1 Which country controlled Eastern Europe between 1945 and 1990?
  1 the Soviet Union   3 the United States
  2 Poland   4 Germany

2 The expansion of Communism into Eastern Europe came about as a result of
  1 World War I
  2 the Vietnam War
  3 World War II
  4 the Boxer Rebellion

3 What happened in the Soviet Union following the coup in August 1991?
  1 the Soviet Union was replaced by independent republics
  2 the Czar returned to power
  3 the Soviet Union merged with Eastern Europe
  4 Eastern Europe was invaded by the Soviet Union

4 Which occurred while Mikhail Gorbachev was leader of the Soviet Union?
  1 The Soviet Union went to war against Iraq.
  2 The decline of the Communist Party began.
  3 The Soviets invaded Western Europe.
  4 The Czar's power was increased.

5 Which was a direct result of the August 1991 Coup in the Soviet Union?
  1 All officials must now be members of the Communist Party.
  2 Only Communist Party members can vote and hold office.
  3 The people vote for their new leaders.
  4 Trade is allowed only with other Communist nations.

6 Since the collapse of the Soviet Union, a major economic trend in Eastern Europe has been
  1 less emphasis on making a profit
  2 increased dependence on the Soviets
  3 the introduction of capitalism
  4 the adoption of Communism

SUMMARIZING YOUR UNDERSTANDING

Directions: Fill in the information in the visual organizer below.

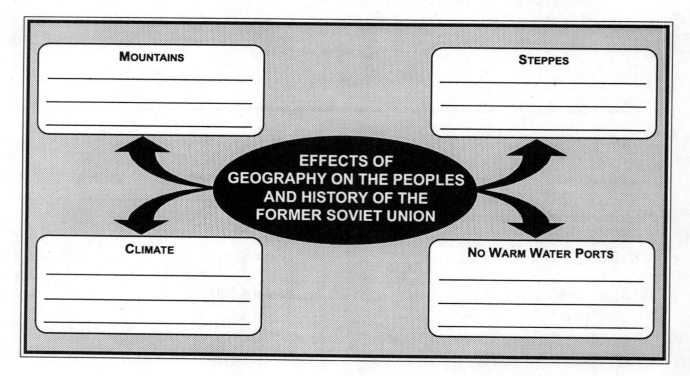

MOUNTAINS

STEPPES

EFFECTS OF GEOGRAPHY ON THE PEOPLES AND HISTORY OF THE FORMER SOVIET UNION

CLIMATE

NO WARM WATER PORTS

WORD CIRCLING

Directions. Use the information in this chapter and other chapters to write each defined word in the shaded boxes; then find each word in the puzzle, and circle it.

L	W	E	S	T	E	R	N	I	Z	A	T	I	O	N
E	S	T	E	P	P	E	S	S	E	O	U	S	T	R
N	M	S	T	A	L	I	N	P	O	B	S	T	J	U
I	N	A	P	E	R	E	S	T	R	O	I	K	A	S
N	E	R	I	N	M	S	T	O	U	L	E	A	N	S
P	C	M	E	A	S	T	E	R	N	N	S	P	T	I
C	O	M	M	U	N	I	S	T	F	E	D	A	C	F
O	U	G	L	G	O	C	M	B	T	M	S	R	L	I
V	P	N	R	B	L	S	T	A	O	E	A	T	A	C
E	S	T	I	O	G	A	X	L	R	P	T	H	N	A
U	P	O	C	S	M	T	S	M	L	X	O	E	D	T
C	C	V	Z	M	P	S	T	N	E	B	D	I	O	I
T	I	A	A	M	E	N	O	R	O	H	U	D	V	O
R	B	S	R	P	T	H	E	N	E	S	U	W	X	N
X	P	L	A	N	N	E	D	R	S	T	T	B	T	C

Government-supported riots against Jews. **P** | | | | | **S** |

Forcing non-Russians to adopt Russian customs. **R** | | | | | | | | | | | | **N** |

Only political party permitted under Stalin and Lenin. **C** | | | | | | **T** |

Gorbachev's economic reforms. **P** | | | | | | | **A** |

Cold area with little vegetation, near the Arctic. **T** | | | **A** |

Slogan of Russian Revolution, "Peace, bread, and _____ ". **L** | | **D** |

Russian plains with the most fertile soil. **S** | | | | **S** |

Russian word for emperor. **C** | | **R** |

Former Soviet Union is now known by these initials. **C** | | (continued on next page)

Policy of "openness" introduced by Gorbachev. G | | | | | | | T

Forcible overthrow of a government. C | | P

Czar Peter's attempt to "Europeanize" Russia. W | | | | | | | | | | | | | N

Brutal ruler of Russia who replaced Lenin. S | | | | N

Economy in which government makes the decisions. P | | | | | D

German thinker who developed the main ideas of Communism. M | | X

Part of Europe controlled by the Soviet Union after W.W. II. E | | | | | N

Leader of the Russian Revolution of 1917. L | | | N

South African policy of racial segregation. A | | | | | D

Directions: Fill in the information in the visual organizer below.

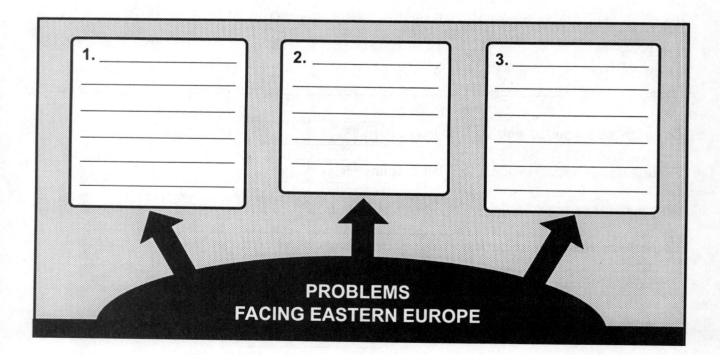

1. _____
_____
_____
_____
_____

2. _____
_____
_____
_____
_____

3. _____
_____
_____
_____
_____

**PROBLEMS
FACING EASTERN EUROPE**

DESCRIBING HISTORICAL EVENTS

Directions: Fully describe the historical event you learned about in this chapter, by filling in the information in the boxes.

WHO was involved?

_____

_____

WHERE did it happen?

_____

THE RUSSIAN REVOLUTION OF 1917

WHOSE ideas inspired it?

_____

WHAT were its causes?

_____

_____

_____

RESULTS:

1. _____

2. _____

3. _____

TEST HELPER — GOVERNING IN A MULTI-ETHNIC WORLD

This Test-Helper section will prepare you to answer questions dealing with different ethnic groups.

WHAT IS ETHNIC DIVERSITY?

"**Ethnicity**" refers to groups of people with a common ancestry and culture. Since all persons share some characteristics and differ in others, ethnic identity depends on which characteristics a society judges as most important. This can be seen by examining some ethnic groups in the United States:

Distinguishing Characteristic	Groups
Race	African Americans, Asian Americans
Religion	Jewish Americans, Mormons
Language	Hispanic Americans, Asian Americans
National Origin	Italian Americans, Irish Americans

GOVERNING STATES: UNITY OUT OF DIVERSITY

Most countries have a mixture of peoples and cultures. A basic problem for many central governments is how to create a single nation in spite of these ethnic differences. Governments have used a number of methods to deal with the problem:

■ **Domination.** The earliest strategy was simply to rule over others by force. The ethnic group to which the king belonged was usually given special privileges. Other ethnic groups were reduced in status and power.

■ **Assimilation.** Some rulers tried to force all groups to adopt the culture of the main group. Local customs were replaced by national laws.

■ **Pluralism.** Under this approach, minorities are accepted and integrated into the mainstream of society. Each group is allowed to keep its own culture and by law is treated the same way as other groups. It does not have to give up its individual ethnic characteristics.

■ **Federalism.** Under federalism, there is a division of power between the central government and local governments. The central government takes care of problems facing the entire country—such as foreign affairs and national defense—while local governments with different ethnic cultures take care of local problems.

THE PROBLEM FACING ETHNIC MINORITIES

In many countries, there is one major group and several smaller ethnic minorities. A **minority** is any ethnic group other than the major group. In the former Soviet Union, for example, every non-Russian group was a minority. Being a member of a minority group causes special problems. The majority group often treats minority members as inferior and uses force to keep them under control. In some societies, minorities are not allowed to own property, use parks or ride on public transportation. Sometimes actions against minority groups are extreme. For example, governments have attempted to eliminate minorities through the policy of **genocide** (*killing off an entire people*). The most famous example of genocide was the Nazi attempt to eliminate the Jews of Europe. Other attempts at genocide include Stalin's subjecting the Ukrainians to starvation, the Khmer Rouge's "Killing Fields" in Cambodia, and Saddam Hussein's war against the Kurds, a minority group in Iraq.

THE EMERGENCE OF NATIONALISM

One way that ethnic groups oppose central control is through **nationalism** — the belief that each nationality or ethnic group should have its own country and rule itself. Historically, nationalism has been a powerful force for unifying groups. For example, after the collapse of Communism in East Germany, German national feeling led East and West Germany to reunite after 45 years of separation. However, nationalism can also divide. This is true when different ethnic groups in a nation decide they want to split apart to form their own states. For example, Czechoslovakia has divided in two on the basis of nationality differences. In Croatia and Bosnia (formerly areas of Yugoslavia), differences among various ethnic groups have led to the worst outbreak of warfare in Europe since World War II.

THE PROTECTION OF MINORITIES

According to the United Nations, human rights are basic rights that all people should have. They include the right to life, equal protection of the laws, and freedom from senseless arrest, enslavement or torture. In the past, members of minority groups have often been targets of human rights violations. There have been several recent efforts to right these wrongs.

■ **International Efforts**. The horrors of World War II led to international attempts to protect human rights. In 1948, the United Nations adopted the **Universal Declaration of Human Rights**. It stated that everyone has the right to life and liberty, and that everyone should have equal protection of the law and the right to a fair trial. Many nations promote human rights as part of their foreign policy. In 1990, for example, the United States intervened in Iraq to protect the Kurds.

■ **Domestic Efforts**. Some groups attempt to overcome their problems by leaving their country, as Soviet Jews did when they emigrated to Israel. Others fight for equal rights within the country, like Blacks have done in South Africa. These groups achieve their goals by spreading information, seeking international support, practicing civil disobedience, and sometimes by terrorist acts. Still others fight for national independence, like the Croats and Bosnians in the former Yugoslavia, and the Palestinians in Israel.

TESTING YOUR UNDERSTANDING

Directions: Circle the number preceding the word or expression that correctly answers the statement or question. Following the multiple choice questions, go on to answer the essay questions.

Base your answers to questions 1 through 3 on the following discussion among speakers from Russia and on your knowledge of social studies.

> **NOTE**: It will help you to answer these three questions if you first read the **Skill-Builder** section on "interpreting speakers," appearing on the next page.

Speaker A: Relations between the Soviet Union and the United States have improved. Since we must live together, we must learn to trust each other.

Speaker B: We need strong armies to prevent an invasion from the nations of Western Europe.

Speaker C: We expect the central government to make our nation powerful. Our leaders know which industries must be developed and improved.

1 In relations between the United States and the Soviet Union, Speaker A would most probably support
1 imperialism   3 an arms race
2 colonialism   4 peaceful coexistence

2 Speaker B's views are most similar to the views of
1 Mohandas Gandhi   3 Josef Stalin
2 George Bush   4 Mikhail Gorbachev

3 Speaker C would most likely support which type of economy?
1 traditional   3 planned
2 capitalist   4 feudal

4 An important function of perestroika was to
1 prevent price increases in Soviet oil
2 ban Soviet nuclear weapons
3 allow factory managers a greater role in decision-making
4 limit all foreign investments in the Soviet Union

5 A major feature of glasnost was to
1 end exports to the United States
2 control Soviet authors
3 limit the spread of religion
4 permit criticism of officials

6 Which geographical feature is correctly paired with its location?
1 Sahara Desert / Pakistan
2 Gobi Desert / Middle East
3 Amazon River / Soviet Union
4 Danube River / Eastern Europe

7 The topics "Bolsheviks," "World War I" and "Nicholas II" would probably be discussed in an essay dealing with
1 the Spanish conquest of Aztec Mexico
2 the Russian Revolution of 1917
3 Indian independence
4 imperialism in Africa

8 Which event occurred first?
1 The Communists took control of Russia.
2 Fidel Castro came to power in Cuba.
3 Mao Zedong introduced Communism into China.
4 Gorbachev introduced Perestroika.

SKILL BUILDER: INTERPRETING SPEAKERS

Occasionally a test contains a speaker-type question. It will be helpful to know what to look for when faced with this type of question.

What Is a Speaker-Type Question?
It presents a series of statements by several speakers. The speakers are identified by letters A, B, C, and D.

The Key to Understanding a Speaker Question
Each speaker's statement is an opinion about a social studies term, concept or situation.

Interpreting a Speaker-Type Question
Start by asking yourself the following questions about each speaker:

- What term, concept or situation is being discussed?
- What is each speaker saying about it?
- Is each speaker in favor or opposed to it?

Notice that the speakers disagree.

- Why do they disagree?
- How well do they support their positions?
- Do their opinions remind you of the views of groups or individuals you are familiar with?

Now that you know what to look for, test your skill at these types of questions by reading what each speaker has to say, and answering the questions that follow:

Speaker A: These colonial peoples have benefited tremendously from the introduction of our government system, laws, and institutions. All we asked is to be able to sell our manufactured goods to these people.

Speaker B: I believe the problems we find today in our homeland are not our doing. We have lived in peace for centuries. When the foreigners came, our people were enslaved, our land was taken and our culture destroyed.

Speaker C: The black majority in our country is not permitted to vote or speak freely. Our people are treated as second class citizens. The government passes laws that separate and isolate us from the white minority.

Speaker D: Our nation has finally achieved independence. We must maintain friendly relations with all nations, being careful to avoid taking sides. It is best if we follow a path of neutrality.

1 Speaker A could best be described as:
    1 an imperialist   3 a Communist
    2 an environmentalist   4 a terrorist

> **Speaker A** could best be described as an **imperialist**, since these arguments are used by imperialist nations. For example, the speaker overemphasizes the advantages to the colony, while stressing the need for the colony to buy manufactured goods from the mother country.

2 Which speaker would favor a foreign policy of non-alignment?
    1 Speaker A   3 Speaker C
    2 Speaker B   4 Speaker D

> **Speaker D**'s views would most favor a foreign policy of non-alignment. Such a policy argues for neutrality with other nations, in order to protect the independence of one's country.

3 Speaker C would most likely be opposed to a policy of
    1 nationalism   3 apartheid
    2 isolationism   4 non-alignment

> **Speaker C**'s views are opposed to apartheid. The statements point out the ways in which blacks are not treated as equal to whites—describing the apartheid policy that existed in South Africa.

ESSAYS

1 Gorbachev's policies of perestroika and glasnost brought about problems and changes in the former Soviet Union.

Part A

Define the policy of glasnost: _____

    State how it changed life in the U.S.S.R.: _____

Define the policy of perestroika: _____

    State how it changed life in the U.S.S.R.: _____

Part B

In your part B answer, you should use information you gave in Part A. However, you may also include different or additional information in your Part B answer.

Explain how Gorbachev's policies of perestroika and glasnost brought about problems and changes in the former Soviet Union.

2 Some individuals have brought about important changes in their countries.

Individuals

Mikhail Gorbachev	Boris Yeltsin
Vladimir Lenin	Peter the Great
Mao Zedong	Mohandas Gandhi

Part A

Select *two* individuals from the list. For *each* one, identify *one* change that the individual brought about in his country.

INDIVIDUAL	CHANGE
1 _____	1 _____ _____
2 _____	2 _____ _____

Part B

In your part B answer, you should use information you gave in Part A. However, you may also include different or additional information in your Part B answer.

Write an essay starting with the topic sentence:

Some individuals have brought about important changes in their countries.

GLOBAL CHECKLIST

THE COMMONWEALTH OF INDEPENDENT STATES

Directions: Before going on to the next chapter, check your understanding of the important people, terms and concepts covered in this chapter. Place a check (✔) mark next to those that you remember. If you have trouble recalling a particular term, refer to the page number following the item.

Food riot during a Russian famine, 1917.

- ❑ U.S.S.R. (204)
- ❑ Tundra (206)
- ❑ Steppes (206)
- ❑ Eastern Europe (206)
- ❑ Czar (208)
- ❑ Westernization (209)
- ❑ Catherine the Great(209)
- ❑ Revolution of 1917 (209)
- ❑ Russification (209)
- ❑ Pogroms (209)

- ❑ Nicholas II (209)
- ❑ Communism (210)
- ❑ Vladimir Lenin (210)
- ❑ New Economic Policy (210)
- ❑ Josef Stalin (211)
- ❑ Collectivization (211)
- ❑ Totalitarianism (211)
- ❑ Cold War (211)
- ❑ NATO (212)
- ❑ Glasnost (213)

- ❑ Perestroika (213)
- ❑ Iron Curtain (214)
- ❑ Planned Economy (218)
- ❑ Peter the Great (221)
- ❑ Mikhail Gorbachev (221)
- ❑ August 1991 Coup (224)
- ❑ Boris Yeltsin (224)
- ❑ Commonwealth of Independent States (224)
- ❑ Berlin Wall (224)

CONCERNS

- **Reunification of Germany**
- **Civil War in Northern Ireland**
- **From Common Market to United Europe**

GEOGRAPHY

- **Size and Location**
- **Geographic Features and Their Effects**

HISTORY

- **Ancient Greece and Rome**
- **Middle Ages**
- **Renaissance**
- **Age of Exploration**
- **Reformation**
- **Age of Absolute Monarchs**
- **Scientific Revolution**
- **Enlightenment**
- **French Revolution**
- **Industrial Revolution**
- **Nationalism and Imperialism**
- **World War I**
- **Totalitarianism and World War II**
- **Postwar Europe**

CHAPTER 9

WESTERN EUROPE

IMPORTANT PEOPLE

- **Ludwig van Beethoven**
- **Albert Einstein**
- **Pablo Picasso**
- **Margaret Thatcher**
- **Helmut Kohl**

SYSTEMS

- **Government**
- **Economy**
- **Religion**
- **Society**
- **The Arts**

What do these pictures show you about Western Europe? _____

_____

_____

_____

1
GEOGRAPHY

In this section you will read about the major geographic features of Western Europe, and how these features have affected its peoples and history.

THINK ABOUT IT

Europe is a continent containing many countries. Name as many Western European countries

as you can: _____

_____

Important Terms: As you read this section, look for the following terms:

◆ **Western Europe**   ◆ **Rhone / Rhine**

SIZE AND LOCATION

Europe, the second smallest of the world's seven continents, shares a large land mass with Asia, the world's largest continent. Some geographers think of Europe and Asia as a single continent called **Eurasia**, since there is no body of water separating these two continents. To the west, across the Atlantic Ocean, lies North and South America. The major countries that
◆ make up **Western Europe** are Great Britain, Ireland, Norway, Sweden, France, Germany, Austria, Belgium, Holland, Spain, Portugal, Italy and Greece. (The countries of Eastern Europe were discussed in the previous chapter.) Europe's location, close to the Middle East and to the continents of Asia and Africa, helps to explain why Europeans borrowed from the cultures of these regions. It is also one of the causes of Europe's frequent involvement in so many wars.

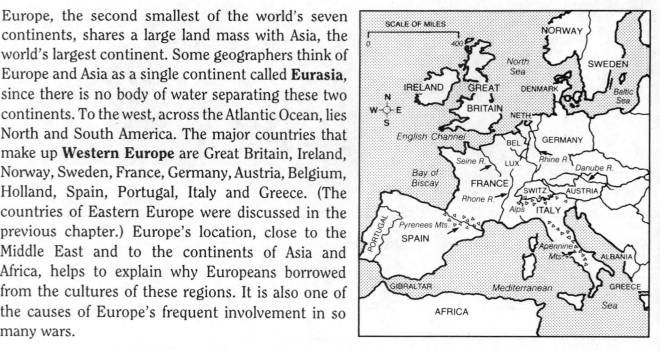

MAJOR GEOGRAPHIC FEATURES AND THEIR EFFECTS

MOUNTAINS

There are many mountain ranges in Europe. They include the Alps, the Pyrenees and the Apennines. These mountains created defensible borders between nations and allowed Europeans to develop many separate nationalities with their own languages and customs. These mountains also limited the land area available for settlement. Because of the continent's small land area and dense population, many different national groups live close to one another. As a result, Europe has been the stage for almost continuous warfare among its nations throughout its history.

SEAS, RIVERS AND COASTLINE

Europe is bordered by several major bodies of water: to the north, the Baltic and North Seas; to the south, the **Mediterranean Sea**; and to the west, the Atlantic Ocean. Europe has many river systems, such as the **Rhone** and the **Rhine**, that crisscross its lands. They allow for easy transportation across ◆ the continent and make fishing a major occupation in some countries. Europe's long coastline has many fine harbors. These factors help explain why so many Europeans depend on the sea to earn a living, and why the sea has played such an important role in European history.

RESOURCES

Europe has a great deal of coal and iron, but very little oil. Coal and iron helped Europe in the early Industrial Revolution, but today the lack of oil makes it dependent on other parts of the world.

SUMMING UP: GEOGRAPHY

Europe's geography helps to explain the ways its people earn their living. Its location accounts for much of its importance to other parts of the world, both today and throughout history.

THINKING IT OVER

How many countries in Western Europe were you able to name? _____ Which ones can you now

add to your list? _____

_____

CHECKING YOUR UNDERSTANDING

Directions: Complete the following cards. Then answer the multiple choice questions that follow.

WESTERN EUROPE

Near which continents is it located? _____

_____

Name some of its countries: _____

_____

RHONE / RHINE

What are they? _____

_____

Why are they important? _____

_____

1 If you were to take a plane from France to the United States, you would be traveling in which general direction?
   1 north   3 south
   2 east   4 west

2 The Mediterranean Sea touches the continents of
   1 Europe and Africa
   2 Africa and North America
   3 South America and Africa
   4 Europe and South America

3 Which two nations are in Western Europe?
   1 Brazil and France   3 India and Israel
   2 Laos and Spain   4 Italy and Germany

4 Which statement about Europe's geography is most accurate?
   1 Its natural boundaries allowed it to develop a single, united culture.
   2 Western Europe lacks any natural resources.
   3 Its mountain barriers led to the development of different nationalities.
   4 The best farmland is found in its mountains.

2
HISTORY

In this section you will read about the history of Western Europe from its origins in Ancient Greece to the French Revolution.

THINK ABOUT IT

European history can be thought of as a series of important developments occurring at different time periods. Try to list the century or centuries in which each of the following occurred.

Greek Civilization _____

Roman Civilization _____

Middle Ages _____

Renaissance _____

Reformation _____

Age of Absolute Kings _____

French Revolution _____

> This "Think About It" deals with historical time periods. If you have trouble understanding historical periods, first read the **Skill-Builder** on pages 242-243 .

Important Terms: As you read this section, look for the following terms:

◆ Crusades   ◆ Renaissance   ◆ Magna Carta
◆ Middle Ages   ◆ Divine Right Theory   ◆ Enlightenment
◆ Feudalism   ◆ Reformation   ◆ French Revolution

GREEK CIVILIZATION (1000 B.C.-150 B.C.)

The ancient Greeks were the first Europeans to develop a civilization. Their culture set standards against which most later cultures measured themselves. Through **cultural diffusion**, Greek culture influenced not only Europe but the rest of the world. Mountainous land caused Greek centers of population to be cut off from one another, and independent **city-states** (*cities that acted as countries*) developed.

Democracy. In a democracy, people participate in their government. Athens, a famous city-state, developed the first democracy. Every citizen had a say in decisions by voting on all issues. However, Athenian women and slaves could not vote, since they were not citizens.

Great Thinkers. The ancient Greeks believed that by using **reason** people could understand how the world worked. Among Greece's greatest thinkers were men whose work we still study today: Socrates, Aristotle and Plato.

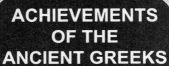

ACHIEVEMENTS OF THE ANCIENT GREEKS

Architecture. The Greeks were great builders. Their temples and other structures were supported by large columns. Some of their buildings, like the Parthenon, still stand today, and modern buildings often copy the classic Greek style.

Math and Science. The early Greeks wondered about many things found in the world and how they came about. Their focus was to try to explain how and why things happened. Their ideas helped to advance fields such as medicine and geometry.

Almost every activity in ancient Greece was related in some way to religion. Gods were an important part of life in Greece. Gatherings such as festivals and Olympic Games were held to honor the Gods. Despite their achievements, the city-states of ancient Greece often fought against each other. This allowed other, larger countries to defeat them.

*Pictured at right: The ruins of the **Parthenon** in Athens, Greece. For this building, Greek sculptors made statues of women to take the place of ordinary columns in holding up the roof.*

SKILL BUILDER: UNDERSTANDING TIMELINES

Sometimes a test will contain a question about a sequence of events, or require you to interpret a timeline. It will be helpful if you know what to look for in this kind of question.

EVENTS IN EUROPEAN HISTORY

509 B.C.	476 A.D.	1215	1517	1789	1914	1933	1957
Roman Republic founded	Fall of the Roman Empire	Magna Carta signed	Luther protests Church practices	French Revolution begins	World War I breaks out	Hitler comes to power	Common Market formed

WHAT IS A TIMELINE?

A timeline lists a series of events in **chronological order** (*from the earliest event to the latest*), along a line. The span of a timeline can be anything from a short period to several thousand years.

KEYS TO UNDERSTANDING A TIMELINE

First, look at its major components:

Title. The title explains the topic. For example, the title of the timeline above is "Events In European History." Important events in Europe's history are listed in the order in which they occurred.

Understanding Dates. Historians divide dates into two groups: **B.C.** and **A.D.** The dividing point is the birth of Christ: B.C. (**B**efore **C**hrist) refers to any time *before* his birth, and A.D. refers to time *after* his birth. (Writers always add B.C. to a date if it occurred before the birth of Christ, but they don't bother to write A.D. if the date is after his birth. For example, if the present year is 1992, we write 1992, not 1992 A.D.) Notice in the following timeline that as time passes, B.C. dates go from higher to lower numbers, while A.D. dates go from lower to higher numbers:

500 B.C.	200 B.C.	1 A.D.	1500 A.D.	1992 A.D.

Special Terms. To understand timeline questions you must be familiar with certain special terms. A **decade** refers to a ten-year period. A **century** is a 100-year period. Thus, the 20th century refers to the 100 years from January 1, 1901 to December 31, 2000. Counting centuries may seem confusing at first. For example, the **1900s** are known as the **20th** century. Let's see why this is so. The first 100 years from the time Christ was born were the years **1** through **100**. That was the **1st century**. Look at the following chart to see how other centuries are identified:

1-100 A.D. _____ First Century
101-200 _____ Second Century
201-300 _____ Third Century
301-400 _____ Fourth Century

What is the present century (1901-2000) called? _____

What will the next century, 2001-2100, be called? _____

Events. Events on the timeline are related to the title. For example, if the title were "Wars in the 20th Century," the events listed would be the wars that occurred between the years 1901 and 2000.

Measuring The Passage of Time. To measure the passage of time from B.C. to A.D., you simply add the dates together. For example, to find out how many years have passed from 500 B.C. to the year 1992, add the two numbers together:

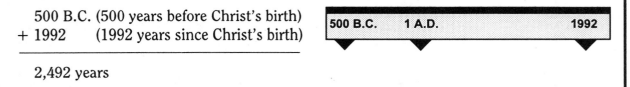

   500 B.C. (500 years before Christ's birth)
 + 1992   (1992 years since Christ's birth)
_____
   2,492 years

Thus 500 B.C. was 2,492 years ago. To measure the number of years from one date to another *within* B.C. or *within* A.D., just subtract the smaller date from the larger date. How long ago was 1500 A.D.? By subtracting 1500 from 1992, we arrive at 490 years ago:

   1992   (1992 years since Christ's birth)
 —1500   (1500 years since Christ's birth)
_____
   492 years ago

INTERPRETING A TIMELINE

Read the title first, to understand the overall meaning. For questions about time span, remember that the events are listed from the earliest to the most recent. Which happened first: the signing of the Magna Carta or the French Revolution? The timeline shows that the Magna Carta (1215) came before the French Revolution (1789). To measure the number of years from the founding of the Roman Republic (509 B.C.) to the fall of the Roman Empire (476 A.D.), add 509 to 476: the answer is 985 years. To measure the number of years from the start of World War I to the founding of the Common Market, subtract 1914 from 1957: the answer is 43 years.

THE ROMAN EMPIRE (27 B.C. - 476 A.D.)

One of the countries that subdued the Greeks was the powerful State that developed around Rome. As a result of trade, the Romans learned many things from the Greeks. These ideas helped Rome to become the most influential civilization in Europe for over 400 years. Its powerful army expanded the Roman Empire to include parts of the Middle East, Northern Africa, Spain, Great Britain and France.

THE ROMAN EMPIRE AT ITS HEIGHT: 117A.D.

A strong central government, led by an all-powerful Emperor, helped run and unify Rome's large empire. One of Rome's major contributions to Western European culture was its belief in a government controlled by laws. Another was the rise of Christianity in the Roman Empire, which eventually had very important effects on Europe. At first, the Romans suppressed and persecuted Christians, but when one of the Roman Emperors converted to Christianity, it became the official religion of the Empire. The Roman Empire lasted for centuries. Eventually it weakened from corruption; it collapsed in 476 A.D. after constant attacks by warlike people from outside the Empire.

THE MIDDLE AGES (500-1500)

◆ The period in history after the fall of the Roman Empire is called the **Middle Ages**. During the early Middle Ages, central governments were so weak that they were unable to maintain law and order. Violence was widespread.

FEUDALISM AND THE MANOR

◆ In order to protect themselves from violence and provide for their needs, Europeans developed **feudalism**. This system helped them survive the collapse of strong central governments. A major characteristic of feudal society in Europe was the development a strict class structure. People were born as serfs, knights or lords, and could not usually change their social position. Like feudalism in

Japan, **lords** (*local rulers*) provided land—since money had no value—in exchange for military service. They had small armies made up of **knights** (*warriors on horseback*). During the feudal period, most people lived on **manors** (*large estates owned by lords*). Each manor produced its own food, clothing and shelter. **Serfs** (*peasants*) gave the lord of the manor part of their harvest in return for the use of the local mill to grind their grain and ovens to bake their bread. The lord protected the serfs from outside attacks.

A TYPICAL MEDIEVAL MANOR

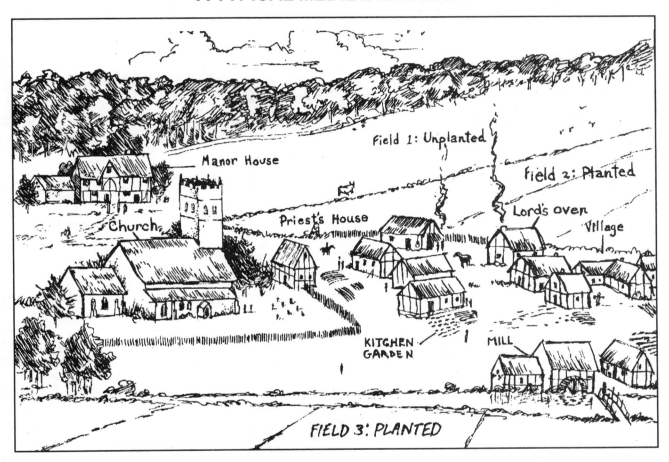

THE ROLE OF THE CATHOLIC CHURCH
During the Middle Ages, Europe had no central government as it did under the Roman Empire. Because of this, the Catholic Church became the most powerful organization of its time. People were extremely religious in those days. They believed that the Church represented God on earth and the key to salvation. The Church was also the main center of learning; churchmen, who learned Latin, were often the only people who could read and write.

THE CRUSADES (1095-1291)
Nothing showed the power of the Catholic Church more clearly than its "holy war" against the Muslims. In the 11th century, the Church called on all Christians in Europe to unite in a series of "Crusades"—wars to capture the area they called the Holy Land (*present-day Israel*) from its Muslim rulers.

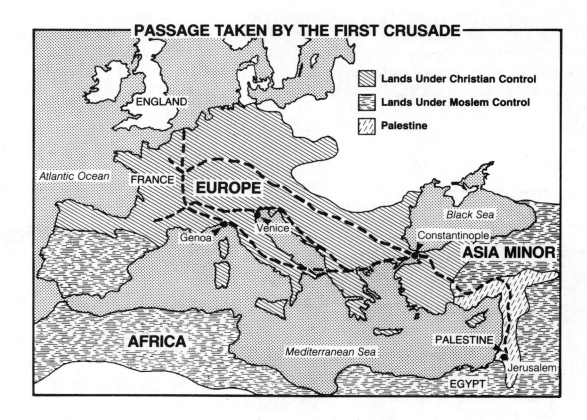

The Crusades, fought over a 200-year period, had many important effects:

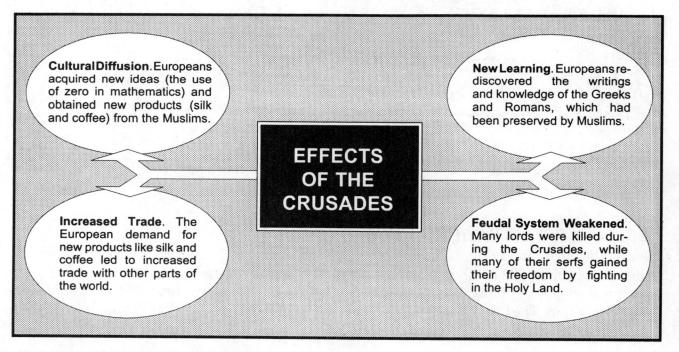

THE END OF THE MIDDLE AGES

Europe began to change in the late Middle Ages because of increased trade. Trade led to the growth of towns, the development of a middle class and an increase in the use of money. A new invention—gunpowder—made knights on horseback less important. In addition, kings with large armies gained new powers over the lords. Serfdom was gradually eliminated, especially after the Black Death (*a disease that swept through Europe in the 1400s*), which created a shortage of labor.

THE RENAISSANCE (1400-1700)

The increase in trade and contact with other peoples led to the period called the **Renaissance**. The ◆ Renaissance refers to a rebirth of learning, based on a re-discovery of ancient Greek and Roman culture. Beginning in Italy in the 15th century, the Renaissance gradually spread to the rest of Europe. **Humanism** was an important influence during the Renaissance, as interest turned away from religion to concern about everyday life. Humanists differed from the traditional thinkers of the Middle Ages in that they gave importance to the uniqueness of the individual. Renaissance thinkers, like the ancient Greeks, had confidence in the power of human reason to explain the world. They looked at individual people as the focus of all things.

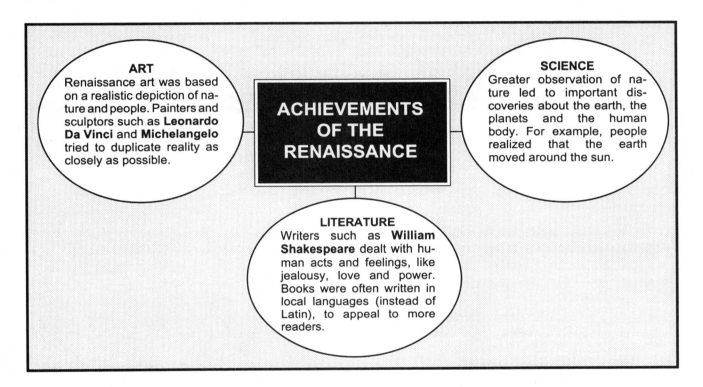

ART
Renaissance art was based on a realistic depiction of nature and people. Painters and sculptors such as **Leonardo Da Vinci** and **Michelangelo** tried to duplicate reality as closely as possible.

ACHIEVEMENTS OF THE RENAISSANCE

SCIENCE
Greater observation of nature led to important discoveries about the earth, the planets and the human body. For example, people realized that the earth moved around the sun.

LITERATURE
Writers such as **William Shakespeare** dealt with human acts and feelings, like jealousy, love and power. Books were often written in local languages (instead of Latin), to appeal to more readers.

THE AGE OF OVERSEAS EXPLORATION (1400-1750)

The Crusades had stirred an interest in goods from Asia such as spices, perfumes and silks. In addition, European missionaries and traders told of the adventure and wealth that awaited Europeans in far-off lands. These factors, combined with a desire to know more about the world, led Europeans to begin overseas explorations. They hoped to increase trade for new products and to gain great wealth for their countries and themselves. The invention of new navigational instruments (such as the compass) allowed explorers to sail farther than ever before. One of these explorers was **Christopher Columbus** (1451-1506). His voyage to the Americas encouraged the entire Age of Exploration. His discoveries of lands unknown to Europeans provided sources of wealth and raw materials that changed the economy of Europe. Other great explorers included **Ferdinand Magellan** (1480-1521) who led the first group of ships to sail around the world, confirming that the earth was round. As a result of these and other overseas explorations, important changes took place.

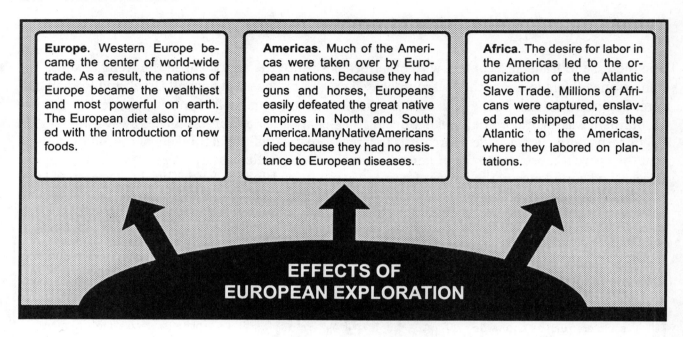

Europe. Western Europe became the center of world-wide trade. As a result, the nations of Europe became the wealthiest and most powerful on earth. The European diet also improved with the introduction of new foods.

Americas. Much of the Americas were taken over by European nations. Because they had guns and horses, Europeans easily defeated the great native empires in North and South America. Many Native Americans died because they had no resistance to European diseases.

Africa. The desire for labor in the Americas led to the organization of the Atlantic Slave Trade. Millions of Africans were captured, enslaved and shipped across the Atlantic to the Americas, where they labored on plantations.

EFFECTS OF EUROPEAN EXPLORATION

THE REFORMATION (1500s)

◆ The Renaissance spirit of individualism soon spread into religion. The **Reformation** occurred during the 1500s. It was a movement, led by **Martin Luther**, to reform several practices of the Catholic Church. Luther's ideas and actions led to the creation of a new form of Christianity, known as **Protestantism** because believers "protested" against the Catholic Church.

PROFILES IN HISTORY

Martin Luther

In 1517 a monk, Martin Luther, posted a list of **Ninety-Five Theses** (complaints) on a church door in Germany, calling for reforms in the Catholic Church. He challenged the right of the **Pope** (*the leader of the Catholic Church*) to sell pardons from punishment for committing a sin. Luther believed that each individual should read and understand the Bible for himself, and that only through one's own faith could one truly be saved. He argued that neither priests nor Popes had any special powers to grant salvation when a person died.

The invention of the printing press helped spread the Reformation to other countries, by making copies of the Bible more easily available to ordinary people. As a result of the Reformation, European Christians became divided into two groups: Protestants and Catholics. These religious differences brought about a century of wars between them. In addition, the Reformation seriously weakened the power of the Catholic Church.

THE AGE OF ABSOLUTE KINGS AND QUEENS (1600-1750)

As a result of new trade, the Age of Exploration and the wars of the Reformation, kings and queens built stronger armies. They paid for these large armies by increasing taxes. The nobles were given special privileges in exchange for their loyalty. Rulers also began to claim that they ruled in the name of God, which they called **Divine Right**. According to this theory, a king or queen was God's chosen deputy on earth. Whatever the he or she decided was the will of God, and no one on earth had the right to question the ruler's power or authority.

PROFILES IN HISTORY

Louis XIV

Absolutism means the total control of people by a king or queen. King Louis XIV of France was a prime example of an absolute ruler. He interfered in the religious and economic life of his subjects. He demanded that Protestants convert to Catholicism or leave the country. Louis XIV spent much of France's wealth on himself and his friends. He built a magnificent palace at Versailles which nearly bankrupted the nation, and fought a series of wars to gain even more power. He claimed that his authority was law and anyone who challenged it would be punished.

ENGLAND: RULERS WITH LIMITED POWER

Unlike Louis XIV, English rulers such as King Henry VIII and Queen Elizabeth I did not have absolute power. Strong limits had been established on the power of the monarchy as early as feudal times.

PROFILES IN HISTORY

Elizabeth I

At age 25 Elizabeth I became Queen of England. Her 45-year reign was marked by a period of great cultural activity. To bring an end to religious disunity, Elizabeth I blended English Protestantism with many Catholic features and practices. In the area of foreign policy, England's peace and security dominated Queen Elizabeth's thinking. She became a national hero by successfully resisting Catholic Spain's attempt to invade England in 1588. In order to encourage trade, Queen Elizabeth granted charters to some businessmen to start the British East India Company and other trading companies. By 1603, the year of Elizabeth's death at the age of 69, England had been transformed into the greatest sea power in the world.

Several of the kings who followed Elizabeth tried to strengthen their powers at the expense of Parliament and the English people. But in two revolutions, first in 1642-1649 and again in 1688, the English overthrew their monarchs and established the supremacy of Parliament.

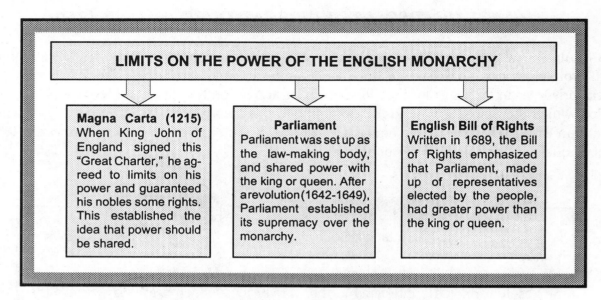

LIMITS ON THE POWER OF THE ENGLISH MONARCHY

| **Magna Carta (1215)** When King John of England signed this "Great Charter," he agreed to limits on his power and guaranteed his nobles some rights. This established the idea that power should be shared. | **Parliament** Parliament was set up as the law-making body, and shared power with the king or queen. After a revolution (1642-1649), Parliament established its supremacy over the monarchy. | **English Bill of Rights** Written in 1689, the Bill of Rights emphasized that Parliament, made up of representatives elected by the people, had greater power than the king or queen. |

THE SCIENTIFIC REVOLUTION (1789)

From the 1500s through the 1750s, new discoveries and scientific theories brought about so many changes that historians call these developments the **Scientific Revolution**. Men of science looked at nature in a new way, rejecting traditional authority and church teachings in favor of direct observation. They observed nature, made **hypotheses** (*educated guesses*), and then tested these hypotheses through experimentation. One of the most influential scientists of the period was Sir **Isaac Newton**. He discovered that every object in our universe behaves according to the law of gravity. This made it possible to calculate the speed of falling objects and the movement of the planets. It raised hopes that the entire universe could be understood by discovering and understanding certain fixed laws.

THE ENLIGHTENMENT (Mid-18th Century)

New ideas about science also began to affect thinking in other fields. The **Enlightenment** brought about a new way of thinking, not only about nature but also about government. Enlightenment thinkers believed that if people used reason and understood the laws of nature, they could improve their lives. These thinkers questioned the Divine Right Theory, believing that people had the right to govern themselves.

John Locke

PROFILES IN HISTORY

John Locke wrote about government in the mid-1600s, but his ideas have been influential far beyond the period in which they were written. His beliefs about government affected the thinking of many people in England and other parts of the world. Locke wrote that the power to rule comes not from God, as the Divine Right theory had asserted, but from the people. Locke defended the people's right to revolt when a government abused its powers or failed to protect its citizens' lives, liberty and property. His ideas greatly influenced the Declaration of Independence, the U.S. Constitution and the French Revolution.

Another important Enlightenment thinker was **Jean Jacques Rousseau**, who believed that government should express the will of the people. Rousseau thought that modern society corrupted man's natural goodness. He wrote, "Man is born free, and everywhere he is in chains." **Voltaire** was a philosopher who poked fun at traditional authority—society, government and the Church. His declaration, "I disapprove of what you say, but I will defend to the death your right to say it" is still quoted today.

THE FRENCH REVOLUTION (1789) ◆

By the end of the 18th century, France was a country ready for a **revolution** (*a rapid, violent change in the way a country is governed*).

CAUSES OF THE REVOLUTION

There was much inequality among social classes in France. The nobles and the clergy continued to receive special treatment, while the common people had few rights. Their labor and taxes helped pay for the luxurious lives of the nobles and church people, as well as France's frequent wars. Eventually the government ran out of money. When King Louis XVI asked his nobles for money, they refused. He then called into session the **Estates General** (*a body like Parliament*). When it assembled, the common people, led by the middle class, demanded more rights. After rioters took the Bastille (*a royal fortress used as a prison*), Louis XVI agreed to many of the demands of the middle class. Later, when word spread that the king changed his mind and would again take absolute power, Louis was arrested and executed.

MAIN EVENTS OF THE REVOLUTION

The slogan of the French Revolution became "**Liberty, Equality and Fraternity** (*brotherhood*)." A struggle began over who would rule France. Violence broke out, and anyone suspected of not supporting the revolution was executed; this period was known as the **Reign of Terror**. Other European kings, claiming to rule by divine right, feared that the ideals of the French Revolution would spread to their countries, so they attacked France. France fought wars with many of these countries to defend its revolution. Under General **Napoleon Bonaparte**, French armies conquered much of Europe. In 1799, Napoleon crowned himself Emperor and attempted to unite all of Europe under his command. After 22 years of continual fighting, Napoleon was defeated at the Battle of Waterloo. He lived his final years as a prisoner on a small island in the Atlantic Ocean. Despite Napoleon's defeat, the French Revolution brought about many important changes in Europe.

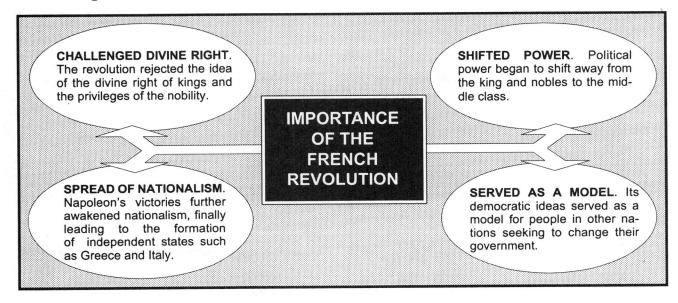

CHALLENGED DIVINE RIGHT. The revolution rejected the idea of the divine right of kings and the privileges of the nobility.

SHIFTED POWER. Political power began to shift away from the king and nobles to the middle class.

IMPORTANCE OF THE FRENCH REVOLUTION

SPREAD OF NATIONALISM. Napoleon's victories further awakened nationalism, finally leading to the formation of independent states such as Greece and Italy.

SERVED AS A MODEL. Its democratic ideas served as a model for people in other nations seeking to change their government.

THINKING IT OVER

Identify something of importance that happened in each of the following periods:

Greek Civilization _____

Roman Civilization _____

Middle Ages _____

Renaissance _____

Reformation _____

Age of Absolute Kings _____

French Revolution _____

Directions: Complete the following cards. Then answer the multiple choice questions that follow.

MAGNA CARTA

What was it? _____

Importance: _____

_____

CRUSADES

What were they? _____

Major effects: _____

_____

MIDDLE AGES

Define it: _____

Main characteristics: _____

_____

FEUDALISM

Define it: _____

Major characteristics: _____

_____

RENAISSANCE

What was it? _____

Main characteristics: _____

_____

DIVINE RIGHT THEORY

Define it: _____

Name a king who ruled under this theory:

_____

ENLIGHTENMENT

Define it: _____

Main ideas: _____

_____

FRENCH REVOLUTION

Major causes: _____

Importance: _____

_____

ANCIENT GREECE AND ROME

1 Which form of government began in the city-state of Athens?
1 monarchy
2 democracy
3 monotheism
4 communism

2 A result of the collapse of the Roman Empire in 476 A.D. was that
1 the emperor's power was eliminated
2 the Crusades started in Europe
3 feudalism developed
4 the power of the Czars ended

3 A major contribution of the Roman Republic to Western Europe was the
1 idea of government by laws
2 rejection of the concept of slavery
3 belief in democracy
4 start of the Industrial Revolution

4 An immediate result of the fall of the Roman Empire was
1 a renewed interest in education
2 a period of disorder and weak government
3 the growth of cities and towns
4 a period of peace and the rise of strong government

MIDDLE AGES, CRUSADES AND FEUDALISM

5 During the Middle Ages, which group or organization was the most powerful?
1 school officials   3 Catholic Church
2 peasants and serfs   4 middle class

6 The Middle Ages in Western Europe were characterized by
1 the manor system and stress on control of land
2 large-scale production by machinery
3 increased central authority
4 decreased emphasis on religion

7 European attempts to free the area Christians considered the "Holy Land" from Muslim rule were known as the
1 Crusades   3 Enlightenment
2 Reformation   4 Renaissance

8 Increased European trade with the Middle East was a direct result of the
1 fall of the Roman Empire   3 Crusades
2 French Revolution   4 Reformation

9 Feudalism is most often characterized by
1 different social classes
2 worship of idols
3 trade with foreign lands
4 women having equal rights

10 The role of the knight in feudal Europe was most similar to the role of
1 an untouchable in India
2 a priest in Latin America
3 a samurai in Japan
4 an artist in the United States

THE RENAISSANCE

11 The Renaissance in Europe is best known for
1 its cultural and artistic achievements
2 machines that replaced hand labor
3 the establishment of democracy
4 the start of World War I

12 Which period was characterized by a renewed interest in Greek and Roman cultures?
1 Middle Ages   3 Renaissance
2 Golden Age of Athens   4 Reformation

13 Which person is correctly paired with his field of achievement?
1 Michelangelo - Sculpture
2 Socrates - Dance
3 Shakespeare - Painting
4 Leonardo Da Vinci - Literature

14 Humanism and concern for the individual were associated with
1 the Crusades   3 feudalism
2 the Renaissance   4 the rule of Russian Czars

15 A major result of the Renaissance was
1 an increased interest in the arts and sciences
2 an increased emphasis on religion
3 a rejection of all central authority
4 the development of Communism

16 Renaissance humanists were most interested in
1 rejecting all ideas having to do with religion
2 emphasizing the importance of the individual
3 studying the religions of India and China
4 strengthening the Catholic Church

THE REFORMATION AND THE AGE OF KINGS

17 Which newspaper headline might have appeared during the Reformation if there had been newspapers at that time?
1 "Rome Falls to Barbarians"
2 "Karl Marx Attacks Capitalism"
3 "Martin Luther Criticizes the Church"
4 "Bismarck Calls for German Unification"

18 A major result of the Reformation was that it
1 ended religious unity in Western Europe
2 caused the decline of the Roman Empire
3 led to European conquest of the Holy Land
4 increased the power of the Popes

19 Which person sought to reform the abuses of the Catholic Church?
1 Vasco Da Gama
2 Leonardo Da Vinci
3 Martin Luther
4 William Shakespeare

20 King Louis XIV believed in theories that led to the practice of
1 absolutism
2 democracy
3 Communism
4 constitutionalism

21 The power of the English kings was limited by the
1 Monroe Doctrine
2 theory of Divine Right
3 Magna Carta
4 Treaty of Versailles

22 Vasco Da Gama, Christopher Columbus and Ferdinand Magellan were famous
1 writers
2 painters
3 politicians
4 explorers

THE ENLIGHTENMENT AND THE FRENCH REVOLUTION

23 Which person believed that rulers get their right to govern from the people?
1 John Locke
2 Napoleon Bonaparte
3 Josef Stalin
4 Louis XIV

24 Which idea developed during the Enlightenment?
1 kings must have absolute power in order to rule effectively
2 the pope is the head of the Catholic Church
3 the power of the king comes from God
4 government gets its power from the people

25 "Governments are instituted among men deriving their . . . powers from the consent of the governed."

These words from the American Declaration of Independence are based largely on the ideas first expressed by
1 John Locke
2 Karl Marx
3 Martin Luther
4 Josef Stalin

26 A major cause of the French Revolution was
1 the fall of the Roman Empire
2 Martin Luther's attack on the Catholic Church
3 inequality among social classes
4 the pollution of the French countryside

27 Using reason to understand the laws of nature is an idea associated with the
1 Middle Ages
2 Crusades
3 Enlightenment
4 French Revolution

28 Which event took place during the French Revolution?
1 the rise of Napoleon to power
2 the bombing of Hiroshima
3 the rise of the Atlantic Slave Trade
4 the fall of the Roman Empire

29 A major result of the French Revolution was
1 the increase in the power of the French King
2 an increase in the number of French colonies
3 the spread of democratic ideals to other nations
4 a split in the Catholic Church

30 Peter the Great of Russia and Louis XIV of France both believed that
1 the support of the people is essential for success
2 government officials must represent the people
3 absolute power is necessary in order to rule
4 rulers receive their power to govern from the people

31 One of these is the main topic, and the other three are sub-topics. Which is the main topic?
1 unfair system of taxation
2 inequality among social classes
3 causes of the French Revolution
4 the common people had few rights

32 The Scientific Revolution promoted the idea that knowledge is based on
1 the experiences of past civilizations
2 experimentation and observation
3 emotions and feelings
4 the teachings of the Catholic Church

In this second section you will read about the history of Western Europe from the Industrial Revolution to the present.

THINK ABOUT IT

Try to identify the century in which you think each of the following took place:

Industrial Revolution _____

Age of Nationalism and Imperialism _____

World War I _____

World War II _____

Post-War Europe _____

Important Terms: As you read this section, look for the following terms:

- ◆ **Industrial Revolution**
- ◆ **Capitalism**
- ◆ **Balance of Power**
- ◆ **World War I**
- ◆ **League of Nations**

- ◆ **World War II**
- ◆ **Holocaust**
- ◆ **United Nations**
- ◆ **NATO**
- ◆ **Marshall Plan**

THE INDUSTRIAL REVOLUTION

◆The **Industrial Revolution** refers to those inventions and ideas which led to new ways of producing goods. It began in Great Britain in the 1750s and slowly spread to other parts of the world. Traditionally, goods were made by hand. As a result of the Industrial Revolution, factories were built where goods were manufactured in large quantities at lower prices. A new invention, the steam engine, was used to run the machines in the factories. Because goods became cheaper to produce, the demand for them increased, and this in turn led to more jobs. However, abuses occurred; factory workers labored long hours for low wages, often under unsafe conditions, and child labor was frequently used. Cities often grew up around factories, as workers sought to live closer to where they worked.

THE DEVELOPMENT OF CAPITALISM

A new group emerged, made up of merchants, landowners and bankers. By investing their money, these
◆people helped to develop the system of **capitalism**. Under capitalism, factories, mines and workshops are owned by private individuals. These individuals risk investing their money in a business, and receive all the profits. The workers provide their labor in return for wages. Under early capitalism, the government did not interfere in the relations between the workers and the capitalist business owners. This policy of government non-interference is known as **laissez-faire**.

Karl Marx

Because conditions for early factory workers were very harsh, capitalism had many critics. A leading critic was Karl Marx, whose ideas became the basis of Communism. According to Marx, the capitalists took advantage of workers by paying them very little. He predicted worker revolutions against the capitalists. Eventually the victorious workers would create a society in which all people would share ownership of the means of production, rather than only the rich. Then the workers would share the profits from their work, according to their needs. It was not until 1917, in Russia, that a Communist revolution based on Marx's ideas took place.

THE AGE OF NATIONALISM AND IMPERIALISM

NATIONALISM

Nationalism is the belief that each distinct group of people, or nationality (*a group which speaks the same language and shares the same customs*), is entitled to its own government and homeland. Napoleon's armies had helped to awaken feelings for a homeland among many national groups. These groups, such as the Italians and Germans, did not have their own independent states. With Napoleon's defeat, the leaders of Europe hoped to prevent the success of nationalistic goals. Austria, a state that included many national groups, felt particularly threatened. Over Austrian objections, however, Italians and Germans finally achieved unified, national states:

➤ **Italy.** In 1860, largely as a result of strong nationalistic feelings stirred up by **Giuseppe Garibaldi** and Count **Camillo Cavour**, Italy became a united nation.

➤ **Germany.** The German leader **Otto von Bismarck** helped to unite a number of small, independent German states into a new unified German nation. Bismarck followed the policy of "**blood and iron**," in which he used diplomacy and war to bring about German unification in 1871.

IMPERIALISM

Imperialism means a stronger nation taking control over a weaker one. It is sometimes called "**colonialism**," because it usually involves the seizing of colonies. In the 1880s, interest in imperialism regained popularity. European nations scrambled for colonies in Africa, Southeast Asia and the Pacific.

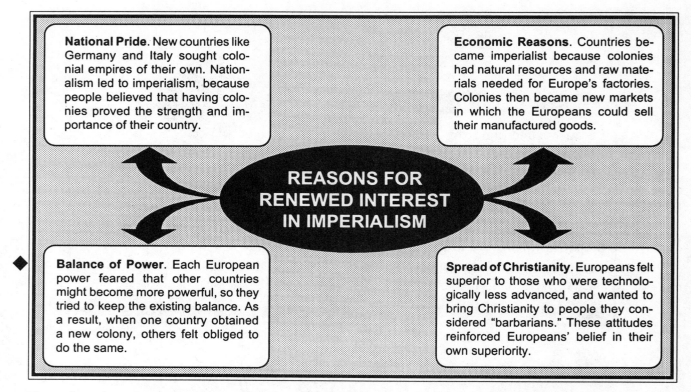

The colonial areas of Africa and Asia were helped and hurt by imperialism. It brought new ideas and technology, but the imperialists took away important resources and treated the local people badly.

WORLD WAR I (1914-1918)

World War I marked a turning point in history. New technologies made war much more destructive, led to the loss of millions of lives and brought down whole systems of government. The war weakened the hold of Europeans on their overseas empires and prepared the way for the rise of dictatorships.

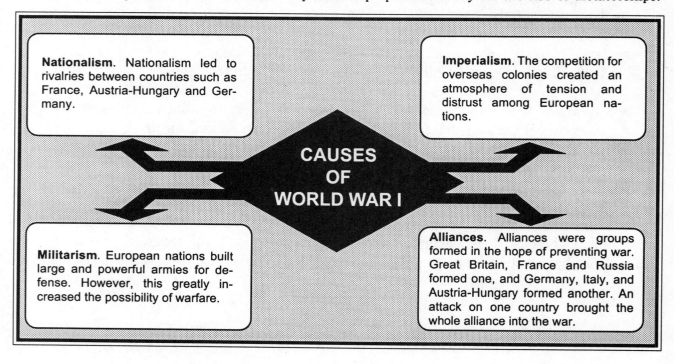

The spark that began the war occurred when Archduke **Francis Ferdinand** of Austria-Hungary was assassinated with the help of the Serbians, who had joined the Russians in the **Triple Alliance**. This started a chain reaction, because an attack on one country in an alliance meant that the rest of the alliance had to come to its aid. Austria-Hungary (part of the other alliance, called the **Triple Entente**) invaded Serbia in revenge. Imperial Russia then attacked Austria, which in turn brought in Germany on the side of Austria. Great Britain and France sided with Imperial Russia. Within a few weeks, all of Europe was at war.

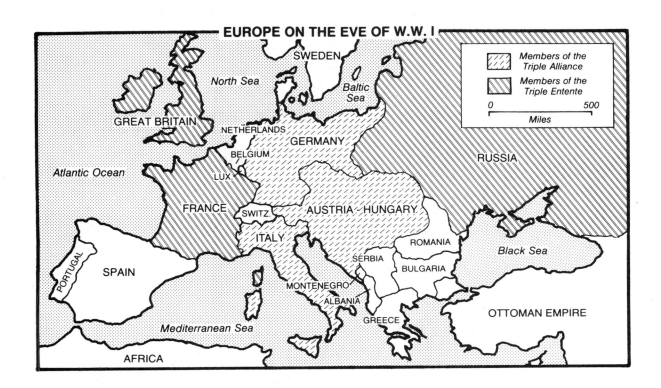

A NEW KIND OF WAR

World War I was unlike any previous wars. New weapons such as machine guns, tanks and poison gas made fighting deadlier than ever. Also, the civilian population was no longer safe from attack by military forces. Submarines changed naval warfare because they could sink ships without warning.

THE END OF WORLD WAR I AND THE PEACE SETTLEMENT

The United States, because it was a neutral nation, had the right to sail the seas freely without being attacked. In 1917, after its ships were attacked by German submarines, the United States entered the war on the side of Great Britain and France. In 1918, weary and worn down by years of fighting, the Germans surrendered. The **Treaty Of Versailles** (1919) ended the war. The terms of the treaty were harsh: Germany had to give up its colonies and greatly reduce its army and navy. In addition, Germany was forced to accept all the blame for starting the war, and to pay Britain and France a large sum of money. The Treaty of Versailles also tried to eliminate future wars by creating a **League of** ◆ **Nations** — an organization of countries that hoped to act together to keep peace. However, when the United States and the Soviet Union refused to join, the League proved too weak to prevent future wars.

Marie Curie

Born in Poland, Marie Sklodowska later moved to Paris, where she married the French scientist Pierre Curie. In 1903 they received the Nobel Prize in Physics for discovering two new radioactive elements—radium and polonium. When her husband died in an accident, she continued her research alone. In 1911, she was again awarded a Nobel Prize, this time in Chemistry, for isolating pure radium. She died in 1934 of leukemia caused by working unprotected with radioactive materials. Curie was the first woman to win a Nobel Prize, and the first person ever to win two of them—at a time when women were not even permitted to vote.

TOTALITARIANISM AND WORLD WAR II (1939-1945)

THE RISE OF TOTALITARIANISM

Totalitarianism is a system of government in which the leader controls all aspects of life, ignoring the people's wishes and needs, and using terror to enforce policies. After World War I, totalitarian governments emerged for similar reasons in the Soviet Union, Italy, Germany and several other European nations. Each country had suffered a great deal from the war. Many people had trouble making a living, and citizens were looking for leadership that would restore pride to their nations.

THE NAZIS TAKE POWER IN GERMANY (1933)

After World War I, Germany became a democracy. However, when the **Great Depression** (*a period of high unemployment*) spread in the 1930s from the U.S. to Germany, it brought serious economic problems. The democratic government was unable to cope. When **Adolf Hitler** promised to restore Germany to greatness, many people supported him. Hitler was a believer in racism and **fascism** (*a system where the State is supreme, the leader decides the needs of the State, and all citizens are expected to make sacrifices for the State*).

Adolf Hitler

Hitler, leader of the Nazi Party, blamed Germany's hard times on the Versailles Treaty and on the Jews. In his book *Mein Kampf*, Hitler wrote that Germans were a superior race who should rule the world. He claimed that Communism was a Jewish plot to control the world, and called the Jews an evil race that should be destroyed (**racism**). Because of his gripping way of speaking, and the anger that Germans felt toward their government, Hitler's ideas were accepted by many Germans. He took power in 1933, and soon afterwards the Germans lost their freedoms of speech, press and assembly. Schools, newspapers and radios had to communicate Nazi ideas. The persecution of Jewish people began.

WORLD WAR II BEGINS (1939)

The chief cause of World War II was Nazi aggression.

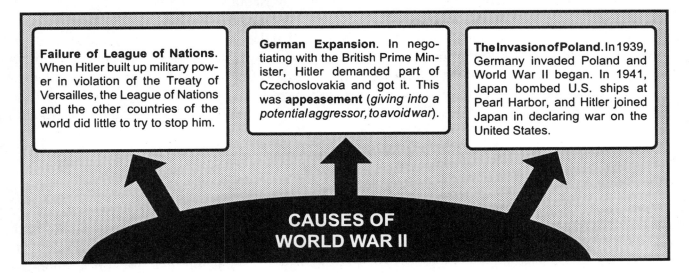

Failure of League of Nations. When Hitler built up military power in violation of the Treaty of Versailles, the League of Nations and the other countries of the world did little to try to stop him.

German Expansion. In negotiating with the British Prime Minister, Hitler demanded part of Czechoslovakia and got it. This was **appeasement** (*giving into a potential aggressor, to avoid war*).

The Invasion of Poland. In 1939, Germany invaded Poland and World War II began. In 1941, Japan bombed U.S. ships at Pearl Harbor, and Hitler joined Japan in declaring war on the United States.

CAUSES OF
WORLD WAR II

THE HOLOCAUST

The Holocaust was an attempt by Hitler to kill all Jewish people. To do this, Germans built special **concentration camps**. Jews from all over Nazi-controlled Europe were sent to these camps to be killed, usually by poison gas, and their bodies were burned in huge ovens. Hitler's "master race" theory and his **anti-semitism** (*hatred of Jewish people*) caused him to murder 6 million Jews and millions of non-German people in the concentration camps. Hitler killed himself just as the war ended, but later many high ranking Nazi leaders were put on trial for their crimes by an international court in the city of Nuremberg. They were accused of starting the war, using slave labor, carrying out experiments on humans, and **genocide** (*attempted murder of an entire people*) against the Jews. At these **Nuremberg Trials**, the Nazi leaders claimed that they were just following government orders. However, the judges rejected this defense, stating that people must disobey orders that are morally wrong. The acts that the Nazis committed were judged to be "crimes against humanity."

THE GLOBAL IMPACT OF WORLD WAR II

Mass Destruction	Defeat of Dictatorships	Decline of Colonialism	Rise of Superpowers
The war was fought in North Africa, East Asia, Europe and the Soviet Union. It left much of Europe completely destroyed and more than 40 million people dead.	Germany was divided into four zones by the U.S., France, Great Britain and the Soviet Union. The postwar governments of West Germany and Japan were democratic.	The European powers had used most of their strength fighting the war. Afterwards they were too weak to prevent their colonies from gaining independence.	The collapse of Europe led to the U.S. and the Soviet Union becoming superpowers. Their differences in viewpoints and economic systems led to the start of the Cold War.

◆ THE UNITED NATIONS

Another effect of World War II was the creation of the **United Nations (U.N.)**. In 1945, the victorious countries set up the United Nations to replace the League of Nations. Its goals are to maintain world peace, to promote international cooperation, and to fight world hunger, disease, and ignorance. A major difference between the U.N. and the League of Nations was that the world's major powers and most other nations decided to join. Each of the major victorious powers in World War II was given a permanent seat in the **Security Council** of the United Nations. The Security Council's major task is to prevent war. Every U.N. member belongs to the **General Assembly**, which makes recommendations to the Security Council. Other U.N. organizations handle special concerns like health, education and human rights.

POST-WAR EUROPE (1945-PRESENT)

After World War II, Europe was divided into two hostile parts: Eastern Europe, which became Communist under Soviet control, and Western Europe, which remained democratic and allied with the U.S. The United States took a number of actions to stop the spread of Communism in Europe and to help develop future U.S.-European trade. In 1947, U.S. Secretary of State **George Marshall** proposed that the United States give money to Western European nations for rebuilding their war-torn economies
◆ and to prevent their falling under Communist control. This became known as the **Marshall Plan**. In
◆ addition, the nations of Western Europe, the U.S. and Canada formed **NATO** (the North Atlantic Treaty Organization) to protect Western Europe from attack by Communist nations. In turn, the Soviet Union and its allies formed the **Warsaw Pact** to defend Communist nations from attack by the West. The Cold War lasted until 1991, when Communism collapsed in Eastern Europe and in the Soviet Union.

SUMMING UP: HISTORY

European history can be studied in many ways. For example, we can see how democracy developed and eventually triumphed, beginning with a study of ancient Greece through to the defeat of dictators like Hitler and the collapse of Communism. Or we can examine the great European technological achievements, the overseas explorations, the Scientific Revolution and the Industrial Revolution. Europe can also be studied by looking at its many wars and revolutions.

THINKING IT OVER

Identify something of importance that happened in each of the following historical periods:

Industrial Revolution _____

Age of Nationalism and Imperialism _____

World War I _____

World War II _____

Post-War Europe _____

CHECKING YOUR UNDERSTANDING

Directions: Complete the following cards. Then answer the multiple choice questions that follow.

INDUSTRIAL REVOLUTION

Where and when it began: _____

What was it? _____

Importance: _____

CAPITALISM

What is it? _____

Main characteristics: _____

_____

BALANCE OF POWER

Definition: _____

Effects: _____

_____

WORLD WAR I

Who fought on each side? _____

Causes: _____

Results: _____

LEAGUE OF NATIONS

What was it? _____

Main purpose: _____

Why it failed: _____

WORLD WAR II

Who fought on each side? _____

Causes: _____

Results: _____

HOLOCAUST

What was it? _____

Describe what happened: _____

_____

UNITED NATIONS

What is it? _____

Main purpose: _____

_____

NATO

What is it? _____

Main purpose: _____

_____

MARSHALL PLAN

What was it? _____

Main purpose: _____

_____

THE INDUSTRIAL REVOLUTION

1 A change to large-scale production occurred during the
   1 Middle Ages   3 Industrial Revolution
   2 French Revolution   4 Russian Revolution

2 Which statement about capitalism is most accurate?
   1 No one may own private property.
   2 The government makes all economic decisions.
   3 The main goal of business is to make a profit.
   4 Exports are always greater than imports.

3 An essential feature of industrialization is
   1 having a democratic government
   2 replacing hand labor with machines
   3 eliminating private property
   4 using nuclear energy

4 A major cause of the Industrial Revolution was the
   1 need to eliminate child labor
   2 development of new machines
   3 development of Communism
   4 desire to obtain foreign colonies

5 A long-range result of the Industrial Revolution was to
   1 decrease the number of people working in factories
   2 encourage people to move from cities to farms
   3 raise the standard of living of most workers
   4 make workers less dependent on employers

6 The invention of machines increased the number of workers in many European industries because
   1 unions required more workers to repair the machines
   2 the demand for goods increased as goods became cheaper to make
   3 laws prohibited women and children from working with machines
   4 machines were less efficient than hand labor

7 A main belief of Karl Marx was that workers
   1 would need foreign help to achieve a revolution
   2 had to work harder to help capitalists make a profit
   3 should unite to overthrow their capitalist bosses
   4 need to become capitalists themselves

8 A main characteristic of laissez-faire capitalism was
   1 government control of the economy
   2 an increased number of government rules
   3 that government did not interfere with businesses
   4 government ownership of business

AGE OF NATIONALISM AND IMPERIALISM

9 Which person played a key role in the unification of Germany?
   1 Nicholas II
   2 Otto von Bismarck
   3 Karl Marx
   4 Adolf Hitler

10 The term "blood and iron" refers to Bismarck's use of
   1 elections to achieve independence
   2 military power to achieve national unification
   3 war to obtain colonies
   4 violence to obtain gold and silver

11 European nations were interested in African colonies for their
1 manufactured goods
2 highly skilled workforce
3 labor-saving machinery
4 natural resources

12 The Industrial Revolution in Europe led to renewed interest in
1 imperialism
2 revolution
3 appeasement
4 isolationism

WORLD WAR I

13 Which was a cause of World War I?
1 nationalism
2 socialism
3 feudalism
4 Communism

14 The "spark" that began World War I was the
1 formation of the Triple Alliance
2 assassination of Archduke Ferdinand
3 shooting of peasants in Russia
4 surprise attack on Pearl Harbor

15 Which was a result of World War I?
1 freedom of the seas ended
2 the Cold War began
3 the League of Nations was established
4 Germany obtained a colonial empire

16 Which was a major goal of the League of Nations?
1 limiting world trade
2 maintaining peace among nations
3 eliminating colonial empires
4 establishing democracy in all nations

TOTALITARIANISM AND WORLD WAR II

17 Which event took place during World War II?
1 the defeat of Napoleon
2 the attack on Pearl Harbor
3 the fall of the Roman Empire
4 the creation of the League of Nations

18 Which was a direct cause of World War II?
1 Germany's invasion of Poland
2 the dropping of atom bombs on Japan
3 the execution of King Louis XVI
4 Napoleon's invasion of Russia

19 Which was a major result of World War II?
1 The Soviet Union lost most of its territory.
2 Germany was divided into two states.
3 Italy obtained a large colonial empire.
4 China took control of Japan.

20 Adolf Hitler of Germany and Joseph Stalin of the Soviet Union were similar in that both were
1 democratically elected to their positions
2 leaders of totalitarian governments
3 concerned about protecting people's rights
4 sought to introduce democratic reforms

21 Which was a belief of Adolf Hitler?
1 Germans are a superior race
2 Jewish people make the best leaders
3 religious differences are unimportant
4 all people are equal under the law

22 The "Holocaust" refers to the
1 effects of overseas explorations
2 killing of Jewish people during World War II
3 rise of nation-states in Europe
4 impact of the writings of Karl Marx

23 Which would be an example of genocide?
　1 the Nazis' attempt to murder all the Jews of Europe
　2 the harsh treatment of workers during the Industrial Revolution
　3 Protestant attempts to halt the spread of the Catholic faith
　4 power of feudal lords over their serfs

24 The policy of appeasement is one of
　1 using new nuclear weapons
　2 granting concessions to a potential aggressor
　3 going to war with enemies that pose a threat
　4 using technology to solve economic problems

25 Which pair of people shared similar ideas about the operation of government?
　1 Adolf Hitler and Mohandas Gandhi
　2 Vladimir Lenin and Michelangelo
　3 Karl Marx and John Locke
　4 Adolf Hitler and Joseph Stalin

26 A student doing a term paper on the "Holocaust," "genocide'" and "concentration camps" is writing about which historical period?
　1 Industrial Revolution　　3 World War II
　2 World War I　　　　　　4 Cold War

27 A major result of the Nuremberg War Trials was that
　1 national leaders were held responsible for their actions
　2 soldiers were required to pay for property damage
　3 Hitler's policies were accepted by most Europeans
　4 German leaders were found not guilty of war crimes

28 The results of World War I and World War II were similar in that in both
　1 Japan attacked the United States
　2 democracies were replaced by the rule of powerful kings
　3 the political boundaries of Europe remained unchanged
　4 Germany was the loser

29 A major goal of the United Nations is to
　1 decrease world trade
　2 increase the size of colonial empires
　3 establish democracy in all nations
　4 maintain peace among nations

POST-WAR EUROPE

30 Which term best describes the economic system in Eastern Europe after World War II?
　1 capitalism　　　　　3 Communism
　2 mercantilism　　　　4 imperialism

31 The emergence of the U.S. and the Soviet Union as superpowers was partly a result of
　1 the Revolution of 1917　3 World War I
　2 World War II　　　　　4 the Gulf War

32 The Marshall Plan was developed to
　1 reduce environmental pollution
　2 build missiles in Europe
　3 rebuild European economies after W.W. II
　4 encourage trade with the Soviets

33 When NATO (the North Atlantic Treaty Organization) was formed, its main function was to
　1 eliminate imperialism
　2 provide for Western Europe's defense
　3 encourage Communist expansion
　4 create an international government

34 A similarity between the League of Nations and the United Nations is that both
　1 had the United States as a member
　2 prohibited Communist nations from joining
　3 sought international peace
　4 conducted elections in democratic nations

In this section you will read about the major political institutions, economic systems, religions and cultural achievements of Western Europe.

THINK ABOUT IT

The peoples of Europe have lived under many different kinds of political systems. Describe as many of these political systems as you can:

Democracy _____

Feudalism _____

Divine Right Monarchy _____

Totalitarianism _____

Important Terms: As you read this section, look for the following terms:

◆ **Socialism**   ◆ **Judeo-Christian Heritage**

GOVERNMENT

Throughout Europe's history, its peoples have lived under many different types of governments.

DEMOCRACY
Democracy (*rule by the people*) first appeared in ancient Greece, in the city-state of Athens. Hundreds of years later, democracy was further developed in Great Britain, where the power of the **monarch** (king or queen) was limited by elected representatives of Parliament. The French Revolution was also fought in large part to turn France from an absolute monarchy into a democracy. Today, all of the countries of Western Europe are democracies. This means that in each of them, citizens have a voice in what government does. They can publish their ideas, give speeches, run for office and most importantly, vote.

FEUDALISM
During the Middle Ages, feudalism developed because there was no strong central government, such as during the Roman Empire. Instead, political power was in the hands of local lords. Kings gave lords the right to exercise political and economic control over the people living on their lands in exchange for pledges of loyalty and military support.

DIVINE RIGHT (ABSOLUTISM)
Kings or queens who ruled by "Divine Right" believed that their absolute power to rule ("*absolutism*") came to them from God. The king's subjects had no rights except those the ruler chose to give them.

TOTALITARIANISM

Totalitarianism might be called a modern form of absolute monarchy, in that all major decisions are made by a **dictator** (*a single national ruler*). The citizens have no right to question or disagree with the dictator. Totalitarianism describes the dictatorships in Germany under Hitler and in the Soviet Union under Stalin. The government controlled all aspects of public and private life.

ECONOMY

European nations have had many different economic systems, which developed over the centuries:

MANORIALISM

In the Middle Ages, most Europeans lived under the manorial system. All economic activity was conducted on the lord's **manor** (*estate*). Land was the most important possession; as part of the **feudal system**, the lord held his land in exchange for his promise to serve his higher lord (or king). The peasants, known as serfs, had no right to leave the land.

CAPITALISM

Western European nations today generally have capitalist economies. Under capitalism people have the freedom to buy from and to sell to anyone they wish. Capitalists believe that allowing people to do what is best for themselves will benefit everybody. People will buy from the producer with the best and cheapest goods. That producer will make a profit and produce more, while less efficient producers will go out of business. Under pure capitalism, the government's role in the economy is very limited.

SOCIALISM AND COMMUNISM

Some people believed that capitalism harmed workers and made many people poor. Thinkers
◆ looked for alternatives. **Socialists** believe that the best way to reduce poverty and treat workers fairly is for the government to own the major means of production (large factories, power companies and mines), with private ownership limited to small businesses and farms. The socialists argue that the change from capitalism to socialism should be gradual and peaceful. Karl Marx, in contrast, believed that a violent revolution was necessary to bring about change. He favored **Communism**—a system in which private ownership of all enterprises and land is replaced by government ownership.

RELIGION

Most Europeans are Christians, but there is a significant minority of Jewish Europeans. There is also a growing number of Muslims, who arrived in the years since World War II. Europeans have benefited from the contributions of these many religious groups. Both Jews and Christians hold certain com-
◆ mon beliefs, known as the **Judeo-Christian heritage**. They both believe in the existence of a single God and the importance of leading a moral life. Historically, however, religious differences have led to many conflicts in Europe. For example, after the Reformation, when Protestants broke away from the Catholic Church, wars developed between the two groups for many years. Also, Jews living in Europe suffered greatly because of their different practices and customs.

SOCIETY

During the early part of European history, the social class to which people belonged played a very important role in their lives. As a rule, these classes were **hereditary** (*being born into a particular class*).

The French Revolution challenged that system; the revolutionaries declared that all people should be considered equal. Later, the Industrial Revolution led to the establishment of a society where people could change their social class much more easily. The Industrial Revolution also gave rise to new kinds of classes: wealthy factory owners and hired workers who lived in cities or towns.

Charles Darwin

PROFILES IN HISTORY

In his book *The Origin of Species*, Darwin theorized that plants and animals slowly evolved over time from simple forms to more complex ones. He thought that differences among species are due to "natural selection," and only the fittest of these species would survive. Animals that were best suited to their surroundings would stay alive, while less suited animals would die at an early age. The superior qualities of the fit would be passed on to their offspring. Some people adopted Darwin's scientific theories to society, claiming that all human groups compete for survival the way other species do. They believed that stronger groups had a natural right to succeed over weaker ones ("Social Darwinism").

THE ARTS

Europeans have produced excellent architecture, sculpture and painting. They also developed their own forms of music and literature.

Statue of Moses, sculpted by Michelangelo

➤ **Greek and Roman Art.** The aim of ancient Greek art was to depict human beauty at its most perfect stage. The ancient Romans excelled in architecture, and were also skilled at sculpting heads of important people, reflecting the Roman concern with individual achievement and dignity.

➤ **The Middle Ages.** In the Middle Ages, the Catholic Church dominated painting, sculpture and architecture. The main concern of art was to glorify God. Most of the giant cathedrals were built during this period.

➤ **The Renaissance.** Renaissance artists observed nature and the human form closely. Their paintings and sculpture achieved a striking realism. The works of Leonardo Da Vinci, Michelangelo, and Raphael remain among the most highly prized art of all time.

➤ **The Modern Period.** With the development of photography, painting became less involved with realism and began moving in other directions. **Impressionism** was an attempt to capture shades of light on canvas. **Cubism** depicted the underlying forms of objects. In **Expressionism** artists used painting as a way to express their deepest feelings.

SUMMING UP: SYSTEMS

GOVERNMENT: Europeans have had many types of governments. Today most European governments are democracies.

ECONOMY: Most Europeans now have capitalist economies.

RELIGION: Western Europeans share a common Judeo-Christian heritage. Most Europeans are Christians, but there are Jewish and Muslim minorities.

SOCIETY: Ever since the French Revolution and the Industrial Revolution, European society has been very mobile in terms of class—similar to the United States.

THE ARTS: European artists have excelled at architecture, sculpture and painting. They have also made notable contributions in music and literature.

THINKING IT OVER

How many of Europe's different political systems were you able to describe? _____ How might you **now** define each of the following?

Democracy _____

Feudalism _____

Divine Right Monarchy _____

Totalitarianism _____

CHECKING YOUR UNDERSTANDING

Directions: Complete the following cards. Then answer the multiple choice questions that follow.

SOCIALISM
What is it?_____
How it differs from Communism: _____
_____

JUDEO-CHRISTIAN HERITAGE
What is it? _____
Beliefs shared by Jews and Christians:_____
_____

1   Which is characteristic of a democratic government?
    1 a dictator makes the important decisions
    2 private ownership of property is forbidden
    3 citizens can exercise their individual rights
    4 all newspapers are state-owned

2   A basic difference between capitalism and Communism concerns the
    1 ownership of the means of production
    2 establishment of labor unions
    3 size of the military
    4 amount of social security benefits

3   An economic system in which employers furnish raw materials, machinery and capital, while workers provide labor, is known as
    1 Communism   3 socialism
    2 mercantilism   4 capitalism

4   Which political system was characterized by an exchange of land for military service?
    1 tribalism   3 feudalism
    2 imperialism   4 nationalism

5   The founder of Communism was
    1 Leonardo Da Vinci 3 Karl Marx
    2 Count Cavour   4 Otto von Bismarck

6   A characteristic of a totalitarian form of government is that
    1 the media is free to print anything
    2 human rights are protected
    3 loyalty to the government is demanded
    4 artistic and literary freedom is encouraged

7   Which event is most closely associated with the Reformation?
    1 the fall of the Roman Empire
    2 Protestants breaking from the Catholic Church
    3 the start of the Crusades
    4 the death of Jews in concentration camps

8   Which ancient civilization first established the basis of Western democracy?
    1 the Egyptians   3 the Greeks
    2 the Chinese   4 the Romans

9   Which historical period is known for its beautiful cathedrals?
    1 Ancient Greece   3 Middle Ages
    2 Roman Empire   4 Renaissance

10 Which historical period is known for the development of Cubism and Expressionism?
    1 Ancient Greeks   3 Middle Ages
    2 Roman Empire   4 Modern Period

4 IMPORTANT PEOPLE

Many of the people who contributed to the development of Western Europe have been described in the History section. Here you will read about other people who have played key roles in Europe's history and culture.

THINK ABOUT IT

In which field and when did each of the following people achieve recognition?

	FIELD	TIME PERIOD
Ludwig van Beethoven		
Albert Einstein		
Pablo Picasso		
Margaret Thatcher		
Helmut Kohl		

 **THE EUROPEAN TIMES**

Volume XXVI   *Number 9*

LUDWIG VAN BEETHOVEN
(1770-1827)

Ludwig van Beethoven is considered one of the greatest musical composers to have ever lived. His concertos and other works, such as the Fifth and Ninth Symphonies, were greatly enjoyed by the people of his time, and continue to please millions of people all over the world. Ironically, Beethoven became deaf in his later years. He was still able to compose, but could not hear the performances of his works.

ALBERT EINSTEIN
(1879-1955)

Albert Einstein is considered one of the greatest scientists of the 20th century. He showed that matter and energy are interchangeable. Einstein demonstrated that a small amount of matter could be made to release tremendous quantities of energy. His theories formed the basis for the development of nuclear energy and atomic weapons.

PABLO PICASSO
(1881-1973)

Pablo Picasso was the leading figure in a new approach to modern art—cubism. His paintings represented familiar objects by breaking them up into their geometric forms, such as cubes, cones, and spheres. Picasso was a pioneer who paved the way for modern abstract art.

MARGARET THATCHER
(1925-Present)

Margaret Thatcher was Prime Minister of Great Britain from 1979 through 1990. Her economic policies included cutting government spending, curbing the power of British trade unions and reducing the role of government in the economy. Opposed to socialism, she sold off many of Britain's government-owned industries, turning them into private, profit-making companies. In 1990, she resigned due to a lack of support from her own political party.

Prime Minister Thatcher addressing the U.N. in 1982

HELMUT KOHL
(1930-Present)

Helmut Kohl was elected Chancellor of West Germany. Under his leadership, West and East Germany were reunited as a single country in 1990. Kohl was able to overcome international resistance by moving rapidly. He reduced East German fears by promising them economic aid. Kohl believes in an economically powerful Germany in a prosperous European common market.

SUMMING UP: IMPORTANT PEOPLE

Different people in a variety of fields have greatly influenced the history of Europe and of the world.

THINKING IT OVER

What did each of the following people do to achieve recognition?

Ludwig van Beethoven _____

Albert Einstein _____

Pablo Picasso _____

Margaret Thatcher _____

Helmut Kohl _____

CHECKING YOUR UNDERSTANDING

Directions: Complete the following cards. Then answer the multiple choice questions that follow.

LUDWIG VAN BEETHOVEN	CHARLES DARWIN
Time period: _____	Time period: _____
Achievements: _____	Achievements: _____
_____	_____

ALBERT EINSTEIN	PABLO PICASSO
Time period: _____	Time period: _____
Achievements: _____	Achievements: _____
_____	_____

MARGARET THATCHER	HELMUT KOHL
Time period: _____	Time period: _____
Noted for: _____	Noted for: _____
_____	_____

1 Which leader is given much of the credit for reuniting Germany in 1990?
   1 Adolf Hitler   3 Otto von Bismarck
   2 Fidel Castro   4 Helmut Kohl

2 Which idea is Charles Darwin most closely associated with?
   1 "divide and conquer"
   2 theory of natural selection
   3 Divine Right theory
   4 nationalism

3 Albert Einstein's theories helped to form the basis for the
   1 invention of the video recorder
   2 building of the first steam engine
   3 development of atomic weapons
   4 creation of abstract art

4 Picasso and Michelangelo are both known for their achievements in the field of
   1 medicine   3 economics
   2 art   4 government

5 CONCERNS

In this section you will read about some of the problems and issues facing Western Europe today.

THINK ABOUT IT

With the end of the Cold War, Europe is facing several problems. What problems do you see in Europe's future? _____

Important Terms: As you read this section, look for the following terms:

◆ **Irish Republican Army**   ◆ **E.E.C. (Common Market)**

THE REUNIFICATION OF GERMANY

After World War II, Germany was divided into occupation zones by the United States, Great Britain, France and the Soviet Union. By 1948, frequent clashes between the Soviet Union and the three Western allies led to the merging of the Western zones into a new Republic of West Germany. The Soviets then established the East German Republic. Thousands of people fled Communist East Germany to the democratic West. In 1961, to stop this flow, the Soviets erected barbed wire and electrified fences along the border, and built the **Berlin Wall**. (The city of Berlin had a Western zone and an Eastern zone, and was the scene of many escapes from the East. The wall divided the city, making it almost impossible to flee East Berlin.) After the Communist system ended in East Germany in 1989, East and West Germany were reunited, and the Berlin Wall was torn down. Some countries fear that a reunited Germany may become too powerful, but German leaders have assured the world that their country is committed to peace. The eastern part of Germany is very poor, and West Germans are paying billions of dollars to modernize it. Recently Germany has been flooded with refugees from Eastern European countries, fleeing from violence among ethnic groups. They are also seeking better job opportunities. Rising unemployment among German youths has led to unexpected outbreaks of violence against these immigrants.

CIVIL WAR IN NORTHERN IRELAND

Protestant Great Britain took control of Catholic Ireland in the 1500s. Religious differences caused many problems between the two peoples. In 1922, the southern part of Ireland gained independence and became the Republic of Ireland. However, Northern Ireland, a majority of whose people were Protestant, chose to remain a part of Great Britain. The Catholic minority in Northern Ireland wants to be part of the Irish Republic and has had violent clashes with the Protestant majority and Great Britain. Some Catholics have formed the **Irish Republican Army (I.R.A.)**, which has used violence and ◆ **terrorism** to try to achieve Northern Ireland's unification with the Irish Republic.

ANALYSIS

Do you think terrorism is ever justified?_____ Explain why, or why not: _____

_____

_____

_____

FROM THE COMMON MARKET TO A UNITED EUROPE

In 1957, several nations formed the **European Economic Community (E.E.C.)** or "**Common Market**" ◆

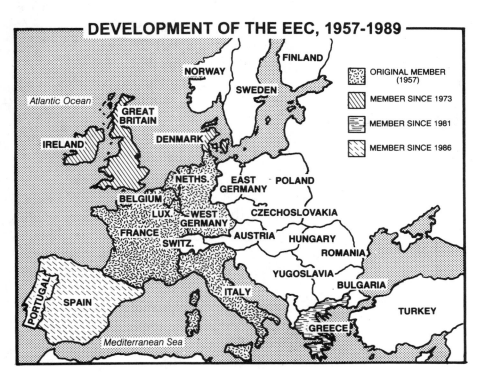

DEVELOPMENT OF THE EEC, 1957-1989

ORIGINAL MEMBER (1957)
MEMBER SINCE 1973
MEMBER SINCE 1981
MEMBER SINCE 1986

Atlantic Ocean
NORWAY
FINLAND
SWEDEN
GREAT BRITAIN
IRELAND
DENMARK
NETHS.
EAST GERMANY
POLAND
BELGIUM
LUX.
WEST GERMANY
CZECHOSLOVAKIA
FRANCE
AUSTRIA
HUNGARY
SWITZ.
ROMANIA
YUGOSLAVIA
BULGARIA
PORTUGAL
SPAIN
ITALY
GREECE
TURKEY
Mediterranean Sea

to eliminate customs duties (*taxes paid when foreign goods are brought into a country to be sold*). The purpose was to make trade easier among E.E.C. nations. Recently its members have moved towards unifying the European economy still further. Eventually all E.E.C. members will use a common currency. There will be no customs officials at the borders; driving from France to Germany will be like driving from New York to New Jersey. E.E.C. members hope to challenge the U.S. and Japan as the world's leading economic power.

SUMMING UP: CONCERNS

Although the Cold War has ended, Europe faces a number of problems. Many people worry about increased German power as a result of reunification. The violence in Northern Ireland has led to many deaths, with no solution in sight. The E.E.C.'s plan to unite Europe may or may not meet with future success. If it does, it could bring great changes to Europe and the world.

THINKING IT OVER

What do you think is the most serious problem for Europe's future? _____

Explain why: _____

CHECKING YOUR UNDERSTANDING

Directions: Complete the following cards. Then answer the multiple choice questions that follow.

IRISH REPUBLICAN ARMY (I.R.A.)

What is it? _____

What is its goal? _____

_____

E.E.C. (COMMON MARKET)

What is it? _____

What are its goals? _____

_____

---

1 Which is a major problem facing Europe today?
   1 increasing birth rates
   2 shortages of investment capital
   3 creating common economic goals
   4 the threat of Communism

2 The major division in Northern Ireland is between
   1 Communists and capitalists
   2 Protestants and Catholics
   3 Muslims and Jews
   4 Hindus and Muslims

3 A major cause of the conflict in Northern Ireland has been over
   1 opposing claims to the Irish throne
   2 economic competition
   3 religious differences
   4 tribal jealousies

4 Which best explains why East and West Germany were reunited in 1990?
   1 the collapse of Soviet Communism
   2 the bombing of Hiroshima
   3 the rise of the Nazi Party
   4 the creation of the United Nations

5 The P.L.O. in the Middle East is similar to the I.R.A. in Northern Ireland in that both are
   1 international peace organizations
   2 political parties
   3 groups that use terrorism
   4 environmental organizations

6 The main goal of the E.E.C. (European Economic Community) is to
   1 eliminate nuclear weapons
   2 create a unified economic force
   3 reduce the growth of population
   4 rebuild war-torn Europe

7 The development of the E.E.C. shows that European nations believe they
1 share common economic goals
2 need to form military alliances
3 seek to create colonial empires
4 want religious unification

8 The Reformation and the civil war in Northern Ireland are similar in that both
1 sought economic reforms
2 involved religious warfare
3 fought against Communism
4 strengthened the Catholic Church's power

SUMMARIZING YOUR UNDERSTANDING

WORD SCRAMBLE

Directions. Use the information you have learned in this and other chapters to unscramble the term being described; spell the word correctly in the shaded boxes.

European writer whose ideas influenced the American Revolution. (**KLOEC**)
L _ _ E

Military efforts to free the Holy Land from Muslims. (**DRAEUCSS**)
_ _ _ _ _ _ S

Total control of a king over his subjects. (**BAOULTSISM**)
_ _ _ _ _ _ _ _ M _

Nazi attempt at genocide of Jews during W.W. II (**CHLOOAUTS**)
H _ _ _ _ _ _ _ _

System based on exchange of land for military service. (**MEUDAFLIS**)
_ _ _ _ _ _ _ M

Political party created by Hitler in Germany. (**ZINA**)
N _ _ _

French Revolution slogan: "Liberty, _____, Fraternity. " (**YETAQUIL**)
_ _ _ _ _ _ _ Y

Rebirth of learning and rediscovery of ancient cultures. (**SRCEENAINSA**)
R _ _ _ _ _ _ _ _ _ _

Leading painter and sculptor of the Renaissance. (**CHALENGLEOMI**)
M _ _ _ _ _ _ _ _ _ _ _

Period following the fall of the Roman Empire. (**DIMDLEGASE**)
M _ _ _ _ _ _ _ _ S

Monk who called for reforms within the Catholic Church. (**THUREL**)
L _ _ _ _ _

Man who seized power and made himself Emperor of France. (**PALONOEN**)
N _ _ _ _ _ _ _

German leader who started World War II. (**THIRLE**)
H _ _ _ _ _

Nation that Otto von Bismarck helped to unify. (**MERANGY**)
_ _ _ _ _ _ Y

Name of treaty that ended World War I. (**SVEALLRSIE**)
_ _ _ _ _ _ _ _ S

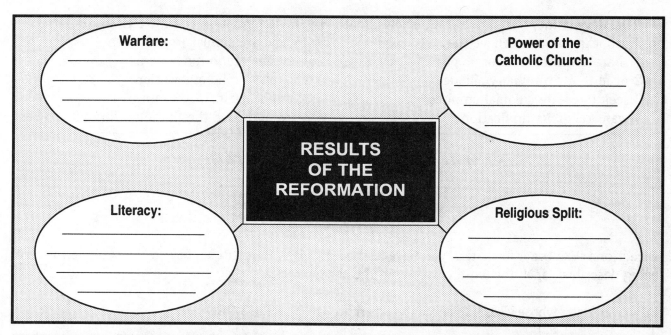

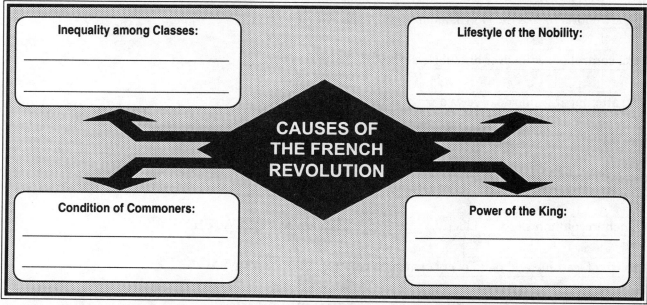

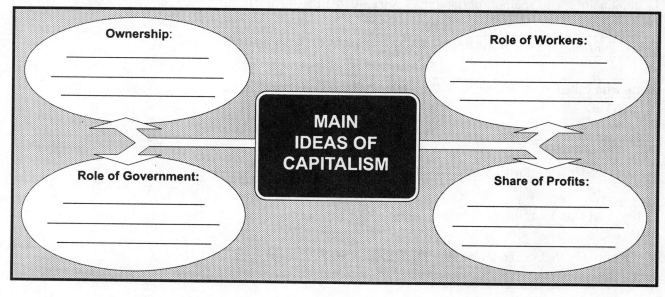

DESCRIBING HISTORICAL EVENTS

Directions: Describe fully an important historical event that you learned about in this chapter. Complete the chart by filling in the information called for in each box.

WHO was involved?

_____

_____

_____

WHEN did it happen?

_____

WORLD WAR II

WHERE was it fought?

_____

_____

_____

WHAT were its major causes?

_____

_____

_____

RESULTS:

1 _____

2 _____

3 _____

4 _____

TEST HELPER — LOOKING AT THE FORCES OF SOCIAL CHANGE

Just as we go through changes in our personal lives, societies also undergo change. The political, social, economic and religious systems of each society are continually changing. The information in this **Test-Helper** section will help you prepare for questions dealing with some of these changes.

MAJOR FORCES OF SOCIAL CHANGE

Historians (*people who study the past*) are especially interested in understanding why and how societies change. The following have been identified as some of the more important causes of major social change:

CONFLICT AMONG GROUPS IN A SOCIETY

Social conflict is one of the basic causes of social change. Many societies are made up of people of different religious and ethnic groups, social classes, ages and backgrounds. Often these groups have conflicting interests. Sometimes these disagreements result in violence or revolution.

NEW IDEAS AND TECHNOLOGY

New ideas can change a society. The introduction of new ways of doing and producing things can also be a powerful factor in historical change. For example, the invention of the printing press helped cause the Reformation by allowing critics of the Catholic Church to communicate their religious ideas widely, through books. Another example is the way British and American ideas about democracy influenced the French Revolution.

CONTACTS WITH OTHER SOCIETIES

Contact with other societies can lead to conflict, war and conquest. It also introduces new ideas through cultural diffusion. The Native American encounter with the Spanish conquistadors, for example, led to the introduction into Europe of new foods like the potato, while horses were introduced into North and South America.

CHANGES IN THE ENVIRONMENT

Changes in the environment can have an impact on society. Today, pollution is suspected of causing a slight warming of the global climate, leading to droughts in Africa and threatening the lives of millions of people.

THE PACE OF CHANGE

Social change can be gradual or very rapid. Gradual change allows different groups and institutions more time to adjust. Rapid changes replace old ways almost overnight. This occurs when new contacts with other societies take place, when new inventions are created, or when new groups challenge the existing order. In a moment of weakness, the existing government collapses and a new group takes charge. For example, the French Revolution was a political revolution in which many changes occurred quickly. Another example of rapid change took place in Japan, when it industrialized soon after re-establishing contact with the West.

TESTING YOUR UNDERSTANDING

Directions: Circle the number preceding the word or expression that correctly answers the statement or question. Following the multiple choice questions, answer the essay questions.

Base your answer to questions 1 through 3 on the timeline below and your knowledge of global studies.

476   **A**   1600   **B**   1915   **C**   1945   **D**   1992

1   Adolf Hitler came to power in the period represented by the letter
   1 A   3 C
   2 B   4 D

2   The Middle Ages were part of the period represented by the letter
   1 A   3 C
   2 B   4 D

3   The invasion of Kuwait by Iraq took place during the period represented by the letter
   1 A   3 C
   2 B   4 D

4   Which geographic feature is paired with its correct location?
   1 Sahara Desert / Pakistan
   2 Gobi Desert / Middle East
   3 Amazon River / Russia
   4 The Alps / Europe

5   Feudalism developed in Europe because it provided
   1 order and stability
   2 a written code of law
   3 a unified European government
   4 a common economic market

6   The role of the knight in medieval Europe was similar to that of the
   1 untouchable in India   3 farmer in Russia
   2 samurai in Japan   4 priest in Vietnam

7   Which headline might appear in a book about the Renaissance?
   1 "Michelangelo Completes Another Painting"
   2 "Karl Marx Attacks Capitalism"
   3 "Adolf Hitler Comes To Power"
   4 "The Industrial Revolution Begins"

8   Divine Right theory was used to justify the
   1 power of the English Parliament
   2 rule of absolute kings
   3 American Revolution
   4 fall of Rome

9   Which phrase is most closely associated with the French Revolution?
   1 "Blood and Iron"
   2 "All men are created equal"
   3 "Peace, Bread, Land"
   4 "Liberty, Equality, Fraternity"

10 The term "Industrial Revolution" refers to
   1 violent uprisings by workers
   2 reforms of the Catholic Church
   3 a movement against kings
   4 changes in the way goods are made

11 Which has been a direct result of the Industrial Revolution?
   1 less emphasis on obtaining an education
   2 increased production by workers
   3 gradual decline in the growth of cities
   4 a decline in the amount of goods

12 Which statement about nationalism is most accurate?
  1 It prevents the rise of militarism.
  2 It leads to greater international cooperation.
  3 It is an idea that can unite a people.
  4 It increases the amount of consumer goods available.

13 Which pair of people shared the same political ideas?
  1 Adolf Hitler and Mohandas Gandhi
  2 Karl Marx and Vladimir Lenin
  3 Josef Stalin and Helmut Kohl
  4 Louis XIV and John Locke

14 A term paper dealing with the topics "Triple Alliance," "League of Nations," and "Archduke Francis Ferdinand" is probably about
  1 Italian unification
  2 Germany under the Nazis
  3 World War I
  4 the life of John Locke

15 Both the manor and the commune are types of
  1 economic organizations
  2 military weapons
  3 terrorist groups
  4 religious buildings

16 Western ideas about democracy were first established by the
  1 Chinese   3 Athenians
  2 Egyptians   4 Mesopotamians

17 Both the Holocaust in Europe and the pogroms in Russia were directed against the
  1 Communists   3 Jews
  2 the Catholic Church 4 Muslims

18 The languages and cultures of Western Europe have been most influenced by
  1 ancient China
  2 the Roman Empire
  3 ancient Mesopotamia
  4 the Mayan Empire

19 The Crusades, the Reformation and the civil war in Northern Ireland are all based on
  1 religious conflicts
  2 the right to vote
  3 economic competition
  4 freedom of speech

20 The Marshall Plan was a program to
  1 end tribal warfare in Africa
  2 rebuild Europe after World War II
  3 reform the caste system in India
  4 increase religious unity in Europe

ESSAYS

1 A nation's political system often affects how its people live.

Political Systems

Democracy   Divine Right
Feudalism   Totalitarianism

Part A

Select *two* political systems. For each one selected, list *two* characteristics of that type of system, and then list *one* effect it might have on people living under that type of system.

POLITICAL SYSTEM	CHARACTERISTICS	EFFECT
A _____	1 _____ 2 _____	1 _____
B _____	1 _____ 2 _____	1 _____

Part B
In your part B answer, you should use information you gave in Part A. However, you may also include different or additional information in your Part B answer.

Write an essay starting with the topic sentence:

A nation's political system often affects how its people live.

2 Revolutions are great events whose impact is often felt world-wide.

Revolutions

Industrial Revolution (1750s)
French Revolution (1789)
Russian Revolution (1917)
Cuban Revolution (1960s)
Iranian Revolution (1979)

Part A
Choose *one* revolution listed above: _____

1 Identify *two* major changes that were brought about by that revolution:

   a _____

   b _____

Part B
In your part B answer, you should use information you gave in Part A. However, you may also include different or additional information in your Part B answer.

Explain how revolutions can have an impact that is felt world-wide.

3   Some people's ideas have influenced the development of the world. Each individual below is paired with a development that is associated with him.

Person / Development

Martin Luther / Reformation
John Locke / Spread of Democracy
Otto von Bismarck / German Unification
Karl Marx / Communism
Pablo Picasso / Modern Art
Adolf Hitler / World War II

Part A

1. Choose *one* person listed above: _____

   State *how* that person was associated with the development with which he is paired:

   _____

   _____

2. Choose *another* person listed above: _____

   State *how* that person was associated with the development with which he is paired:

   _____

   _____

Part B

In your part B answer, you should use information you gave in Part A. However, you may also include different or additional information in your Part B answer.

Write an essay explaining how some people's ideas have greatly influenced the historical development of the world.

GLOBAL CHECKLIST

WESTERN EUROPE

Directions: Before going on to the next chapter, you should check your understanding of the import-ant people, terms and concepts covered in this chapter. Place a check (✔) mark next to those that you remember. If you have trouble recalling a term, refer to the page number following it.

A meeting of the United Nations General Assembly

❑ Eurasia (238)
❑ City-states (243)
❑ Roman Empire (244)
❑ Feudalism (244)
❑ Middle Ages (244)
❑ Crusades (245)
❑ Manor (245)
❑ Renaissance (247)
❑ Reformation (248)
❑ Martin Luther (248)
❑ Absolutism (249)
❑ Divine Right (249)

❑ Enlightenment (250)
❑ French Revolution (251)
❑ Capitalism (256)
❑ Industrial Revolution (256)
❑ Balance of Power (258)
❑ League of Nations (259)
❑ Treaty of Versailles (259)
❑ Totalitarianism (260)
❑ Adolf Hitler (260)
❑ World War II (261)
❑ Holocaust (261)
❑ Nuremberg Trials (261)

❑ Marshall Plan (262)
❑ United Nations (262)
❑ NATO (262)
❑ Warsaw Pact (262)
❑ Socialism (268)
❑ Charles Darwin (269)
❑ Ludwig van Beethoven (272)
❑ Pablo Picasso (272)
❑ Albert Einstein (272)
❑ Margaret Thatcher (272)
❑ I.R.A. (275)
❑ E.E.C. (275)

CHAPTER 10

GLOBAL CONCERNS

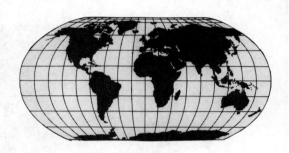

1
GLOBAL PROBLEMS

Only a few hundred years ago, people rarely traveled outside their own village. Each culture had little contact or knowledge about others. Now, new methods of communication and transportation have changed all this. The television and telephone bring us even closer together. Such changes have helped bring about a world that is more **interdependent**, where each nation depends on other nations. As a result, what happens in one part of the globe has world-wide effects. This section takes a look at some of these global problems.

THINK ABOUT IT

The world today faces many serious problems. Can you name some of them?

1. _____   3. _____

2. _____   4. _____

Important Terms: As you read this section, look for the following terms:

- ◆ AIDS
- ◆ Desertification
- ◆ Deforestation
- ◆ Population Growth

AIDS

THE PROBLEM. Acquired Immune Deficiency Syndrome (**AIDS**) is caused by a virus that prevents the body's immune system from fighting disease. People with AIDS then die from catching other infectious diseases they cannot fight off. It is rapidly becoming one of the most serious problems facing modern society. It has been estimated that AIDS may affect more than 100 million people world-wide.

POSSIBLE SOLUTIONS. There is no known cure. To fight the disease, governments have set up educational programs to make people aware of steps they can take to prevent the spread of AIDS. In addition, many nations are increasing their spending on research to try to find a cure. While some progress has been made, scientists fear the AIDS virus will also appear in new forms.

POPULATION GROWTH

THE PROBLEM. The world's population is increasing at a rapid rate. If this continues, the world's population will be well over 10 billion people by the 21st century. Such growth threatens to create severe housing, fuel, food and water shortages. The problem is particularly serious in developing countries, since they are often unable to grow enough food to feed their present population. Despite this, many families continue to have many children. Large families often represent a form of status for the parents. In addition, children carry on the family name, provide a source of labor and give support to parents when they become too old to work.

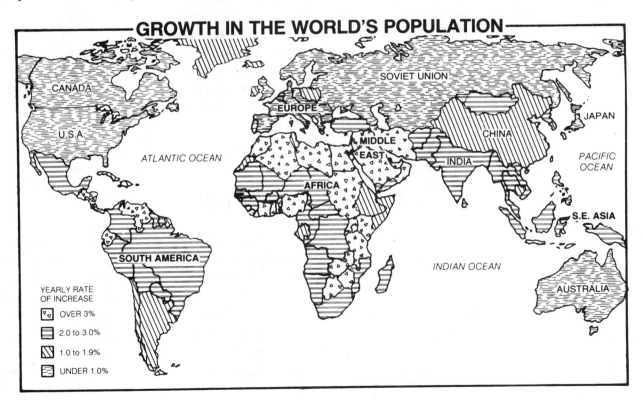

GROWTH IN THE WORLD'S POPULATION

YEARLY RATE OF INCREASE
- OVER 3%
- 2.0 to 3.0%
- 1.0 to 1.9%
- UNDER 1.0%

POSSIBLE SOLUTIONS. Suggestions for lowering the birth rate include increased efforts to educate people about **family planning** — teaching birth control methods, introducing new forms of birth control and giving rewards to those who have smaller families. China has been especially strict in enforcing its family planning policies (see page 161).

HUNGER AND MALNUTRITION

THE PROBLEM. Only a few nations are able to produce more food than they need. These few nations contain only a small part of the world's total population. For the rest—especially the developing nations of Asia, Africa, Latin America and the Middle East—hunger and **malnutrition** (*a condition caused by not eating enough proper foods*) are daily facts of life. In some areas, conditions are made worse by serious **droughts** (*lack of rainfall*). As a result, large numbers of people die from hunger each year.

POSSIBLE SOLUTIONS. Better ways of growing food are being introduced, including the planting of high-yield crops which need shorter growing periods and produce much bigger harvests. However, ending widespread hunger cannot come about until some other problems are solved: civil wars, religious and cultural clashes, and rapid population growth in many parts of the world pose great obstacles to growing and distributing more food.

Jehan Sadat

PROFILES
IN
HISTORY

Jehan Sadat grew up in an area traditionally dominated by men. Her husband, Anwar Sadat, was a revolutionary hero 15 years older than she who became the leader of Egypt, Mrs. Sadat was the first wife of a Muslim leader to travel outside her own country and to have her photo appear in a newspaper. Jehan Sedat is a women's rights advocate; she helped reform Egypt's divorce laws, became a spokesperson for family planning, and has campaigned against gender discrimination. To emphasize women's need for education, she enrolled in college and received a Ph.D at age 41. Asserting the need for women in politics, she ran for office as an independent candidate. She has dedicated her life to breaking traditional barriers and winning increased rights for Muslim women.

ENVIRONMENTAL POLLUTION

THE PROBLEM. As the countries of the world have become more developed, pollution of the earth's air, water, soil and natural resources has become an even greater threat. Although the problem affects every corner of the globe, it is particularly serious in highly industrialized nations. Industrial growth often brings an increase in the amount of pollutants released into the air. These toxic (*poisonous*) substances create such problems as **acid rain**, which puts harmful chemicals into waterways and forests, harming or killing trees and fish. Another problem is the thinning out of the **ozone layer** that protects the earth from the harmful effects of the sun's radiation. Some scientists predict that because of harmful pollutants in the air, the earth may become several degrees warmer in the future. This "**greenhouse effect**" (*global warming trend*) may have serious consequences. Because it will cause changes in the world's weather patterns, local climates will be affected; places where much of the world's food is now grown may become hotter and more desert-like, and ocean levels may rise, causing serious flooding.

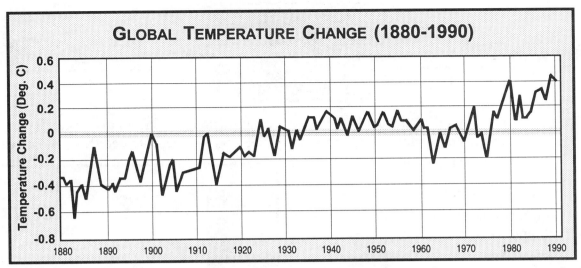

Source: NASA Goddard Institute for Space Studies

POSSIBLE SOLUTIONS. It important to educate people about the results of pollution. Once they understand the problems, private individuals and governments can agree on the steps needed to begin to restore a healthy world environment. Governments can ban chemical dumping into streams and oceans, limit the amount of pollutants that lead to acid rain, and prohibit the use of **fluorocarbons** (*chemicals that wear away the ozone layer*). Even nations that are leaders in educating their citizens about pollution have not yet taken the steps needed to reduce it—because in the short run, it is cheaper to pollute than worry about its effects. However, the earth's environment must be preserved for future generations. For this reason, world leaders met at an international conference in Rio de Janeiro, Brazil, in the summer of 1992 to try to decide on measures to reduce global pollution.

Having trouble understanding the following bar graph? It will help if you first read the **Skill Builder** section on bar graphs that appears on the next page.

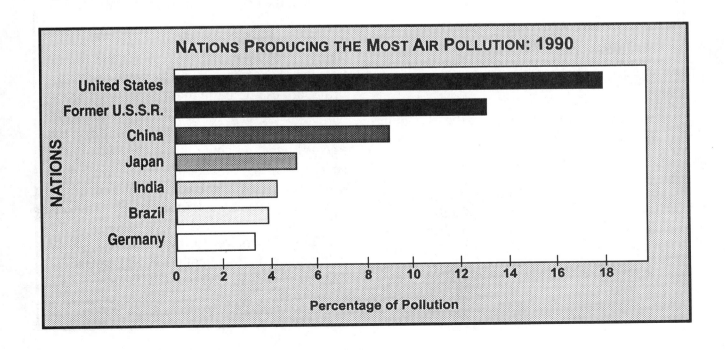

Sometimes tests contain questions based on a bar graph. This section explains bar graphs and how to answer this type of question.

What Is A Bar Graph?
A bar graph is a chart showing parallel bars of different lengths. Its main function is to compare several items.

Keys to Understanding a Bar Graph
First, look at its main components:

Title. The title states the overall topic. In the bar graph on the *previous page*, the title is "Nations Producing the Most Air Pollution: 1990." Thus the graph shows which nations emitted the most air pollution in the year 1990.

Legend. If more than one type of bar is used, the legend explains what each type of bar represents. However, since there is only type of bar in our graph (showing percentages of air pollution), no legend is needed.

Vertical and Horizontal Axis. Bar graphs are composed of a *vertical axis* (which runs from top to bottom) and a *horizontal axis* (which runs from left to right). In our graph, the vertical axis indicates the *items* that are being compared (the nations); the horizontal axis shows the *amount* of each of these items (the percentage of air pollution).

Note: Some bar graphs show the bars running up and down instead of sideways. In that case, the vertical axis indicates the amount being compared, and the horizontal axis shows the items. For instance, the infor-

mation on air pollution in our graph on page 289 could be represented this way instead:

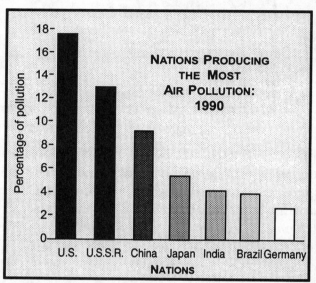

The only difference between an up-and-down type bar graph and a sideways bar graph is what the vertical and horizontal axes represent. In the small graph above, the horizontal axis shows the items (nations), while the vertical axis shows the amount (percentage of pollution by each nation).

Interpreting a Bar Graph
Start by looking at the title, to get the overall meaning of the information. To find specific information, examine the individual bars. For example, how large a share of global pollution was caused by Brazil? *Do this on the bar graph on the previous page*: go down the vertical axis to the bar representing Brazil. Next, run your finger across to the end of the bar. If you look at the percentage scale at the bottom, along the horizontal axis, you'll see that the bar ends at about 4%. Thus, the answer to the question — How large a share of global pollution was caused by Brazil in 1990? — is about 4%.

DEFORESTATION ◆

THE PROBLEM. The rain forests of South America, Africa, and Southeast Asia provide much of the world's oxygen. They are also home to over half of our planet's animal and plant species, and provide 25% of our medicines. However, countries are clearing their rain forests (**deforestation**) at the rate of 96,000 acres a day—selling wood for much-needed cash and making the land available to grow more food. For example, the government of Brazil is building a long highway through the Amazon rain forest. To make it easier for people to get there, the land is being cleared. However, once the trees are cut down, heavy rains wash away nutrients and the quality of the soil becomes so poor that it will produce only a few crops. Then the people have to move to a new area and cut down still more trees.

The World's Tropical Rainforests

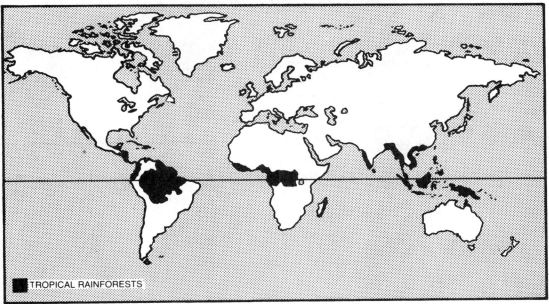

TROPICAL RAINFORESTS

POSSIBLE SOLUTIONS. An international campaign is taking place to save the world's rain forests. Measures such as educating farmers about soil erosion, replanting trees, and restricting cattle grazing are also being encouraged. At the international conference on world environment at Rio de Janeiro in 1992, most countries signed a treaty aimed at preserving **biological diversity** (*the variety of species of plants and animals*). More than half of these species are found only in the world's rain forests, and governments are developing ways to protect them from extinction.

DESERTIFICATION ◆

THE PROBLEM. In some areas, especially in Africa just south of the Sahara Desert, attempts have been made to increase food production by clearing large areas of land. The cut trees are then used for firewood. This practice of clearing the land, along with many years of drought, has led to **desertification** (*an expansion of desert land*).

POSSIBLE SOLUTIONS. Ways must be found to halt the erosion of the soil. Possible solutions include **reforestation** (*planting new trees*), limiting cattle grazing and educating people about the causes of desertification.

HUMAN RIGHTS VIOLATIONS

The Problem: Human rights have been defined as basic rights that all people need. They include the right to life, equal protection of the laws, freedom from arrest without reason, and laws against torture and enslavement. In some countries, governments do not permit people to have basic rights. Military governments and dictatorships are often the worst abusers of human rights.

Possible solutions: Many nations have signed the Universal Declaration of Human Rights. Groups such as Amnesty International expose human rights violations. Some governments make the promotion of human rights an important part of their foreign policy.

SUMMING UP: GLOBAL PROBLEMS

Problems like overpopulation, hunger, pollution, deforestation and AIDS, while occurring more in some areas than others, have become world problems affecting everyone.

THINKING IT OVER

Were you correct in identifying some of the major problems facing the world?_____ Which do you *now* think is the most serious problem? _____

_____

CHECKING YOUR UNDERSTANDING

Directions: Complete the following cards. Then answer the multiple choice questions that follow.

AIDS

What is it? _____

Why is it a problem? _____

_____

Suggested solutions: _____

_____

DEFORESTATION

What is it? _____

Why is it a problem? _____

_____

Suggested solutions: _____

_____

```
┌─────────────────────────────────┐
│        DESERTIFICATION          │
│                                 │
│ What is it?  _____  │
│                                 │
│ Why is it a problem? _____  │
│ _____│
│                                 │
│ Suggested solutions: _____  │
│ _____│
└─────────────────────────────────┘
```

```
┌─────────────────────────────────┐
│       POPULATION GROWTH         │
│                                 │
│ What is it? _____  │
│                                 │
│ Why is it a problem? _____  │
│ _____│
│                                 │
│ Suggested solutions: _____  │
│ _____│
└─────────────────────────────────┘
```

1 "Fluorocarbons" "greenhouse effect," and "wearing away of the ozone layer" are phrases most closely associated with
1 the environment
2 the population explosion
3 hunger and malnutrition
4 nuclear weapons

2 One reason for the concern about future energy shortages is because
1 there is a decreasing demand for energy
2 there is a lack of investment capital
3 government regulations are increasing
4 the earth's resources are limited

3 In an outline, one of these is a main topic and the other three are sub-topics. Which is the main topic?
1 World Problems   3 Deforestation
2 Desertification   4 Population Growth

4 Which global problem is a cause of the other three?
1 not enough land for growing crops
2 hunger and malnutrition
3 energy shortages
4 population growth

5 Which is a feature most commonly associated with deforestation?
1 an increased foreign debt
2 a loss of plant and animal life
3 an increased oxygen supply
4 an increase in AIDS

6 The term "desertification" is often used when referring to
1 military actions used by absolute rulers
2 killing of Jewish people in Nazi Germany
3 racial policies used in South Africa
4 growth of wastelands from drought

2 GLOBAL TRENDS For centuries, nations were mainly self-sufficient (*producing themselves most of what they needed*). Contact between nations was limited by great distances and the difficulties of travel. Revolutions in technology, transportation and other fields have changed the world. Today, most nations have come to realize how truly interconnected we all are.

Name one important change that has occurred during your lifetime in each of the following areas.

Computers: _____

Space Exploration: _____

Automation: _____

Communications: _____

Important Terms: As you read this section, look for the following terms:

◆ **Technology**   ◆ **Automation**

TECHNOLOGY IN A CHANGING WORLD

We live in a world that is undergoing constant change. One major reason for this change is the improvements brought about by **technology** (*putting science to practical uses*). In the 20th century, technology has increased the pace of cultural diffusion. Some societies face serious problems adjusting to these technological advances. For example, in Iran, Islamic Fundamentalist leaders oppose the influence that Western ideas and modern technology have on their traditions. However, technology can have many positive effects on a society.

THE COMPUTER REVOLUTION

When first developed, the computer needed a large building to house its memory unit. Today, with the invention of **silicon chips**, computers can perform millions of calculations in seconds, and are small enough to hold in the palm of your hand. Computers free people from paperwork that once took thousands of hours. They make possible all kinds of modern conveniences, like automatic banking, compact disks, and calculators. However, some people are concerned that large amounts of information stored in computers might lead to abuses of people's rights to privacy.

◆AUTOMATION

Automation (*the use of machines to replace human labor*) has helped make many tasks much easier. This helps societies make products at lower cost, but it also reduces the number of workers needed to make most products, reducing jobs. Some economists believe that new jobs are created in different fields just as quickly as old ones are eliminated. Workers trained for simpler tasks, however, may not be able to easily change over to new jobs which require different skills.

TRANSPORTATION

When industry adapted the engine to power automobiles, ships and airplanes, the impact on people's lives was enormous. Cars allow people to travel quickly to places that once took days to reach. However, the increased use of cars has brought smog, pollution and clogged highways in many cities.

COMMUNICATIONS

Inventions such as the telephone, radio, television and fax machines now permit almost instant communication between people thousands of miles apart. As a result, some people now call the world a **global village** as a result. People are better informed today, but some find it difficult to cope with ever-increasing amounts of information.

SPACE: THE NEXT FRONTIER

In 1957, the Soviets launched an artificial satellite, **Sputnik I**. This began a contest between the United States and the Soviet Union to see which country could put people on the moon first. These efforts became known as the "**space race**." In 1969, the United States placed the first person on the moon. The United States and the Soviet Union carried out many other important space projects, sending astronauts and satellites deep into space with greater frequency. However, space exploration is very costly. Some argue that the money could be better spent on such things as medical research, improving education and helping the poor. Others disagree: they point out that space exploration has contributed to the development of many new products, such as improved computers.

SUMMING UP: GLOBAL TRENDS

The world is constantly undergoing change. Many of these changes have had both positive and negative effects. Certain societies have not been in agreement with some of the changes brought about by advances in technology.

THINKING IT OVER

In your lifetime, which single change in the world do you think has had the greatest impact?

_____ Why? _____

_____

CHECKING YOUR UNDERSTANDING

Directions: Complete the following cards. Then answer the multiple choice questions that follow.

TECHNOLOGY
What is it? _____
How has it changed the world?_____
_____

AUTOMATION
What is it?_____
Advantages:_____
Disadvantages:_____

1 Technology in the 20th century has
   1 eliminated famine and disease in the world
   2 delayed progress in developing nations
   3 increased the rate of cultural diffusion
   4 decreased political reforms

2 A newspaper article about silicon chips would mainly deal with
   1 computers
   2 politics
   3 music
   4 the environment

3 Global problems, such as environmental pollution and hunger, reflect a need for
   1 increased international cooperation
   2 policies of economic nationalism
   3 reduced foreign aid to developing nations
   4 increased military spending by all nations

4 Technology is often viewed as a threat by traditional societies because it
   1 may bring changes in traditional values
   2 threatens to bring Communism
   3 lowers standards of living
   4 prevents cultural diffusion

SUMMARIZING YOUR UNDERSTANDING

WORKING WITH A MAP

Part A. Place the number of each item in its proper location on the outline map below. If you have trouble locating an item, check some of the maps found throughout this book.

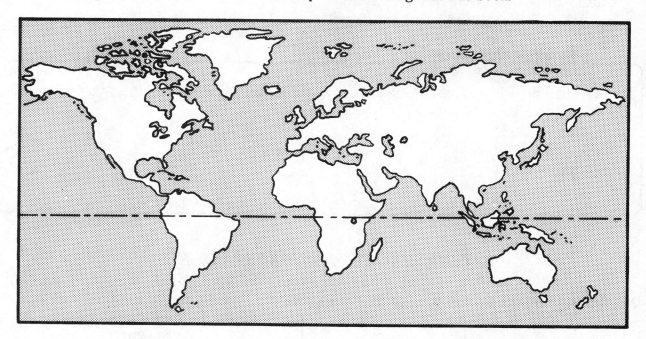

OCEANS	SEAS	NATIONS	LANDFORMS
1. Atlantic 2. Pacific 3. Indian	4. Mediterranean 5. Caribbean 6. North 7. Red 8. Arabian	9. China 10. India 11. South Africa 12. U.S. 13. C.I.S.	14. Himalayan Mts. 15. Sahara Desert

Part A. On the map on page 296, first locate and then write the letter identifying each country or region listed below. Then indicate a problem or concern facing that area.

COUNTRY OR REGION	PROBLEM OR CONCERN FACING THAT AREA
A. (_Africa_)	_____ _____ _____
B. (_Latin America_)	_____ _____ _____
C. (_Europe_)	_____ _____ _____
D. (_Asia_)	_____ _____ _____
E. (_C.I.S._)	_____ _____ _____
F. (_Middle East_)	_____ _____ _____

Directions: Describe below four causes of hunger in the world today.

Directions: Describe below the trends occurring in the four areas listed.

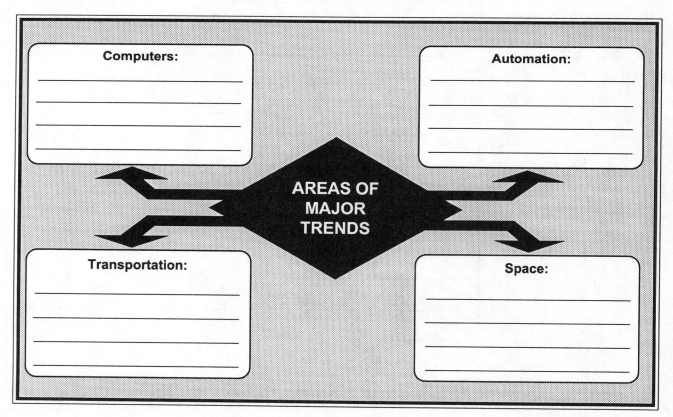

LOOKING AT TECHNOLOGY

TEST HELPER

Technology (*the use of knowledge and skills to make and do things*) makes it possible for us to change and adapt to nature, and to enjoy better standards of living. This **Test-Helper** section will help you to answer questions dealing with technology.

MILESTONES IN THE HISTORY OF TECHNOLOGY

Each generation builds on the achievements of the past. We can therefore begin by looking at the historical development of technology.

THE NEOLITHIC REVOLUTION (about 8000 B.C.)

The Neolithic Revolution first occurred in Mesopotamia and Egypt about 10,000 years ago when people discovered how to grow crops by planting seeds. They also learned how to tame and use animals to do work. These developments allowed people to live in one place, establish villages and to have a settled way of life.

THE RISE OF CIVILIZATIONS (about 3000 B.C.)

A "civilized" society is one where people live in organized communities and some people know how to read and write. Early civilizations invented the sailboat and the wheel; mined metals; built palaces, temples, tombs and monuments; developed religion, philosophy, calendars and alphabets; and produced magnificent works of art, literature and poetry.

THE CHINESE ACHIEVEMENT (1st century A.D. through 13th century)

The Chinese originated many major inventions we still use today. They developed paper, invented water clocks to measure time, and built the Great Wall in the northwest part of China. In addition, they developed early ironwork, fine porcelain, silk, the magnetic compass, block printing and gunpowder.

IMPROVEMENTS IN EUROPE (14th century through early 18th century)

A number of important technological advances occurred in Europe as a result of contacts with the Middle East and China. One important invention was the printing press. This allowed the printing of newspapers, pamphlets and books, which led to an information explosion. During the "scientific revolution" and the Enlightenment of the 1600s and 1700s, thinkers developed new ways of looking at the world. They believed they could discover fixed laws of nature and use this knowledge to change their environment for the benefit of humankind.

THE INDUSTRIAL REVOLUTION (late 18th century through 19th century)

The Industrial Revolution began in Great Britain at a time when Britain was the world's leading imperialist power. A series of important inventions made it possible for British factory owners to apply steam power to run machines for spinning and weaving cotton cloth. This allowed them to produce more cloth at a much cheaper price than handmade cloth. Steam power was next used to build railroads and steamships.

THE AGE OF RAPID CHANGE (20th Century)

By the beginning of the 20th century, there was a conscious effort to promote scientific research and technology. The result has been an almost continuous stream of major inventions throughout the century: the airplane, automobile, radio, television, radar, antibiotics, nuclear energy, missiles, and the computer. Each of these has had a major impact on our social and cultural development.

FACTORS BEHIND THE DEVELOPMENT OF TECHNOLOGY

Sociologists (*people who study society*) believe that some of the main factors affecting the pace of technological development are:

THE ROLE OF TRADITION

Many societies pride themselves on following ancient ways. These traditional societies are not interested in technological progress, and they attempt to preserve traditions. In these societies, technological progress is slow.

EXCHANGE OF THOUGHT AND EXPRESSION

Progress is helped by the exchange of ideas. In societies where the government controls the thoughts and expressions of individuals, technological advances are difficult. Technological progress is greatest when a society promotes the work of inventors and scientists by providing a system of rewards.

CULTURAL DIFFUSION AND ADAPTATION

An important factor in technological progress has been **cultural diffusion** (*the spread of ideas and technologies from one culture to another*). During the Crusades, new products, ideas and techniques were exchanged between the Islamic world and the Europeans. Sometimes groups oppose contacts with other cultures because they fear that new ideas will threatens their traditional order. For example, Japan limited contact with Europe from the 17th to the 19th centuries. Other groups, however, welcome foreign ideas because they believe their society will be improved by them. In Imperial Russia, Peter the Great borrowed Western European technologies to develop the country.

THE CHALLENGE OF MODERN SCIENCE

Technology is a tool placed in our hands. The existence of this tool does not guarantee that humans will put it to good use. For example, improvements in technology have made weapons much more destructive than before. Thus technology can be compared to a hammer. We can use a hammer to drive nails into wood to build a house, or use the same hammer to destroy our neighbor's house — the choice lies with each nation and its people, not with the hammer.

TESTING YOUR UNDERSTANDING

Directions: Circle the number preceding the word or expression that correctly answers the statement or question. Following the multiple choice questions, answer the essay questions.

Base your answer to questions 1 through 3 on the following bar graph and on your knowledge of global studies.

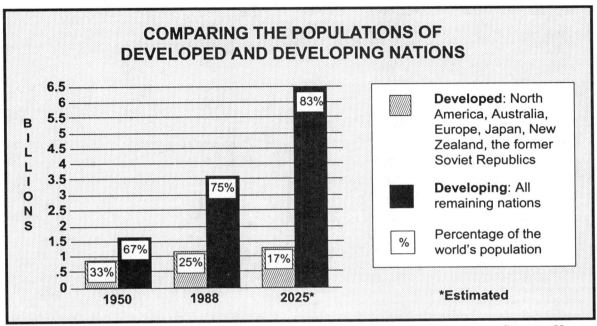

Source: Unesco

1 According to the graph, the total population of the world in 2025 will be
   1 almost 6.5 billion people
   2 exactly 4.8 billion people
   3 about 1.3 billion people
   4 nearly 7.8 billion people

2 According to the graph, which statement is correct?
   1 The population in developing nations is increasing faster than in developed nations.
   2 The population in developed nations is expected to double in the next 25 years
   3 The population in developing and developed nations has remained unchanged.
   4 The population in developing nations is decreasing.

3 If the current trend shown in the graph continues, a likely result will be that
   1 most people in developed countries will move to the countryside
   2 traditional family values in developed countries will decline
   3 housing and food shortages will occur in developing nations
   4 developing countries will refuse to accept foreign aid

4 Cultural diffusion occurs most rapidly in societies that
   1 follow traditional social values
   2 have frequent contact with other societies
   3 have extended families
   4 lack a written language

5 Which statement concerning world hunger to-day is most accurate?
1 Hunger exists in only the industrialized nations of the West.
2 Hunger has been eliminated in almost every nation.
3 Rapid world population growth continues makes it difficult to end hunger.
4 Because the world's population is decreasing, hunger is no longer a problem.

6 Damage from acid rain and the wearing away of the earth's ozone layer indicates a need for
1 the elimination of international trade
2 greater international cooperation over the environment
3 an increase of military alliances
4 the nationalization of all small industries

7 An appearance of the Moscow Ballet on Broadway would be an example of
1 social mobility   3 cultural diffusion
2 overpopulation   4 desertification

8 Which environmental problem is currently facing many nations?
1 cultural diffusion   3 ethnic diversity
2 religious differences   4 acid rain

9 Global interdependence is best illustrated by
1 an increase of nationalism in developed nations
2 the rise of democratic governments in the world
3 one nation buying needed items from a nation in another area
4 a colony breaking all ties with its former "mother country"

10 "The world is moving closer to becoming a global village." Which statement best explains the meaning of this quotation?
1 Most people today live in villages.
2 Problems in one part of the world often affect other parts of the world.
3 The world is moving towards a single government.
4 People are moving from cities to villages.

ANSWERING ESSAY QUESTIONS ABOUT GLOBAL PROBLEMS

Often a test will have questions about problems facing the world. Although the specific questions will vary, they generally focus on:

A. **Defining the Problem.** Here you are expected to describe the nature of the problem. It is very helpful to go through a mental checklist — **who, what, where, when** — in describing or defining the problem. For example, you may be asked to describe how new technology can cause serious problems in developing areas. You could write something like:

> Deforestation occurs when nations cut down their forests. Brazil is using modern machinery to cut down some of the Amazon rain forest. This leads to **soil erosion** (*heavy rains washing away the soil*) and depletes the soil's nutrients.

B. **Identifying the Causes.** Causes deal with the **reasons** that led to the problem. You are expected to explain **why** something came about. For example, you might explain:

> People have longer lives now than at any time in history, as a result of advances in modern medicine. This has led to overpopulation by decreasing the death rate.

C. Explaining the Effects. You are expected to explain the effects or impact that the problem is having on a nation or the world. For example, you might write:

> Environmental pollution is causing acid rain. This is killing trees in forests throughout parts of Canada and the United States.

D. Providing Some Solutions. You are expected to discuss **some actions** that have been taken by governments or private groups to solve the problem, or you might be expected to make some recommendations of your own to help solve the problem. For example, you might write:

> Educational programs about safe sex are being used to help combat the spread of AIDS.

A HELPFUL SUGGESTION

To get better results from studying, think about all four aspects of each problem: *defining* the problem, identifying its *causes*, explaining its *effects*, and providing some *solutions*.

Now answer the following practice essay question on global problems.

1 There are many problems facing the world today.

Problems

AIDS Epidemic	Deforestation
Desertification	Hunger and Malnutrition
Energy Shortages	Environmental Pollution

Part A

Select a problem: _____

State why this has become a problem: _____

> Note that the question asks you to state *why* something came about. You are expected to give the *reasons* that led to the problem.)

Select another problem: _____

State why this has become a problem: _____

Part B

In your part B answer, you should use information you gave in Part A. However, you may also include different or additional information in your Part B answer.

Write an essay beginning with this topic sentence:

There are many problems facing the world today.

ANSWERING ESSAY QUESTIONS ABOUT GLOBAL TRENDS

A **trend** is a pattern of change that points in some direction. Several trends occurring throughout the world today have had an important impact on our future, and will continue to do so. Often a test will have questions about current trends. Again, the specific questions vary, but they generally focus on:

A. **Defining the Trend**. Here you are expected to describe the trend or development. Again, it is very helpful to go through a mental checklist — **who, what, where, when** — in defining the trend. For example, when answering a question on how the role of women has recently changed in many developing countries, you might write:

> The traditional role of women is changing. Women who used to stay home to take care of their children now go off to work, study at colleges, and run for political office.

B. **Predicting the Effects**. Here you are expected to discuss the effect or impact on society that the trend has had or is likely to have. For example, you might write:

> As the role of women changes, there has also been a change in traditional life-styles. The father is no longer the only provider, and women are sharing in important decisions within the family. In some homes, men now share the household tasks.

A HELPFUL SUGGESTION

To get better results from studying, make sure you can *define* the trend or development and can **predict** its effects.

Now answer the following practice essay question on global trends.

2 The rapid rate of change in many areas is affecting life-styles all around the world.

Areas of Change
Communications   Transportation
Computers   Space Exploration

Part A

Select *two* areas of change from the list. State *one* specific change that has taken place in that area and *one* effect of this change on the life-style anywhere in the world.

> Note that you are asked to *describe* the changes taking place, and their *effects* (what is happening because of them).

Area of Change	Change Taking Place	An Effect of the Change
A _____	1. _____ _____	1. _____ _____
B _____	2. _____ _____	2. _____ _____

Part B

In your part B answer, you should use information you gave in Part A. However, you may also include different or additional information in your Part B answer.

Write an essay explaining how changes in many areas are affecting life-styles around the world.

GLOBAL CHECKLIST

GLOBAL CONCERNS

Directions: Check your understanding of the important people, terms and concepts covered in this chapter. Place a check (✔) mark next to those that you remember. If you have trouble recalling a particular term, refer to the page number following the item.

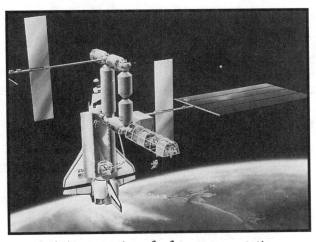

Artist's conception of a future space station

- ❏ Interdependent (286)
- ❏ AIDS (287)
- ❏ Malnutrition (280)
- ❏ Family planning (287)
- ❏ Drought (288)
- ❏ Jehan Sedat (288)
- ❏ Ozone layer (288)
- ❏ Acid rain (288)
- ❏ Greenhouse effect (288)
- ❏ Global warming (288)
- ❏ Deforestation (291)
- ❏ Biological diversity (291)
- ❏ Desertification (291)
- ❏ Reforestation (291)
- ❏ Fossil fuels (292)
- ❏ Technology (294)
- ❏ Computer Revolution (294)
- ❏ Silicon chips (294)
- ❏ Automation (294)
- ❏ Global Village (295)
- ❏ Space race (295)

CHAPTER 11

A FINAL REVIEW

This chapter is divided into two sections. The first section helps you to bring together everything you have learned and to prepare for a comprehensive test in global studies. The second section provides you with a review of the concepts and terms used in this book—the key items that you must know in order to do well on any final examination in global studies.

FORMS OF GOVERNMENT

Throughout history, nations have created different types of government. These forms of government are usually characterized by some leading idea or belief. Summarize your knowledge of the different types of governments about which you have read by completing the following chart (*the last column indicates the page where you can read about the item if you have trouble recalling it*):

Note: We have started the first chart for you.

GOVERNMENT	ITS MAJOR IDEA OR FEATURES	EXAMPLE	PAGE
DEMOCRACY	*People have control over government, either directly or indirectly by electing representatives.*	*City-State of Athens*	57
FEUDALISM			244
DIVINE RIGHT			249
ABSOLUTISM			249
TOTALITARIANISM			260

IMPORTANT HISTORICAL PERIODS

History is often divided into special time periods, to make it easier to study past events. Historical periods are usually characterized by some leading idea or belief. Summarize your knowledge of important historical periods about which you have read by completing the following chart:

TIME PERIOD	MAJOR IDEA OR FEATURE	PAGE
ANCIENT EGYPT (3000 B.C.-100 B.C.)		85
MIDDLE AGES (500-1500)		244
AGE OF EXPLORATION (1500-1600)		247
RENAISSANCE (1400-1600)		247
REFORMATION (1500-1600)		248
ENLIGHTENMENT (1700-1800)		250
AGE OF ABSOLUTISM (1600-1750)		249
AGE OF IMPERIALISM (1880-1945)		257
COLD WAR (1945-1991)		211

DESCRIBING HISTORICAL EVENTS

Directions: Fully describe an important historical event about which you learned by filling in the information called for in each box.

WHO was involved?

_____

_____

WHEN did it happen?

_____

_____

WORLD WAR I

WHERE was it fought?

_____

_____

WHAT were its main causes?

_____

_____

RESULTS:

1. _____

2. _____

3. _____

4. _____

TYPES OF ECONOMIC SYSTEMS

Throughout history, people have organized their economic systems to help them meet their needs. These economic systems are often based on some major idea or goal. Summarize your knowledge of the various economic systems about which you have read by completing the following chart:

ECONOMIC SYSTEM	ITS MAJOR IDEAS OR FEATURES	EXAMPLE	PAGE
TRADITIONAL			90
MANORIALISM			244
CAPITALISM			57
IMPERIALISM			18
COMMUNISM			153

MAJOR GROUPS AND ORGANIZATIONS

Letters often represent the names of organizations. Summarize your knowledge of the various organizations you have studied by completing the following chart:

GROUP OR ORGANIZATION	WHAT ITS LETTERS STAND FOR	ITS MAJOR GOAL	PAGE
U.N.			262
O.P.E.C.			99
O.A.S.			65
O.A.U.			20
I.R.A.			275
P.L.O.			98
A.N.C.			30
E.E.C.			275

IMPORTANT EVENTS IN THE 20TH CENTURY

The following timeline contains two completed events. Fill in the remainder by selecting important events that occurred between 1900 and 1992. See how much you can remember. Be sure to include at least *one* event from *each* geographic area (Africa, Latin America, Middle East, etc.). Indicate when the event took place, and a brief description about why it is important.

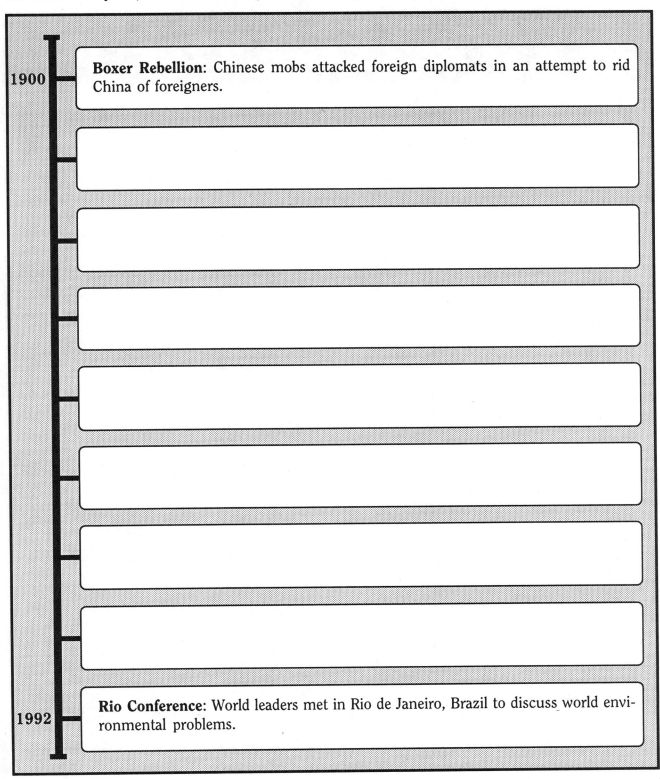

1900

Boxer Rebellion: Chinese mobs attacked foreign diplomats in an attempt to rid China of foreigners.

1992

Rio Conference: World leaders met in Rio de Janeiro, Brazil to discuss world environmental problems.

MAJOR RELIGIONS OF THE WORLD

Religions have had a major impact on the lives of many people as well as on the history of the world. Summarize your knowledge of the world's major religions by completing the following chart:

RELIGION	WHERE IT IS FOUND	MAJOR BELIEFS	PAGE
ANIMISM			24
BUDDHISM			154
CHRISTIANITY			92
HINDUISM			123
ISLAM			92
JUDAISM			91
SHINTOISM			187

COMPARING AND CONTRASTING HISTORICAL FIGURES

Directions: Select a pair of names from the list below, and write the required information.

Historical Figures

Mohammed / Martin Luther
Mao Zedong / Louis XIV
Mohandas Gandhi / Karl Marx
Josef Stalin / Adolf Hitler
Nelson Mandela / Otto von Bismarck

Pair selected: _____

HOW WERE THEY ALIKE?

_____

_____

_____

_____

HOW DID THEY DIFFER?

_____ **Where they came from** _____

_____ **Goals** _____

_____ **Beliefs** _____

_____ **Tactics** _____

_____ **Impact** _____

IMPORTANT REVOLUTIONS

Important revolutions not only change the society in which they occur, but they have an impact on the rest of the world. Summarize your knowledge of the most important revolutions about which you have read by completing the following chart:

REVOLUTIONS	LEADERS	MAJOR CHANGES BROUGHT ABOUT	PAGE
Scientific Revolution (1500-1700)			250
Industrial Revolution (1750s-1850s)			256
French Revolution (1789)			251
Russian Revolution (1917)			209
Chinese Revolution (1949)			149
Cuban Revolution (1959)			65
Iranian Revolution (1979)			99

MAJOR WORLD LEADERS AND THINKERS

Throughout history, certain key individuals have had a great influence on their people, their nation and the world. Summarize your knowledge of these world figures by completing the following chart:

INDIVIDUAL	HAD MOST IMPACT ON	MAJOR IDEAS/ ACHIEVEMENTS	PAGE
Louis XIV			249
Peter The Great			209
Catherine The Great			209
Napoleon Bonaparte			251
Vladimir Lenin			210
Mohandas Gandhi			117
Joseph Stalin			211
Mao Zedong			148
Deng Xiaoping			150
Adolf Hitler			260
Mikhail Gorbachev			213
Saddam Hussein			95

MAJOR GLOBAL PROBLEMS

Throughout the world there are many important problems that confront nations. Summarize your knowledge of these problems by completing the following chart:

PROBLEM	DESCRIBE THE PROBLEM	EFFECTS	POSSIBLE SOLUTIONS	PAGE
AIDS Epidemic				287
Overpopulation				287
Pollution				288
Hunger and Malnutrition				288
Deforestation				291
Desertification				291
Energy Shortages				292

GLOSSARY OF KEY TERMS AND CONCEPTS

Bold numbers in brackets [   ] indicate where the item is first discussed.

Absolutism: The total control by a monarch or king over his subjects. For example, Louis XIV of France was an absolute ruler. His rules were law, and critics who challenged his authority were punished. **[249]**

African National Congress (A.N.C.): An organization in South Africa whose goal is to end apartheid and gain political power for South African Blacks. At one time the A.N.C. supported the use of violence to achieve this goal, but it is now cooperating with the government for non-violent change. **[30]**

AIDS: Acquired Immune Deficiency Syndrome is a virus that prevents the body's internal defense system from fighting disease. AIDS is becoming an increasing health threat throughout the world. **[287]**

Animism: A religious belief that every object in nature has its own spirit and that people's ancestors in the spirit world watch over them in the living world. Many traditional African religions were animist. **[24]**

Apartheid: The former policy of the Republic of South Africa that legalized racial segregation (*separation of the races*) and oppression of South African blacks. This policy led to widespread conflict and violence. **[29]**

Appeasement: Granting concessions to a potential aggressor in order to avoid a conflict. For example, British Prime Minister Chamberlain appeased Hitler at the Munich Conference in 1938 by giving in to Hitler's demand for an area in Czechoslovakia inhabited by a large German population, in an attempt to avoid war. **[261]**

Atlantic Slave Trade: African tribes brought captives from other tribes to Africa's coast, where they were traded to European and American slave traders in exchange for guns and ammunition. The enslaved people were then shipped like cargo across the Atlantic Ocean for sale in North America and Latin America, where they worked as forced labor on plantations. The Atlantic Slave Trade encouraged tribal warfare, destroyed a rich African culture, and resulted in the loss of millions of lives. **[16]**

Balance of Power: A system of international relations aimed at preventing any one country from becoming so powerful that it could dominate other countries. The European Great Powers kept a balance of power among themselves for most of the 19th century. Whenever any of them gained new colonies, the others did the same. When some of them formed an alliance to make themselves stronger, the others formed an opposing alliance. In this way the power of each of them, compared to the others, stayed the same. **[258]**

Berlin Wall: Constructed in 1961 to prevent East Berliners from escaping into the free city of West Berlin. The wall came to symbolize Soviet control and domination in Eastern Europe. It was knocked down in 1989. **[224]**

Big Stick Policy: In 1904 President Theodore Roosevelt expanded the Monroe Doctrine by announcing that European powers would be prevented from intervening in any Latin American nation, even if that nation owed debts. Roosevelt's policy led to increased U.S. influence in Latin America. **[64]**

Boxer Rebellion (1899-1900): An unsuccessful uprising by a group of Chinese that sought to remove all foreign influences from China. The rebellion led to increased foreign interference in China. **[148]**

Buddhism: A religion based on a philosophy of self-denial and meditation. Buddhism teaches that because of human desires, life is filled with pain and suffering. The only way to end these desires is to give up searching for material things. Buddhism started in India and has spread into Southeast Asia, China and Japan. **[154]**

Capitalism: An economic system characterized by private ownership of property and the desire to make money (*the profit motive*) as the main stimulus to production. Under this system capital is invested in the hope of creating more wealth for the entrepreneur (*the individual who risks his or her money*). **[57]**

Caste System: In traditional India, society was organized into hereditary social classes known as "castes." One's caste determined whom one associated with, and what occupations one could enter. Hindus believe that each person is born into a particular caste based on that person's behavior in a previous life. **[123]**

Christianity: A religion founded by the followers of Jesus Christ and now the main religion in Europe, the Commonwealth of Independent States, Australia, and North and South America. Large numbers of Christians also live in Asia and Africa. Christians believe that Christ was the son of God and savior of mankind. **[92]**

Civil Disobedience: A policy in which people refuse to obey laws that they believe are unjust, in order to get the government to change them. For example, Mohandas Gandhi encouraged Indians to disobey British laws by holding peaceful demonstrations, boycotts and sit-ins. **[117]**

Civilization: An advanced form of culture in which people build cities, use writing and other technical skills, and are able to produce enough food to feed themselves. **[16]**

Cold War (1945-1990): A conflict that developed after World War II between Communist nations led by the Soviet Union and Western nations led by the United States. It was called the "Cold War" because no actual shooting took place as in a "hot war." The Cold War ended when the Soviet Union abandoned the Communist system. **[211]**

Collectivization: A policy in which privately-owned lands were taken from peasants and merged into large farms owned and operated by the government. This was a policy used by Stalin in the Soviet Union. **[211]**

Communism: An economic, political and social system that emphasizes that the needs of the group are more important than those of the individual. Communists hoped that doing away with private property would lead to the ideal society. In practice, Communism has been characterized by government agencies running all aspects of production and planning in the economy. The Soviet Union was the world's first Communist country. Today, the leading Communist countries are China, Vietnam and Cuba. **[153]**

Confucianism: A system of beliefs based on the teachings of Confucius, a Chinese philosopher. The main message of his teachings was that a person can achieve peace and harmony by fulfilling his or her proper role in the family and society. Confucianism has had a great influence on China and countries in East Asia. **[158]**

Conquistadors: Spanish soldiers of the 16th century who conquered lands in the Americas. They used horses and cannon (which were unknown to the native peoples) to conquer them. **[51]**

Crusades (1095-1291): A call to arms by various Popes for an army of Christian knights to capture what Christians believed was their "Holy Land" (Jerusalem) from the Muslim Turks. The Crusades greatly increased trade between the East and West. **[86]**

Cuban Missile Crisis (1962): When Soviet missiles were discovered in Cuba, President Kennedy ordered a blockade of Cuba by the U.S. Navy to force the Soviets to withdraw the missiles. Many feared a nuclear war might result. The Soviets agreed to withdraw the missiles in exchange for a pledge that the U.S. would not invade Cuba. **[65]**

Cuban Revolution of 1959: Fidel Castro overthrew the previous dictator, and introduced Communism to the island of Cuba. **[65]**

Cultural Diffusion: The exchange of different ideas and goods between cultures. **[17]**

Cultural Diversity: Differences in the religion, language, traditions and culture among members of a population. For example, there are over 15 different official languages spoken in India, illustrating its cultural diversity. **[131]**

Cultural Revolution: An attempt by Mao Zedong of China to create a society more in keeping with Communist beliefs and ideology. Students called "Red Guards" attacked the urban professional classes throughout China. Mao later recognized the failure of the Revolution, and in 1969 it was ended. **[149]**

Culture: A group's language, attitudes, customs and beliefs. Every society has its own culture, which explains why each group of people lives somewhat differently. **[16]**

Deforestation: Destruction of forests to increase farmland. Since rain forests produce oxygen, deforestation decreases the amount of this important element. Destruction of rain forests also means the loss of many forms of animal and plant life. Deforestation is now a major problem in some countries in Latin America, such as Brazil. **[66]**

Democracy: A system in which citizens of a society participate in the decisions of government by voting directly on issues brought before them, or by electing people to represent them in the legislature. Democracy was first developed in ancient Athens. **[57]**

Desertification: When land turns into desert through erosion and drought. An example of desertification is the loss of land taking place in the Sahel region of western Africa. **[31]**

Dictatorship: A system in which citizens have no power and the government is controlled by an undemocratic leader or dictator. Dictatorships exist in such countries as Syria, Iraq and Cuba. **[57]**

Divine Right: A European concept based on the idea that all political power comes from God. According to this theory, each king was God's deputy on earth, and royal commands expressed God's wishes. For example, King Louis XIV of France claimed to rule his country by divine right. **[249]**

Encomienda System: The Spanish created vast plantations which were controlled by a small, privileged class in Latin America. This system led to the use of enslaved peoples by the landowners. **[52]**

Enlightenment: A European movement begun in the mid-18th century in which writers and philosophers believed that government decisions and social arrangements should be based on the laws of nature, reason and science. **[250]**

Ethnocentrism: Belief that the culture of other peoples is inferior to one's own culture. For example, the Chinese traditionally believed that their culture was superior, and that other peoples were barbarians. **[144]**

European Economic Community (E.E.C.) ("Common Market"): In 1957, six European nations agreed to eliminate custom duties, lower trade barriers, and increase trade among themselves. Today, Common Market members hope to eliminate all barriers between themselves. Their goal is to compete against their economic rivals, the United States and Japan. One problem the E.E.C. faces is reaching agreements on how much power each country should give up to the E.E.C. as a whole. **[275]**

Extended Family: A family containing three or more generations (grandparents, parents, and children) living together under one roof. In China, the traditional home contained an extended family. **[23]**

Fascism: The belief that the state is supreme, that an absolute leader expressed the needs of the state, and that citizens should make sacrifices for the state. War was viewed as making a people noble, and democracy was looked down upon. For example, Nazi Germany under Hitler's rule was a fascist state. **[260]**

Feudalism: A political, social, and economic system which had a rigid class structure and in which land was exchanged for military service. The social systems in Europe during the Middle Ages and Japan in the 1600s and 1700s are examples of feudalism. **[244]**

Free Market Economy: An economic system in which producers set their prices based on what they think consumers will pay. Consumers, interacting with producers, help determine what is produced, how it is produced, and for whom. **[57]**

French Revolution (1789-1799): In 1789, a revolution broke out in France against the King because of the inequalities among classes, an unfair tax system, and overspending by a bankrupt government. The revolution eventually resulted in a shift in political power away from the King and nobles to the bourgeoisie (*upper middle classes*). **[251]**

Genocide: Policy of mass murder carried out against a racial, ethnic or religious group. An example of genocide was the extermination of European Jews by the Nazis. **[119]**

Glasnost (1985-1990): Policy introduced into the Soviet Union by Mikhail Gorbachev allowing for a greater "openness" in Soviet society: especially the right to criticize public officials who commit errors or wrongdoing. **[213]**

Global Interdependence: The mutual dependence of two or more nations on each other. Each buys and sells goods to the other. Most nations in the world today are economically interdependent. **[193]**

Global Warming: When pollutants in the air act to block heat from escaping harmlessly out into space. Some scientists predict global warming will result in a permanent rise in temperatures. This may be enough to cause farmlands to become deserts, polar ice caps to melt, seas to rise to dangerous levels, and existing rivers to dry up. **[288]**

Good Neighbor Policy: In the early 20th century, the United States frequently intervened in Latin American affairs. In 1933, President Franklin D. Roosevelt stated that the United States would no longer do so. As a result, relations between the United States and Latin American nations improved. **[64]**

Great Leap Forward: Proposed by Mao Zedong of China, the main goal of the Great Leap Forward was to increase industrial and agricultural production. It was a political and economic disaster leading to a severe crisis in China. **[153]**

Green Revolution (1960-1980): In the 1960s and 1970s, the Indian government attempted to improve agricultural production by applying modern science and technology. The Green Revolution had some success in increasing farm yields in India; it was less successful in spreading to other countries where farmers were simply too poor to make use of the new seeds, fertilizers and equipment. **[122]**

Gulf War (1990-1991): A war fought after Iraq invaded the oil-rich kingdom of Kuwait. A coalition force, led by the United States, sent troops into Kuwait and Iraq and brought about the total withdrawal of Iraqi forces from Kuwait. The war was an important example of international cooperation against aggression. **[100]**

Hinduism: A religion followed by millions of people in South Asia. Hindus believe in reincarnation (*a person's soul never dies, but leaves the body to be reborn again in another living thing*). Hindus also believe in many gods and goddesses. **[123]**

Hiroshima: A Japanese city attacked by the United States with an atomic bomb. The bombing of Hiroshima and a second Japanese city named Nagasaki ended World War II and marked the start of the Atomic Age. **[180]**

Holocaust (1939-1945): The attempted genocide of the Jewish people in Europe by the Nazis during World War II. It is estimated that over 6 million Jewish people were killed. **[261]**

Human Rights Violations: Violations against people's civil rights and liberties by governments. Such violations may include the denial of free speech, arrests and executions without trial, and torture and enslavement. **[292]**

Imperialism: The political and economic control of one area or country (known as a "colony") by another country (known as the "mother country"). In the late 19th century, European imperialism led to the colonization of most of Africa by European nations. **[18]**

Industrial Revolution (late 18th-19th centuries): Begun in England in the 1750s, this was a basic change in the way goods were produced. Instead of people working at home making goods by hand, people now produced them in factories with the help of large machines. An important result was that the structure of society changed to include a growing working class and middle class. **[256]**

Iranian Revolution (1979): A popular uprising that overthrew the Shah of Iran and replaced him with the Islamic fundamentalist leader Ayatollah Khomeini. **[99]**

Irish Republican Army (I.R.A.): A Catholic terrorist organization which uses violence to achieve its goals of ending the Protestant control of Northern Ireland and unifying it with the rest of Ireland. **[275]**

Iron Curtain: The Soviets claimed they were surrounded by hostile nations following World War II. In an attempt to protect themselves they created an "Iron Curtain" (border barriers, and the Berlin Wall) to separate the nations of Eastern Europe and the Soviet Union from the West. **[214]**

Islam: A major religion of the world established in Arabia by Mohammed. Followers of Islam (*Muslims*) believe in Allah, the all-powerful God, who determines each person's fate and who will judge all people at the end of the world. **[92]**

Isolationism: The policy of a nation that avoids becoming involved in the affairs of other nations. In extreme cases, isolationist nations avoid all contact with the outside world. Japan was isolationist in the 17th and 18th centuries. **[179]**

Judaism: One of the world's major religions. Judaism was the first religion to be based on monotheism (*belief in one God*). Jews believe that God wants people to act justly toward their fellow human beings and that God will protect those who obey God's commandments. **[91]**

Judeo-Christian Heritage: A set of common beliefs held by followers of the Jewish and Christian religion. Both believe in the existence of one God and the importance of leading a moral and just life. **[268]**

Khmer Rouge: A group of Communist rebels who seized power in Cambodia in 1975. They used terrorism and other brutal and violent methods to further their revolutionary goals. The Khmer Rouge have been accused of attempted genocide of millions of their own people. **[119]**

Koran: The sacred book of the Islamic religion, which is said to reveal the word of God as received by Mohammed. **[92]**

League of Nations (1919-1939): An organization of nations, created by the Versailles Treaty of 1919. People believed this new organization would prevent future wars. However, the League had no army and depended on the will of its members to stop aggression. One cause of its failure was that some of the major powers, such as the United States and Russia, refused to join. **[259]**

"Liberty, Equality, Fraternity:" The phrase that expressed the ideals of the French Revolution: "liberty" for those who were oppressed under the King: "equality" for all social classes; and "fraternity" or brotherhood for all citizens. **[251]**

Machismo: A term used in Latin America to justify male dominance, in which the physical, psychological, and moral strength of men are glorified. Although the term "machismo" is used mainly in Latin America, many other traditional societies share similar beliefs. **[58]**

Magna Carta (1215): A "Great Charter" signed by King John of England, which limited the power of the English monarchy. The Charter promised that the King would not imprison English nobles or townspeople except according to the laws of the land and after a fair trial. **[250]**

Meiji Restoration (1868): When rule by the Shoguns collapsed in 1868, the Emperor of Japan, who had been acting as a puppet ruler like his ancestors did for a thousand years, was "restored" to power in Japanese government. Emperor Meiji used his new power to modernize and industrialize Japan. **[179]**

Mercantilism: An economic theory that a nation's wealth is measured by the amount of its gold and silver. Mercantilists urged European rulers to acquire colonies in the 17th and 18th centuries. **[52]**

Middle Ages: The period in Europe that followed the fall of the Roman Empire in 476 A.D. and lasted until about 1500. The early Middle Ages were marked by a complete collapse of central authority, replaced by weak local government under the system called feudalism. **[244]**

Monotheism: A religion that believes in one God, rather than many gods and goddesses. Judaism, Christianity, and Islam are monotheistic. **[92]**

Monroe Doctrine (1823): A policy announced by President Monroe, in which he warned European nations not to intervene in the Western Hemisphere to restore newly independent nations of Latin America to European control. It halted further European imperialism in the Western Hemisphere, but was used to justify frequent U.S. intervention in Latin American affairs in the early 20th century. **[64]**

Monsoons: Seasonal winds that blow across Asia. In summer, these winds bring heavy rains; while in winter they bring hot, dry weather. Monsoons can cause flooding, property damage and death. If they come too late, crops can die from a lack of water. **[113]**

Nationalism: The belief that each ethnic group or "nationality" is entitled to its own government and national homeland. An important characteristic is that such a group of people have some beliefs and values in common that make them want to join together to form a nation. Nationalism is strongest among people with a common language, customs and history. **[19]**

Nationalized: When a government seizes the private property of businesses, banks and industries. For example, Fidel Castro nationalized all U.S. industries when he came to power in Cuba. **[23]**

Nazism: A form of totalitarianism developed in Germany after World War I, by Adolf Hitler. Nazism glorified Germany and blamed the Jews for all the world's problems. Nazism also taught that the state was supreme and that the "leader" (Hitler) expressed the will of the state. When the Nazis took power, they controlled all aspects of German life, started World War II, and murdered Jews and political opponents. **[260]**

Ninety-Five Theses: In 1517, Martin Luther posted a list of reforms which questioned the role and power of the Pope in the administration of the Catholic Church. Eventually, Luther broke with the church and established the Lutheran Church. Luther's list of reforms provided a model for other religious leaders that led to the Protestant Reformation. **[248]**

Nonalignment: A foreign policy during the Cold War period in which developing nations did not take sides with either the United States or the Soviet Union. Usually they sought foreign aid from both sides. **[213]**

North Atlantic Treaty Organization (N.A.T.O): A military alliance between the U.S. and Western European nations, formed after World War II. N.A.T.O. member nations provided for their mutual defense against the threat of Communism. With the collapse of Communism in Eastern Europe, N.A.T.O. is now seeking a new role. **[212]**

Nuremberg Trials (1945): Allied leaders, following the defeat of Germany in World War II, put leading Nazis on trial for "Crimes against Humanity." These trials showed that national leaders would be held personally responsible for criminal actions committed during a war. **[261]**

"One-Child" Policy: A policy attempting to limit China's growing population by permitting families to have only one child. This program met with resistance because peasant farmers seek large families to help with farm work. **[161]**

Open Door Policy (1899-1900): A U.S. policy at the turn of the last century to preserve China as an independent country by keeping it open to trade with all nations. It prevented the total division of China by foreign powers. **[148]**

Organization of American States (O.A.S.): This organization of states in the Western Hemisphere was created in 1948 to provide a peaceful means for settling regional disputes among its members. **[65]**

Organization of Petroleum Exporting Countries (O.P.E.C.): Organization formed in the 1970s to give its members more influence in setting oil prices in world markets. Important results of its formation have been increases in oil prices and the use of oil as a political weapon by its members. **[99]**

Overpopulation: An enormous increase in population in some countries. Unless such population growth is halted, it can threaten to outrun a nation's ability to provide housing, food, and fuel. For example, overpopulation is a problem in India and China. **[66]**

Palestine Liberation Organization (P.L.O.): A political organization that seeks to establish a home state for Palestinian Arabs, carved out of part of Israel. Other Arab countries recognize the P.L.O. as the representatives of the Palestinians. For many years, the P.L.O. supported the use of terrorism against Israel, but has recently shown a willingness to give up terrorism to achieve an independent state. **[98]**

Passive Resistance: A non-violent approach used to achieve political objectives. For example, Indians peacefully suffered British beatings and violence but refused to obey what they considered unjust laws, making it impossible for the British to govern India. This led to Indian independence in 1947. **[117]**

"Peace, Bread, Land:" The slogan used by Communists in attempting to gain power in Russia. "Peace" meant the need for Russia to end to its war with Germany, "Bread" the need to feed the workers, and "Land" the need for a fairer distribution of land among all the people. **[210]**

Pearl Harbor: In 1941, Japan hoped to strike a "knock-out blow" against the U.S. by conducting a surprise air attack against U.S. forces in the Pacific stationed in Hawaii. The attack brought the United States into World War II against Japan. **[180]**

Perestroika (1985-1990): The economic program developed by former Soviet leader Mikhail Gorbachev. Perestroika means "restructuring." It created economic reforms, but failed to go far enough in the direction of a free market economy. **[213]**

Planned Economy: An economic system in which decisions are made by a central authority. For example, in a planned economy, what to produce, how it will be produced, and who gets what is produced are made by the ruling party, government or leaders. This system is most often found in Communist economies such as Cuba and North Korea. **[218]**

Population Density: Refers to the number of people living in a square mile of land. **[45]**

Racism: A contempt for other races in the mistaken belief that one race is superior to others. Racism was used by Hitler to victimize Jews in Europe. Racism also affected British attitudes towards native cultural achievements in British India. **[260]**

Reformation (16th century): The breaking away of a large number of Europeans from the Catholic Church. The Reformation ended the religious unity of Western Europe and led to a century of religious wars. **[248]**

Renaissance (15th and 16th centuries): The word literally means "rebirth." The Renaissance began in Italy and was marked by important contributions to art and the rediscovery of ancient cultures. **[247]**

Roman Empire: A period in history in which parts of Africa, Europe, and Asia were under the control of the Roman army. The Roman Empire was overthrown in 476 A.D. As a result, Europe went through a period of disorder and weak central governments lasting hundreds of years. **[244]**

Russian Revolution (1917): A series of revolutions that first overthrew the Russian Czar and then established the world's first Communist government. One cause of the revolution was the existence of sharp economic differences between the social classes of Russia. **[209]**

Russification: The policy of Russian Czars that forced non-Russian people under their control to adopt the Russian language, culture, and religion. **[209]**

Russo-Japanese War (1904-1905): Japan went to war against Russia in an attempt to limit Russia's influence in the Far East. Japan won the war, and emerged as a strong military power in Asia. Europeans were shocked to see an Asian nation defeat a great European power. **[148]**

Sepoy Mutiny (1857): A mutiny is a rebellion of soldiers or sailors. In 1857, Indian soldiers known as sepoys rebelled against the British practice of using animal grease for loading their rifles, because this practice violated their religious beliefs. **[117]**

Serfs: Peasant farmers who worked land owned by noble landlords. The nobles maintained absolute power over the lives of their serfs, who were bought and sold with the land. **[208]**

Shintoism: The official religion of Japan. Shintoism teaches that spirits or gods are found throughout nature. Japanese Emperors claim to be the spiritual leaders of the Shinto religion. **[187]**

Shogun: The chief general or military governor of Japan. The Shogun became more important than the Emperor and was the real governmental ruler. However, the Emperors re-asserted their power and eliminated the Shogun during the Meiji Restoration in the 19th century. **[179]**

Single Cash Crops: A form of agriculture in which a nation relies on producing a single crop such as sugar or coffee. Found in some Latin American nations, this form of agriculture usually characterizes a nation lacking modern farming methods. It often leads a nation to become highly dependent on other nations. **[46]**

Sino-Japanese War (1894): A war between China and Japan over the control of Korea. The war resulted in Japan's victory, and alerted the world to its new military strength. **[148]**

Social Mobility: An ability to move from one social class to another. Societies differ in their degree of social mobility. In traditional India, there was almost no social mobility between castes. The United States today provides an example of a society with a great deal of social mobility. **[123]**

Spanish-American War (1898): This war between the United States and Spain began because of the brutal Spanish treatment of Cubans. A result was that the United States acquired Puerto Rico, and gained a controlling interest in Cuban affairs. **[64]**

Sphere of Influence: An area of a country under the political and economic control of a foreign nation. For example, areas of China that fell under foreign control in the mid-19th century were known as "spheres of influence." **[147]**

Steppes: Grasslands, where the soil is rich and fertile and the climate is moderate. Steppes are found in southern Russia and the Ukraine (countries in the new Commonwealth of Independent States). **[206]**

Subcontinent: A large piece of land smaller than a continent. India is an example of a subcontinent. **[112]**

Subsistence Farming: A system of agriculture in which a farmer produces only enough food to meet the family's immediate needs. **[23]**

Superpowers: Countries that are militarily more powerful than other countries. Because of the size of their military forces around the world, the United States and the former Soviet Union were considered superpowers. However, since the breakup of the Soviet Union, it is no longer considered a superpower. **[213]**

Technology: The use of tools and methods ("techniques") to produce goods and services. Human technology has consistently improved through the centuries. However, modern technology has led to a weakening of traditional values and family patterns. **[294]**

Terrorism: The use of violence against civilians to achieve a political end. It is used to frighten governments into making concessions and to draw attention to a group's grievances. **[275]**

"Third World" Nations: An expression referring to developing nations of the world. People in many of these nations suffer from hunger, illiteracy and poverty. For example, Bangladesh is considered a developing nation of the Third World. **[71]**

Tiananmen Square Protests (1989): In China, students conducted a peaceful demonstration for democratic reforms. They were fired on by soldiers, which brought an end to their protest. The suppression of the protest showed that China's leaders would use force to prevent certain reforms. **[150]**

Totalitarianism: A system in which the government controls all aspects of life — education, ideas, the economy, music, art, etc. The government ignores the rights of individuals. One of the important characteristics of totalitarianism is that loyalty is measured by the extent to which a person agrees with government policy. Totalitarianism was used by Stalin in the Soviet Union and Hitler in Nazi Germany. **[260]**

Traditional Economy: An economic system in which custom, tradition, and time-honored methods are followed by children as they learn the same trades as their parents. **[90]**

Treaty of Versailles (1919): The peace treaty that concluded World War I. It was noted for its harsh treatment of Germany and its creation of the League of Nations. **[259]**

Tribe: Members of a group who speak the same language and share the same customs form a tribe. In present-day Africa, many Africans feel a greater loyalty to their tribe than to their nation. **[23]**

Tribalism: The allegiance of a group of people to their tribe rather than to their country. One example is the stronger allegiance of African Zulus to their own tribe than to the Republic of South Africa. Tribalism has resulted in political disunity in many African countries. **[30]**

Tundra: The marshy, treeless plains of northern Russia and north America just below the Arctic Circle. The climate is extremely cold and there is little vegetation, since the land is frozen most of the year. **[206]**

United Nations (U.N.): An international peace-keeping organization that was formed after World War II. Its aim is to provide international harmony, peace, and economic development. Most countries now belong to the United Nations. The U.N. Security Council gives a special role to the world's leading economic and military powers. **[262]**

Urbanization: The movement of peoples from rural areas to cities, primarily in search of jobs or a better economic situation. **[23]**

Vietcong: Vietnamese Communists who fought a guerrilla war against the South Vietnamese government and Americans in the 1960s and 1970s, in order to unify Vietnam under Communist rule. **[119]**

Westernization: A policy of adopting Western customs, values and technology used by non-Western societies. Westernization was first introduced into Russia by Czar Peter the Great in an attempt to turn Russia into a modern military power. The Japanese also adopted a policy of Westernization at the end of the 19th century. Some countries have actively opposed Westernization as a threat to local, traditional values. Ayatollah Khomeini opposed Westernization in Iran. **[209]**

World War I (1914-1919): A global war that began after the assassination of Archduke Francis Ferdinand. Conflicting nationalist aims in Europe led to its outbreak. New weapons like the machine gun led to large casualties on the battlefield. A major result was that Germany and Austria-Hungary lost their empires. **[258]**

World War II (1939-1945): A global war caused by the aggression of Germany in Europe and of Japan in Asia. World War II was the most destructive war in human history, killing 40 million people and destroying whole countries. After the war, the United States emerged as a superpower. **[260]**

CHAPTER 12

A FINAL PRACTICE TEST

Now that you have learned the various test-taking strategies and reviewed the content areas, you should take this practice test to measure your progress. It is similar to actual final examinations given in some schools and states, and it will help you identify any areas that you might still need to study. The test has two parts: Part I has 50 multiple choice questions (of which you must answer all questions) and Part II, which has 4 essay questions (from which you must answer 2).

We recommend that you take this practice test under "real" test conditions. Take the whole test at one time, either in class or on your own in a quiet place. Do not talk to anyone while you are taking the test. Time yourself. Finally, show your practice essays to your teacher or tutor and get their opinion about them. Good luck on this practice test!

PART I (Answer all questions in this part.)

Directions: For each statement or question, *circle* the number of the word or expression that, of those given, best completes the statement or answers the question.

1 The term "culture" is most often used when discussing
   1 a nation's economic system   3 the central government of a nation
   2 the beliefs and habits of a people   4 increased foreign trade

Base your answer to question 2 and 3 on the following map and your knowledge of social studies.

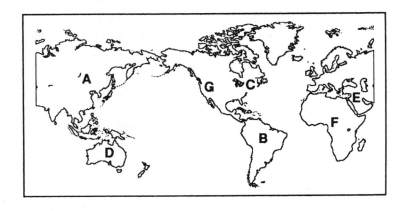

2 Which location is closest to where you live?
   1 A   3 C
   2 B   4 D

3 In which area are Palestinian Arabs clashing with Israelis?
   1 A   3 D
   2 C   4 E

4 Which person is correctly paired with his or her country?
1 Nelson Mandela - South Africa
2 Mao Zedong - Japan
3 Mikhail Gorbachev - Cuba
4 Margaret Thatcher - Bangladesh

5 The fact that the U.S. has many ethnic restaurants is an example of
1 nationalism   3 imperialism
2 cultural diffusion   4 social mobility

6 In an outline, one of these is a main topic; the other three are subtopics. Which is the main topic?
1 World Religions   3 Christianity
2 Buddhism   4 Confucianism

7 Feudalism developed when
1 educational standards were raised
2 a central government failed to protect people
3 high tariffs were created by a government
4 workers tried to improve production

8 Which term describes the seasonal winds that blow over India and Southeast Asia?
1 tundras   3 steppes
2 monsoons   4 grasslands

9 An important belief of Hinduism is that
1 all people are equal
2 one should be in harmony with nature
3 a person's soul never dies
4 there is only one God

10 Which term describes the hereditary social classes of India?
1 castes   3 tribes
2 communes   4 serfs

11 Which phrase best reflects the basic ideas of Mohandas Gandhi?
1 "Power flows from the barrel of a gun."
2 "Non-violence can overcome the use of force."
3 "Divide and conquer your enemies."
4 "Peace, bread and land."

Base your answer to questions 12 and 13 on the following cartoon and your knowledge of social studies.

W. A. Rogers in *Harper's Weekly*, November 18, 1899

Uncle Sam: "I'm out for commerce, not conquest."

12 Uncle Sam in the cartoon is shown trying to hold back
1 U.S. colonies   3 Latin American leaders
2 colonial powers   4 private corporations

13 The events shown in the cartoon eventually led to the issuance of the
1 Monroe Doctrine
2 Open Door Policy
3 Good Neighbor Policy
4 Camp David Accords

14 Which statement is a fact, not an opinion?
1 Chinese civilization contributed more to mankind than any other civilization.
2 The world's oil supply will probably be used up by the year 2000.
3 Catherine the Great of Russia came to power in 1762.
4 The Mayan civilization had the most advanced culture in Latin America.

15 The purpose of apartheid was to
1 increase farm production
2 segregate people by race
3 decrease urban population
4 eliminate government corruption

16 Which factor could best be regarded as a cause of European imperialism in both South America and Africa?
1 a desire to learn from foreign peoples
2 the need for natural resources
3 the fear of Communism
4 a wish to preserve native cultures

17 Which two nations were created out of the partition of India in 1947?
1 Pakistan and Laos
2 India and Pakistan
3 Bangladesh and Cambodia
4 the Philippines and India

18 Which event took place during World War II?
1 the fall of the Roman Empire
2 the unification of Germany
3 the Holocaust
4 the formation of the E.E.C.

19 Chiang Kai-shek, Sun Yat-Sen and Anwar Sadat are best known as
1 political leaders
2 economic theorists
3 social reformers
4 religious leaders

20 Which statement best expresses views held by Mao Zedong?
1 Respect should be given to Americans.
2 Each person is born into a hereditary social group.
3 Ethnic racial groups should be separated.
4 Group interests should come before individual interests.

21 If a report contained the topics "Meiji Restoration," "Emperor worship" and "the Constitution of 1947," the report would most likely be about the government of
1 India
2 France
3 Japan
4 China

22 Which pair of terms is associated with different types of political arrangements?
1 the Reformation and the Marshall Plan
2 democracy and the Renaissance
3 feudalism and absolutism
4 totalitarianism and castes

23 • Japan is smaller than the state of California.
• Japan has over 120 million people, while California has 25 million people.

Based on this information, which statement would be a correct conclusion?
1 Japan and California are both located in Asia.
2 California is located near Japan.
3 Japan has a higher population density than California.
4 California has more fishing than Japan.

Base your answer to question 24 on the following cartoon and your knowledge of social studies.

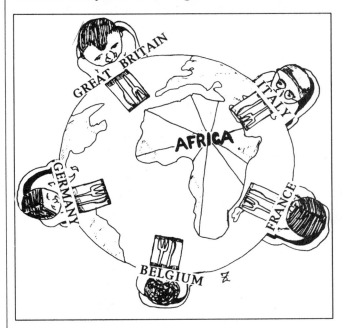

24 The cartoon depicts the
1 ethnocentrism of African nations
2 military aid given to African nations
3 division of Africa into colonies
4 spread of the Cold War to Africa

25 The term "sub-Saharan Africa" refers to countries in Africa that are
1 located south of the Sahara Desert
2 not a part of Africa
3 located in northern Africa
4 largely made up of desert

26 The term "imperialism" refers to the
   1 division of a nation into smaller states
   2 unification of a people under a central government
   3 political and economic control of one nation by another
   4 political system in which people voice their personal opinions

27 Which nation is a part of the region known as Central America?
   1 Brazil   3 Spain
   2 Nicaragua   4 Argentina

28 Which statement best describes the role of Fidel Castro?
   1 He introduced democracy into Cuba.
   2 He sought more U.S. investments in Cuba.
   3 He introduced Communism into Cuba.
   4 He is a strong ally of the United States.

29 The Middle East is a crossroads for which three continents?
   1 Asia, Antarctica, and Europe
   2 Australia, Asia, and Europe
   3 Australia, Asia, and Africa
   4 Africa, Europe, and Asia

30 One similarity between Judaism, Christianity and Islam is their common belief in
   1 animism   3 polytheism
   2 monotheism   4 Communism

31 The PLO, religious clashes, and water shortages are often associated with
   1 Southeast Asia
   2 South America
   3 the Middle East
   4 sub-Saharan Africa

32 Which was a major result of World War II?
   1 division of Germany by the Allies
   2 division of India and Pakistan
   3 creation of the League of Nations
   4 China taking control of Japan

33 Which geographical feature is correctly paired with its location?
   1 Sahara Desert / China
   2 Nile River / India
   3 Ganges River / Latin America
   4 Andes Mountains / South America

34 Mohandas Gandhi and Nelson Mandela are similar in that both
   1 sought to adopt Christianity
   2 protected British economic rights
   3 worked to achieve political rights for their people
   4 represented their countries in the League of Nations

35 The term "passive resistance" refers to
   1 violent uprisings against the government
   2 movements to overthrow democratic reformers
   3 changes in the way goods pass from businesses to consumers
   4 attempts to bring about political change without using violence

36 A major result of the Monroe Doctrine was that
   1 Iraq was prevented from invading Kuwait
   2 European powers did not take control of Latin America
   3 China continued to trade with all nations
   4 India became an independent nation

Base your answer to questions 37 and 38 on the following bar graph and on your knowledge of global studies.

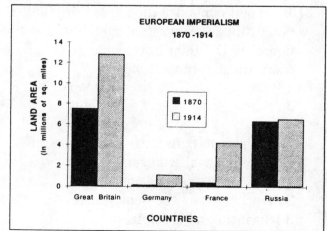

37 Which European nation controlled the largest colonial area in 1914?
1 Great Britain   3 France
2 Germany   4 Russia

38 Which statement is best supported by the data in the bar graph?
1 European imperialism ended in 1870.
2 European colonial expansion increased from 1870 to 1914.
3 European powers were unhappy with imperialism.
4 Europe's birth rate led to increased overseas expansion.

39 Which best describes the Communist view of history?
1 class struggles lead to violent revolution
2 private property ownership brings about an end to religion
3 peaceful social change brought on by a free press
4 social mobility leads to a free market economy

40 Confucianism is primarily concerned with
1 learning about God
2 learning about suffering
3 following God's commandments
4 respecting and honoring others

41 On which two continents is Russia located?
1 Asia and Africa
2 Australia and Asia
3 South America and Europe
4 Europe and Asia

42 The adoption of Western ideas and culture in Russia came about mainly through the
1 efforts of Peter the Great and his successors
2 invasion of Russia by Germany
3 imitation of China
4 influence of Byzantium

43 Which person was the first to write about the idea of a classless society?
1 Nicholas II   3 Peter the Great
2 Karl Marx   4 Otto von Bismarck

44 A major result of the Reformation was that it
1 ended the religious unity of Western Europe
2 led to the European conquest of the Holy Land
3 caused the decline of the Roman Empire
4 increased the power of the Popes

Base your answers to questions 45 and 46 on the following table and on your knowledge of global studies.

SELECTED STATISTICS FOR AFRICAN NATIONS

Nation	Literacy Rate	Life Expectancy	Yearly Income
Mali	10 %	40 years	$40
Sudan	20 %	44 years	$370
Uganda	25 %	49 years	$240
Zaire	30 %	47 years	$127

45 Based on the information in the table, which nation needs to do the most to improve health care for its people?
1 Mali   3 Uganda
2 Sudan   4 Zaire

46 According to the information in the table, which statement is most accurate?
1 The ability to read is the same in Mali and Zaire.
2 Uganda has the longest life expectancy.
3 Sudan has the lowest yearly income.
4 Zaire has the lowest life expectancy.

47 "Subsistence farming" refers to growing
1 enough crops for export
2 enough food to feed your own family
3 crops that yield a high income
4 citrus fruits such as oranges

48 The main purpose of OPEC is to
1 limit nuclear weapons
2 save the rain forests
3 regulate oil production and prices
4 insure world peace and stability

49 Which two nations are located in Western Europe?
   1 Brazil and France   3 India and Israel
   2 Laos and Spain   4 Italy and Germany

50 Which system of government allows its citizens the right to vote on issues?
   1 totalitarianism   3 democracy
   2 absolutism   4 monarchy

PART II

ANSWER TWO QUESTIONS IN THIS PART

1 A nation's political system influences how its people live.

Political Systems

Democracy
Divine Right Kingships
Feudalism
Totalitarianism

Part A

Choose *one* political system listed above: _____

   State how that political system works and influences society. _____

   _____

Choose *another* political system listed above: _____

   State how that political system works and influences society. _____

   _____

Part B

In your part B answer, you should use information you gave in Part A. However, you may also include different or additional information in your Part B answer.

Write an essay beginning with the following topic sentence:

The political system of a country influences how its people live.

2 Scientific and technological developments can often have important effects on a society.

Scientific and Technological Developments

Invention of the printing press	Use of nuclear power
Development of the scientific method	Use of the computer
Invention of the steam engine	Advances in transportation

Part A

Select *two* developments from the list. For *each* development chosen, state *one* way it helped change a society.

DEVELOPMENT	HOW IT CHANGED A SOCIETY
1. _____	1. _____
2. _____	2. _____

Part B

In your part B answer, you should use information you gave in Part A. However, you may also include different or additional information in your Part B answer.

Write an essay explaining how scientific and technological developments have affected a society.

3 The way people live is often influenced by an area's geography and climate.

Features

Deserts	Rivers and river valleys
Location	Mountains
Coastline	Climate

Part A

Select *two* features from the list. For *each* geographic feature you select, identify *one* effect of this feature on the way people live in a specific country or area.

FEATURE	COUNTRY/AREA	EFFECT ON THE WAY OF LIFE
1. _____	_____	1. _____
2. _____	_____	2. _____

Part B

In your part B answer, you should use information you gave in Part A. However, you may also include different or additional information in your Part B answer.

Write an essay explaining how people's lives are influenced by the geographic features of their area.

4 Events in one part of the world often affect other parts of the world.

Events
French Revolution (1789)
Russian Revolution (1917)
Hitler comes to power in Germany (1933)
Independence of India and Pakistan (1947)
Castro's takeover of Cuba (1949)
Gorbachev reforms the Soviet Union (1985-1991)

Part A

Select *two* of the events listed. For *each* event selected, identify one specific way the event affected another nation or region of the world.

EVENT	EFFECT ON ANOTHER NATION OR REGION
1. _____	1. _____ _____
2. _____	2. _____ _____

Part B

In your Part B answer, you should use information you gave in Part A. However, you may also include different or additional information in your Part B answer.

Write an essay describing how events in one part of the world often affect other parts of the world.

INDEX

ILLUSTRATION CREDITS

Chapter 2: Sub-Saharan Africa

Page 9: (top, left) National Museum of African Art, (middle, right) United Nations 157137, (middle, left) United Nations 176005, (bottom, left) National Museum of African Art; **13:** Library of Congress; **24:** (middle, right) National Museum of African Art (bottom, left) National Museum of African Art; **27:** (top, right) United Nations 167298 (middle, left) United Nations 176007 (bottom, right) United Nations 157273; **41:** National Museum of African Art.

Chapter 3: Latin America

Page 43: (top, left) United Nations 148001, (top, right) Library of Congress (middle, left) United Nations 150382, (bottom, left) United Nations 122635; **51:** Library of Congress; **53:** Library of Congress; **54:** Library of Congress; **58:** National Gallery of Art; **61:** (top, left) Library of Congress (top, right) United Nations 142117 (bottom, right) United Nations 169681; **77:** Library of Congress.

Chapter 4: Middle East

Page 79: (top, left) United Nations 158010, (top, right) United Nations 158130, (middle, left) United Nations 88320, (bottom, right) United Nations 158212; **85:** United Nations 152159; **93:** Israeli Minstry of Tourism; **95:** United Nations 122838.

Chapter 5: South and Southeast Asia

Page 111: (top, left) United Nations 93614, (middle, right) India Tourist Office, (bottom, left) India Tourist Office, (bottom, right) India Tourist Office; **113:** India Tourist Office; **116:** Library of Congress; **117:** United Nations 155010; **119:** Amnesty International; **124:** India Tourist Office; **127:** (middle, left) Consulate General of India, (middle, right) United Nations 174207 (bottom) United Nations 168346; **141:** India Tourist Office.

Chapter 6: China

Page 143: (top, left) Freer Gallery of Art, (top, right) Library of Congress, (bottom, left) United Nations 150680, (bottom, right) Paul and Beverly Jarrett; **150:** Amnesty International; **155:** United Nations 161042; **158:** (middle, left) Library of Congress (bottom right) Library of Congress; **160:** Library of Congress; **171:** United Nations 154944.

Chapter 7: Japan

Page 173: (top, left) Japanese National Tourist Office, (top, right) Japanese National Tourist Oficce, (bottom, left) Library of Congress, (bottom, right) Japanese National Tourist Office; **179:** National Archives; **187:** Japanese National Tourist Office; **190:** Library of Congress.

Chapter 8: C.I.S. and Eastern Europe

Page 203: (top, left) Library of Congress, (top, right) Library of Congress (bottom, left) Library of Congress, (bottom, right) United Nations 67223; **218:** (top) Library of Congress (bottom) Library of Congress; **221:** (left) Library of Congress, (right) United Nations 172547; **235:** Library of Congress.

Chapter 9: Western Europe

Page 237: (top, left) Library of Congress, (top, right) Library of Congress (bottom, left) Library of Congress, (bottom, right) Library of Congress; **241:** Library of Congress; **269:** Milstein Collection; **272:** United Nations 149877; **285:** United Nations 176105.

Chapter 10: Global Concerns

Page 305: NASA (84-8C-16)